(Continued from front flap)

tent, especially in his satirical use of the persona, but the rhetoric of his earlier poetry in general has been ignored. By focusing on six of his earlier poems this study brings us closer to a more comprehensive description of his rhetorical art.

Rhetorical treatments of his earlier poems have focused primarily on his couplet art, on tropes and figures, often neglecting larger designs generated by his couplets. When we consider his verse paragraphs (rather than couplets) as poetic units, structural elements become visible and we can perceive a paradigmatic relationship between Pope's own design and the rhetorical processes and modes within traditional and metamorphosed genres. This enables us to locate an imaginative center for each poem based on his rhetorical art.

Literate Culture: Pope's Rhetorical Art demonstrates how Pope's rhetoric merges with his poetics, producing a mimetic art that fuses form and content, sound and sense, creating a public poetry seeking to enchant and move his reader. His methods of selecting, combining, shaping, and refracting test the limits of the poetic text—and its intertextuality—by consciously striving to take hold of his reader. Poetry becomes for Pope "a powerful rhetoric" (Kenneth Burke's phrase) if for no other reason than that the triadic relationship of poet, poem, and reader persistently abides. To instruct, delight, or simply impress ideas on his reader, Pope must in some way sustain this relationship. Thus, in each of Pope's poems may be found a unique purpose revealed by its rhetorical methods.

Literate Culture won the University of Delaware Press Award for best manuscript in Eighteenth-Century Studies.

LITERATE CULTURE

University of Delaware Press
Manuscript Awards
for Eighteenth-Century Studies

The Moral Animus of David Hume
Donald T. Siebert

Literate Culture
Ruben Quintero

LITERATE CULTURE
Pope's Rhetorical Art

Ruben Quintero

Newark: University of Delaware Press
London and Toronto: Associated University Presses

© 1992 by Associated University Presses, Inc.

All rights reserved. Authorization to photocopy items for internal or personal use, or the internal or personal use of specific clients, is granted by the copyright owner, provided that a base fee of $10.00, plus eight cents per page, per copy is paid directly to the Copyright Clearance Center, 27 Congress Street, Salem, Massachusetts 01970. [0-87413-433-1/92 $10.00 + 8¢ pp, pc.]

Associated University Presses
440 Forsgate Drive
Cranbury, NJ 08512

Associated University Presses
25 Sicilian Avenue
London WC1A 2QH, England

Associated University Presses
P.O. Box 39, Clarkson Pstl. Stn.
Mississauga, Ontario,
L5J 3X9 Canada

The paper used in this publication meets the requirements of the American National Standard for Permanence of Paper for Printed Library Materials Z39.48-1984.

Library of Congress Cataloging-in-Publication Data

Quintero, Ruben, 1949–
    Literate culture : Pope's rhetorical art / Ruben Quintero.
    p.   cm.
    Includes bibliographical references and index.
    ISBN 0-87413-433-1 (alk. paper)
    1. Pope, Alexander, 1688–1744—Technique.
  2. Rhetoric—1500–1800. I. Title.
PR3637.T4Q56 1992
821'.5—dc20   90-50939
                                                                       CIP

PRINTED IN THE UNITED STATES OF AMERICA

To Evelia

Contents

Acknowledgments	9
1. Pope's Rhetorical Art	13
2. Rhetoric and Poetics in *An Essay on Criticism*	19
3. Design in *Windsor-Forest*	40
4. *Persona*, Drama, and Epic in *The Rape of the Lock*	65
5. Expression, Emotion, and Forsaken Women	88
6. Rhetorical Irony in *The Dunciad Variorum*	116
Appendix A: The Dionysius Rhetoric	136
Appendix B: Juno's Dressing Scene in Pope's *Iliad* Translation	139
Appendix C: Pope's Translation of Longinus	141
Appendix D: Sapphic Sublimity	145
Notes	147
Works Cited	174
Index	183

Acknowledgments

I wish to thank Walter Jackson Bate and James Engell for providing generous criticism of this study in its early stages as a Harvard University dissertation; Steven Shankman for sharing his ideas on Pope and Pindar and for reading a rough draft of chapter 3; and Charles Beckwith, Peter Brier, Herbert Landar, and Gregory Maertz for commenting on aspects of my work. I also appreciate the detailed advice and criticism of my anonymous reader at the University of Delaware Press, and am grateful to John Cleman, chairman of the Department of English, California State University, Los Angeles, for helping me obtain time for research and revision.

My notes reflect my deepest admiration for the many scholars who have increased our understanding of Pope and of the history of rhetoric.

As Seneca the philosopher tells us, "He who receives a benefit with gratitude repays the first installment on his debt."

Acknowledgment is granted by the following: *The Twickenham Edition of the Poems of Alexander Pope*, edited by John Butt et al., reprinted by permission of Methuen & Co. Ltd.; *The Correspondence of Alexander Pope*, edited by George Sherburn, *Critical Essays of the Seventeenth Century*, edited by J. E. Spingarn, and *The Spectator*, edited by Donald F. Bond, reprinted by permission of Oxford University Press; *The Prose Works of Alexander Pope*, vol. 1, edited by Norman Ault, and vol. 2, edited by Rosemary Cowler, reprinted by permission of Basil Blackwell, Ltd., and vol. 2 reprinted by permission of The Shoe String Press, Inc.; The Loeb Classical Library, Aristotle, *The Poetics*, and Longinus, *On the Sublime*, vol. 23, translated by W. Hamilton Fyfe (1927), and Quintilian, *Institutio Oratoria*, vols. 1–4, translated by H. E. Butler (1920–22), reprinted by permission of Harvard University Press; and lastly, *The Critical Works of John Dennis*, edited by Edward Niles Hooker, reprinted by permission of The Johns Hopkins University Press.

LITERATE CULTURE

1
Pope's Rhetorical Art

This study attempts a reconstruction of the rhetorical sensibility that Alexander Pope expected of his eighteenth-century reader and seeks a revision of our own understanding of his poetry as modern readers. More specifically, it examines the rhetorical art of Pope's early poetry by focusing on six major poems published from 1711 to 1729: *An Essay on Criticism, Windsor-Forest, The Rape of the Lock, Elegy to the Memory of an Unfortunate Lady, Eloisa to Abelard,* and *The Dunciad Variorum.* Rhetorical strategies explored in some detail are Pope's use of generic expectations in either traditional "poetic kinds" or in his own metamorphosed versions; underlying structures of argument patterned after classical oratorical models; his methods of appeal through rational argument, character, or emotion; his reliance on *personae*; and his variations of expressive *transparency* and *opacity* correlating with classical views of formalistic refinement and poetic distance—of "light" and "shadow."

The Dunciad Variorum (1729) roughly divides Pope's poetical career. In 1729 Pope began his serious planning for an "*opus magnum,*" which later became his *Moral Essays* and *An Essay on Man,* and shortly thereafter he turned his attention to the composition of his Horatian satires.[1] It appears that the satirical muse of his *Moral Essays* prepared him for the crucial inspiration of his friend Lord Bolingbroke around 1733.[2] The prevailing satirical character of his later poetry, setting apart *An Essay on Man,* suggests a major shift in rhetorical strategies deserving more attention than this study could afford. I have alluded to some of these strategies in discussing his earlier poems. Moreover, Pope's later satires and *An Essay on Man* have been explored rhetorically to some extent, especially in his satirical use of the *persona,* but the rhetoric of his earlier poetry in general has been ignored, though there have been some exceptions.[3] By focusing on six of his earlier poems, this study brings us closer to a more comprehensive description of his rhetorical art.

Pope's intimacy with the works of Aristotle, Dionysius of Halicarnassus, Cicero, Longinus, and Quintilian and the arduous task of translating the Homeric poems provided him with an available store of rhetorical tools for composing original poems. His command of these works and his eclectic method of composition enabled him to create his own powerful rhetoric by interlacing many of their ideas within the fabric of his poetry.[4] Rhetorical treatments of his earlier poems have focused primarily on his couplet art, on tropes and figures, often neglecting larger designs generated by his couplets.[5] When we consider his verse paragraphs, rather than couplets, as poetic units, structural elements become visible, and we can perceive a paradigmatic relationship between Pope's own design and the rhetorical processes and modes within traditional and metamorphosed genres, enabling us to locate an imaginative center for each poem based on his rhetorical art.

By the term *rhetoric*, I refer to Pope's applied strategies and conventional literary practices drawn either directly from classical theorists and poets or from the Renaissance tradition that subsumed them in merging rhetoric with poetics.[6] A rhetorical situation begins when Pope consciously seeks to move his reader in a specific manner; and as a public poet—one of those poets who wish to be understood (paraphrasing Robert Frost)—he writes consciously with an audience in mind.[7] Though his couplets consistently reveal an element of rhetorical play in their figurative richness, his use of rhetoric is not merely stylistic. Genre, *personae*, and methods of appeal also belong to the broader spectrum of his rhetoric, which subserves his poetic objective of delighting and instructing or simply impressing his ideas "without action or goal" on his reader.[8] Recognizing this creative dimension of his rhetorical art provides us a fuller understanding of his poetry.

Pope's rhetorical technique partially relies on literary convention to move his reader. Traditional topics, patterns of arrangement, and figures and tropes have garnered a forcefulness through repeated and successful use, and Pope creatively refashions them in his poetry. For him, convention offers a common ground for a community of readers to begin that precarious act of communication. His use of genre, or "poetic kind," serves such a purpose. While genre imposes a disciplined starting point for his poetry, it also functions as a liberating device to transform the familiar into the unfamiliar and further realize his imaginative vision in language. At the same time, he has a strong historical sense of the permissible and scorns the injudicious use of poetic conventions that garnish rather than improve on the ground laid by past poets. Genre, therefore, enables Pope's poetic discourse to proceed in a recognizable direction, orienting his reader and making accessible his unique mode of perception.

Traditional poetic practices—his use of metaphor and simile, imitation, repetition of sound, to name a few—can evoke predictable responses, arousing and predisposing his reader's mind and spirits, or can establish larger kinetic structures of syllogistic, qualitative, or repetitive progression, also generating stock responses. Formulaic elements or movements mediating between poet and reader, as a form of literary currency within a literate culture, serve to guide Pope's reader to new poetic prospects.

In such ways, Pope's rhetoric merges with his poetics, producing a mimetic art that fuses form and content, sound and sense, creating a public poetry seeking to enchant and move his reader. His methods of selecting, combining, shaping, and refracting test the limits of the poetic text—and its intertextuality—by consciously striving to take hold of his reader. Poetry becomes for Pope "a powerful rhetoric" (Kenneth Burke's phrase) if for no other reason than that the triadic relationship of poet, poem, and reader persistently abides. To instruct, delight, or simply impress ideas on his reader, Pope must in some way sustain this relationship. Thus, in each of Pope's poems may be found a unique purpose revealed by its rhetorical methods.

Pope's *psychagôgia*, his art of influencing souls, has now lost much of its suasive effect because of a general shift in rhetorical sensibility. Kenneth Burke brilliantly sums up this "difference between the 'old' rhetoric and a 'new'" in distinctly aesthetic terms: "The key term for the old rhetoric was 'persuasion' and its stress was upon deliberate design. The key term for the new rhetoric would be 'identification,' which can include a partially 'unconscious' factor in appeal."[9]

Rather than a displacement of the "old" rhetoric by a "new," Northrop Frye perceives "a recurrent opposition of two views of literature," a historical dialectic between two methods of appeal, "the Aristotelian and the Longinian, the aesthetic and the psychological, the view of literature as product and the view of literature as process." At least for the present, the Longinian view has preempted: "In our day we have acquired a good deal of respect for literature as process, notably in prose fiction."[10]

Frye describes a polarity between two impulses, "the aesthetic and the psychological," between product and process in art. But does Longinus really argue against the formalism of rhetorical practice, which Frye's opposition implies? Indeed, Longinus does express an early concern with the psychological effects of literature, as seen in his *On the Sublime:*

> For the effect of genius is not to persuade the audience but rather to transport them out of themselves. Invariably what inspires wonder casts a spell upon us and is always superior to what is merely convincing and pleasing. For our convictions are usually under our own control, while such passages exercise an irresistible power of mastery and get the upper hand with every member of the audience.[11]

But Samuel H. Monk reminds us: "It is evident that Longinus is well within the tradition of ancient rhetoric when he treats the sublime style as emotive in purpose and as capable of being expressed both in ornamental and in simple language."[12] Recalling the originally rhetorical nature of his sublime, which suffered a conceptual disfiguration and revision in the eighteenth century, enables us to recognize how Pope sought a now neglected form of Longinian sublimity in his poems *Elegy to the Memory of an Unfortunate Lady* and *Eloisa to Abelard* (see chap. 5).

The eighteenth century is the transitional period for what Kenneth Burke calls the "old" and the "new" rhetoric, occurring roughly between two distinctive poetic sensibilities, seen in Sir Philip Sidney's *An Apology for Poetry* (1595) and Percy Bysshe Shelley's *A Defence of Poetry* (1821; published 1840). Sidney's *Apology* stands clearly within the classical tradition in which rhetoric and poetics merged.[13] For Sidney, the poet sees through a glass darkly in a postlapsarian world, where nature is brazen and only "the poets can deliver a golden."[14] The poet's metaphor, as Sidney himself uses it, serves to enhance and to ornament the world, but not fundamentally to change it. Language functions in a quite different way for Shelley's poet:

> Their [poets'] language is vitally metaphorical; that is, it marks the before unapprehended relations of things and perpetuates their apprehension, until the words which represent them become, through time, signs for portions or classes of thoughts instead of pictures of integral thoughts; and then if no new poets should arise to create afresh the associations which have been thus disorganized, language will be dead to all the nobler purposes of human intercourse.[15]

Shelley's poetics are committed to a psychological world of discovery—of Prometheus. Pope's poetics, however, like Sidney's, belong to a rhetorical world of humanism—of Adam. Just so, we find that Pope's use of metaphor will "presume not God to scan," subserving instead the purposive design of his poetry.[16]

The rhetorical nature of Pope's poetry has contributed more than its share to the historical controversy over his merits as a poet. This controversy devolves from, among other sources, a romantic reaction to the classical capaciousness of his poetic medium, which may range from quotidian domesticity to sublime elevation. The romantic revision of the poet and his purpose entailed rejecting not only stylistic conventions, but also kinds of poetry that had become too familiar, too artificial, or too mundane to accommodate the newness of poetic material. *What* a poet said, rather than *how* he said it, had tipped the balance, and the poetic language of eighteenth-century poets like Pope was perceived as purely ornamental and even deceptive by severer critics. The classical conception of invention, with its commonplaces and topics, was superseded by a desire for originality. In 1821 Byron, another master of the satirical couplet, declared in one of his letters: "To the question, 'Whether the description of a game of cards be as poetical, supposing the execution of the artists equal, as the description of a walk in a forest?' it may be answered, that the *materials* are certainly not equal; but that 'the *artist*,' who has rendered the 'game of cards poetical,' is *by far the greater* of the two."[17] Pope's use of the couplet as a multipurposed vehicle and his preoccupation with conventional themes required that he be Byron's supreme artist of expression to succeed as a poet.

An impulse to "make it new" prompted poets to attack the preeminent poet of the early eighteenth century, who most represented a tradition they considered stifling. For these younger poets eager to assert themselves, the past could only become a burden. Maybe, as Harold Bloom argues, such reactions or revisions are essential to poetic creation.[18] But even if each generation must proclaim its independence with its own poetic voices and modes of expression, it will be our loss as readers (or Bloom's misreaders) of poetry if we fail to recognize and to appreciate those suasive aspects of a classical tradition in which poetics and rhetoric merged. Samuel Johnson bears repeating: "If Pope be not a poet, where is poetry to be found?"[19]

"For all a rhetorician's rules," writes Samuel Butler in

Hudibras, "Teach nothing but to name his tools." I have not concerned myself with simply naming those tools within Pope's "*Rhetorical Chest of Drawers,* consisting of three Stories," but have sought to show how they function and affect our understanding of his poetry.

2
Rhetoric and Poetics in *An Essay on Criticism*

In 1925 I. A. Richards declared: "It is absurd to read Pope as though he were Shelley, but the essential differences cannot be clearly marked out unless such an outline of the general form of a poetic experience . . . has been provided. The psychological means employed by these poets are demonstrably different."[1] However obvious Richards's declaration may seem, many readers of Pope judge his poetry without giving adequate attention to their own poetic expectations and how they might differ from those of Pope's contemporary reader, who was more conversant in traditional rhetoric. It is the reader, after all, who privileges the poet; a lack of rhetorical knowledge can be as significant as an ignorance of historical background in accounting for Pope's lack of immediacy. Only through a knowledge of Pope's rhetoric can we begin to realize "the psychological means" by which he crafts his poetry. Regardless of Richards's warning, we can see for ourselves how Pope's poetry is radically distinct from Shelley and other Romantics; and Pope's critical declarations in *An Essay on Criticism* show as well as tell us exactly in what ways.

As already suggested in the first chapter, in *A Defence of Poetry* Shelley lays bare his desire to pierce through dispiriting garnitures of conventional language and acquire a poetic hyperperception; and he seeks fresh metaphors to describe that newly seen world. Pope, however, uses his poetic medium in an altogether different way. He strives instead for a *strength* of perception accomplished through, among other means, changing points of view. By establishing within his poetry a variety of angles of perception, he has his reader see semblances and differences in words, images, and concepts, representing the *same* variegated world but with different illuminations:

> But true *Expression*, like th' unchanging *Sun*,
> *Clears*, and *improves* whate'er it shines upon,
> It *gilds* all Objects, but it *alters* none.
> (*Essay on Criticism*, 315–17)

Unless he consciously seeks a satirical counterpoint, as in *The Rape of the Lock* (see chap. 4) or *The Dunciad* (see chap. 6), he strictly avoids the fantastic novelty of his bathetic poet in *Peri Bathous*: "The circumstances which are most natural are *obvious*, therefore not *astonishing* or peculiar. But those that are far-fetch'd or unexpected, or hardly compatible, will surprise prodigiously."[2] Yet, as his Twickenham editor states, he prefers "the complications rather than the simplifications of artistic truth," and "[the] result of such a preference is a poem like *An Essay on Criticism*, where the antithetical reality is not obscured but emphasized."[3]

Pope directs his reader's imagination with a highly disciplined art of technical variation, and his reader is expected to recognize his command of the poetic surface and marvel at his control. What allows him to be a virtuoso of expression is his idiom, one that subscribes to a general rhetoric first seen in the Homeric poems, described by later Greek and Roman authors, and recovered, modified, and sustained by European literary culture. His precise control of expression and his conscious eloquence thrives on the classicism of his educated reader.

Pope gives classical writers in *An Essay on Criticism* the highest form of praise by turning their rhetorical strategies to his own poetical use; and evidence of such appropriation is to be found in the *Essay*'s structure, which has been generally overlooked.[4] In fact, *An Essay on Criticism* in several ways resembles paradigms for deliberative and forensic speeches in Quintilian's *Institutio Oratoria*, and it appears that Quintilian's work provides a guiding spirit for the organization of the poem.[5] Furthermore, we will see how Pope's method of *talking* his reader into "sense" is indebted to Aristotle's *Rhetoric*.

Rhetorical Structure

In *An Essay on Criticism*, we detect an emphatic tone of youth piercing through Pope's *persona*, an unyielding idealism not yet mollified by painful trials of experience. We also perceive an unmistakable maturity. Pope expresses in his poem the touchstones that will guide him throughout his poetical career: the relationship between nature and poetry, critic and poet; critical pitfalls to be avoided; standards to be embraced; techniques to write as well as read a poem; veneration of the ancients; and means to improve on them. All of these critical issues arise. *An Essay on Criticism* encapsulates his poetical intentions, and he wishes to prepare his most influential reader, the literary critic, for them. In fact, there is something almost too sober, too mature, in the prophetic lines: "Now Length of *Fame* (our *second* Life) is lost, / And bare Threescore is all ev'n That can boast" (479–80). *An Essay on Criticism* concerns Pope's future, as well as the future of poetry. His interest in the just conduct of his arbiters, the literary critics, reveals a deliberative purpose in Pope's effort to invoke prudent criticism. But the poem also functions as an *apologia* spoken through Pope's idealistic *persona*, describing for us his own poetics and rhetoric.

Lamenting the apparent lack of structure in *An Essay on Criticism* has become commonplace. In his influential *Life of Pope*, Samuel Johnson complains:

> Almost every poem, consisting of precepts, is so far arbitrary and immethodical, that many of the paragraphs may change places with no apparent inconvenience; for of the two or more positions, depending upon some remote and general principle, there is seldom any cogent reason why one should precede the other. But for the order in which they stand, whatever it be, a little ingenuity may easily give a reason.[6]

As with Johnson, so with other eighteenth-century readers, *An Essay on Criticism* appeared an interchangeable mosaic and has suffered since from a neglect of its formal qualities, a fate similar to that of *Windsor-Forest* (see chap. 3).[7] Perceiving an order in the poem, however, has not been left to the ingenuity of the reader, for the poem possesses a structure, we shall soon observe, determined in part extratextually.

Underlying Johnson's remarks is a desire to perceive within the poem an internal logic accounting for its order. We might consider Johnson's inclination here as evidence for a "new" rhetoric more clearly emerging in the latter half of the century; with a psychological impulse for discovery, Johnson expects to be guided by interstitial connections, logical or emotional, not quite in the manner of Coleridge's "organic" poetry but something near. Johnson's criticism also demonstrates just how far apart rhetoric and poetics had moved, for the poem is ordered by both internal logic and rhetorical convention. Johnson's failure to recognize or to appreciate that convention suggests how much the effectiveness of Pope's rhetoric of presentation had dissipated even in his own century.

The "arbitrary and immethodical" order described by Johnson actually reflects a malleability in a rhetorical formula Pope employs poetically; in this case, a six-part oration consisting of an opening (*exordium*), a statement of facts (*narratio*), a proof (*probatio*), a confutation (*refutatio*), a digression (*egressio*), and a conclusion (*peroratio*). This particular structure is a rhetorical stroke in itself, modifying Quintilian's forensic model for Pope's poetical deliberation on the future of criticism. But before this can be further discussed, we must examine how the poem conforms to these oratorical parts.

Pope divides his poem into three parts to demarcate his order of argumentation. Each of his parts establishes a logical point of departure, a poetic version of a rhetorical *basis* (or *stasis*), described by Quintilian, that invites us to follow his poet into the next part.[8] Resorting to an outline, we can see how Pope's division encompasses the parts of his modified version of a deliberative oration.[9] (I describe the *basis* of argument for each of Pope's parts to show how one division logically initiates the next):

Part 1 (1–200). Basis: What is the issue, and what are the facts with which to assess that issue?

    A. The opening, or *exordium*, contains Pope's proposition, the danger of erroneous critical judgement (1–8): "less dang'rous is th' Offence, / To tire our *Patience*, than mislead our *Sense*."

    B. The statement of facts, or *narratio*, declares what Pope regards as self-evident grounds on which to base criticism (9–200):

> 'Tis with our *Judgments* as our *Watches*, none
> Go just *alike*, yet each believes his own.
> . . . . (9–18)
> Yet if we look more closely, we shall find
> Most have the *Seeds* of Judgment in their Mind;
> . . . . (19–35)

["half-learn'd Witlings" are opposed to the noble
critic, 36–51]
Nature to all things fix'd the Limits fit,
. . . . (52–67)
First follow NATURE, and your Judgment frame
By her just Standard, which is still the same:
. . . . (68–87)
Those RULES of old *discover'd*, not *devis'd*,
Are *Nature* still, but *Nature Methodiz'd*;
. . . . (88–91)
[with examples of Greece and Rome, 92–140]
Some Beauties yet, no Precepts can declare,
For there's a *Happiness* as well as *Care*.
. . . . (141–68)
. . . Those oft are *Stratagems* which *Errors* seem,
Nor is it *Homer Nods*, but *We* that *Dream*.
(169–80)
. . . To teach vain Wits a Science *little known*,
T' *admire* Superior Sense, and *doubt* their own!
(181–200)

Part 2 (201–559). Basis: What, therefore, has misled critics?

C. The proof, or *probatio*, opens up the issue of faulty judgment and clarifies its particular sources and problems (201–559):

Of all the Causes which conspire to blind
Man's erring Judgment, and misguide the Mind,
What the weak Head with strongest Byass rules,
Is *Pride*, the *never-failing Vice of Fools*.
. . . . (201–14)

1. He with "A *little Learning*" is opposed to "A perfect Judge" (215–88); in the example of "La Mancha's Knight" (267–84).
2. "Some to *Conceit*" are opposed to the "*True Wit*" (289–304).
3. Those "Others for *Language*" are opposed to those with "true *Expression*" (305–36).
4. Judging "by *Numbers*" is opposed to the proper use of representative meter (337–83).
5. Those who "Avoid *Extreams*" (384–93) are opposed to those favoring either ancients or moderns (394–407);

the famous (408–23); schisms (424–29); fashion (430–51); one's ownself (452–73); yet, "Be thou the *first* true Merit to befriend" (474–93).
6. "*Sacred Lust of Praise*" is opposed to "*Good-Nature* and *Good-Sense*" (494–525).
7. True satire is opposed to "*Dulness* with *Obscenity*" (526–33); with past examples of vicious satirical wit (534–59).

Part 3 (560–744). Basis: What, then, should a critic do to avoid these errors and insure proper judgment?

D. The confutation, or *refutatio*, reveals ways to prevent mistakes in judgment (560–630):

> LEARN then what MORALS Criticks ought to show,
> For 'tis but *half* a *Judge's Task*, to *Know.*
> . . . . (560–65)

1. "Be *silent* always when you *doubt* your Sense" (566–71).
2. "Without *Good Breeding, Truth* is disapprov'd" (572–77).
3a. "Be Niggards of Advice on no Pretence" (578–83); and the example of Appius, who cannot bear honest criticism (584–95).
3b. " 'Tis best sometimes your Censure to restrain" (596–99); as with poetasters, who cannot profit from criticism (600–609), and criticasters, their counterparts (610–30).

E. The digression, or *egressio*, provides illustrative examples of the ideal critic, for the purpose of amplifying the previous exposition and adding lustre to critical achievement (631–732). The sequence by chronology and by quality is traditional:

> But where's the Man, who Counsel *can* bestow,
> Still *pleas'd* to *teach*, and yet not *proud* to *know?*
> . . . .
> (631–42)

[with historical examples of great critics from Aristotle to Walsh, 643–732]

F. In the conclusion, or *peroratio*, the poet's emotional elevation arouses and prepares the reader for a brief summation (733–44):

> The Learn'd reflect on what before they knew:
> Careless of *Censure*, nor too fond of *Fame*,
> Still pleas'd to *praise*, yet not afraid to *blame*,
> Averse alike to *Flatter*, or *Offend*,
> Not *free* from Faults, nor yet too vain to *mend*.

In his essay "'First Follow Nature': Strategy and Stratification in *An Essay on Criticism*," John M. Aden recognizes a rhetorical structure in Part 1 of the poem. He fails to see, however, how Parts 2 and 3 follow: "Whatever may be said of the last two parts of the poem (and the charges of want of method seem valid enough there), it is clear that Pope designed his first part, that he did so on the analogy of the classical oration, and in so doing he conferred peculiar emphasis upon the 'follow Nature' passage."[10] Aden does not see a continuity because he overlooks Pope's primary deliberative purpose, which determines the succeeding progression of thought. A competent orator never employs a formula willy-nilly but always has a purpose in mind that informs his approach. In reading Quintilian, Pope would have known this basic oratorical rule. A recognition of *An Essay on Criticism* as deliberative in nature suggests immediately how Parts 2 and 3 relate to and function along with Part 1.[11]

A student of Quintilian also would know that it was customary—moreover, essential—to adjust the parts of an oration according to an orator's immediate purpose; as Quintilian reminds his orator: "We must remember that *arrangement* is generally dependent on expediency."[12] That Pope's poetic texture remains so prominent demonstrates how gracefully he has managed to submerge his argumentative method within his poem, improving on Horace in his *Ars Poetica*, who according to Pope "still charms with graceful Negligence, / And without Method *talks* us into Sense" (653–54) and allows us to forget that "Those oft are *Stratagems* which *Errors* seem" (179). To some extent Pope anticipated Johnson's kind of criticism, and whether or not one recognized in his poem "grave *Quintilian's* . . . justest *Rules*, and clearest *Method* join'd" (669–70), Pope insured that verve and wit instill pleasure in his reader. In subordinating rhetoric to poetry, he inverted his own description of Quintilian's suasive method, which aimed "less to please the Eye, than arm the

Hand" (673), by emphasizing graceful expression without sacrificing principles of sound argument.[13]

The poet speaking in *An Essay on Criticism* manifests the same concerns of an orator in his clear sense of purpose and conscious consideration of his audience. An orator's purpose regulates how he fashions his speech and suggests to him which parts of traditional oratory would be useful. Most rhetoricians follow Aristotle in describing the three modes of argument according to purpose. These three modes (or kinds)—*forensic* (or judicial), *demonstrative* (or epideictic), and *deliberative*—were generally accepted among later rhetoricians and varied among them primarily in questions of execution. For Aristotle, these modes are characterized according to the speaker's subject and his audience, "to whom the end or object of the speech refers"; he describes them further in his *Rhetoric:*

> Now the hearer must necessarily be either a mere spectator or a judge, and a judge either of things past or of things to come. For instance, a member of the general assembly is a judge of things to come; the dicast, of things past; the mere spectator, of the ability of the speaker. Therefore there are necessarily three kinds of rhetorical speeches, deliberative, forensic, and epideictic.[14]

Though Pope's poet describes the past through precepts and examples and involves himself with praise of the exemplary critic, his primary concern is with the future of criticism, "with things to come."

Reviewing the *bases* of Pope's three parts in the outline above, we perceive a temporal sequence of argument: Part 1 concerns the pervasive order of Nature and its present relation to poetry and criticism; Part 2 describes rather specifically past violations of Nature in criticism; and Part 3 turns pragmatically to the future by suggesting what can be done in the present and how it has been done in the past. The temporal dialectic of Parts 1 and 2 is compressed in Part 3, as major and minor movements from present to past to present are syncopated to underscore the emotional emphasis of the poet's deliberative message.

Quintilian declares that "there are three points which must be specially borne in mind in advice or dissuasion: first the nature of the subject under discussion, secondly the nature of those who are engaged in the discussion, and thirdly the nature of the speaker who offers them advice."[15] Pope wishes to make a case for sensible action in judging poetry, therefore, *An Essay on*

Criticism engages its reader primarily through reasoning and, in fact, opens with a rational appeal declaring the danger of ill judgment:

> 'Tis hard to say, if greater Want of Skill
> Appear in *Writing* or in *Judging* ill;
> But, of the two, less dang'rous is th' Offence,
> To tire our *Patience*, than mis-lead our *Sense*.

This appeal establishes the tone of much of the poem. Reasonable, yet wittily expressed, the internal rhymes, feminine ("Writing," "Judging") and leonine ("Patience," "Sense"), immediately suggest to the reader the crucial symbiosis between writer and critic. Pope's poet gives ground to the critic in admitting the folly of writers like himself, declares how important is the duty of the critic, and establishes through a subtle union of sound and sense that he too has a stake in the issue, reinforcing his own credibility.

Lacking the authority that "carries greatest weight in deliberative speeches," Pope adopts a *persona* of humility.[16] As Quintilian suggests: "If on the other hand he has none of these advantages [distinguished birth, age, or fortune] he will have to adopt a humbler tone."[17] This posture becomes apparent in the direct speech of elevated passion at the end of Part I:

> Oh may some Spark of *your* Cœlestial Fire
> The last, the meanest of *your* Sons inspire,
> (That on weak Wings, from far, pursues *your* Flights;
> *Glows* while he *reads*, but *trembles* as he *writes*).
> (195–98)

And again at the end of the poem: "This humble Praise, lamented *Shade!* receive, / This Praise at least a grateful Muse may give!" (733–34).

Furthermore, the exclamatory tone of these culminating lines in the *peroratio* (Part 3.F) not only expresses the poet's humility, it also appeals to the emotions of the reader, a strategy for the *peroratio* that Quintilian describes in considerable detail. This emotional appeal then prepares the reader for the summation following (739–44), which is another function of the *peroratio* according to Quintilian: "This final recapitulation must be as brief as possible . . . and summarize the facts under the appropriate heads."[18]

Though this rhetorical design contains many of the strategies found in Quintilian's *Institutio Oratoria*, Pope's ingenious transformation of such methods into his own rhetoric demonstrates how he is not "a Slave to Authority and Opinion," as John Dennis alleges.[19] For example, Pope follows essentially the paradigm of a forensic oration described by Quintilian, an oratory concerned with persuading a jury about past events, but employs it for a deliberative purpose; Quintilian distinguishes between their methods: "the task of oratory must either be concerned with the law-courts or with themes lying outside the law-courts."[20] The forensic paradigm has a more complex sequence of argumentation than Quintilian's deliberative oration and allows Pope greater poetical versatility without relinquishing cohesive argument. Judging critical follies of the past not only enhances the poetic texture, but reinforces Pope's deliberative message. Pope also clearly violates one of Quintilian's proscriptions in forensic speech by including a major digression (Part 3.E) before ending the poem. The virtue of this addition is at once aesthetic and purposive. Finally, Quintilian underplays the need for an exordium in a deliberative speech,[21] which we see Pope employ to considerable advantage (Part 1.A). Thus, Pope adjusts a rhetorical model to his needs and manages a fructifying union between his aesthetic and rhetorical concerns, creating a poem distinctively *sui generis*.

Methods of Appeal

In *An Essay on Criticism*, Pope uses three rhetorical methods for appealing to his reader, rational argument *(logos)*, character *(ethos)*, and emotion *(pathos)*. The most important source of appeal lies in the poet's power of reasoning, his own evident wit and judgment. Pope's Twickenham editor notices how Pope's broad use of "wit" resembles that of Quintilian's "invention."[22] For Quintilian, invention and, in fact, all matters of rhetoric require strong powers of judgment.[23] The poet's use of maxims, precepts, and examples also serves to strengthen his chain of argument.

Pope's use of a *persona*, a poetic mask, is essential to his use of *ethos* as an appeal. Depending on his poetic purpose, this *persona* will reflect differing degrees of dissociation from Pope, the author behind the mask. The convention of a *persona*, a common device among classical writers, appears to have roots in the nature of art itself. Yeats, who would sometimes quote Mill's

"Oratory is heard, poetry is overheard," nevertheless, captured the rhetorical essence of the use of *personae* in his *Autobiography:*

> If we cannot imagine ourselves as different from what we are and assume that second self, we cannot impose a discipline upon ourselves, though we accept one from others. Active virtue as distinguished from the passive acceptance of a current code is therefore theatrical, consciously dramatic, the wearing of a mask. It is the condition of arduous full life. One constantly notices in very active natures a tendency to pose, or if the pose has become a second self a preoccupation with the effect they are producing.[24]

Since Pope himself and, thereby, his poet *persona* lack authority in speaking to critics, care must be taken not to distance the reader from the outset through a presumptuous posturing. This requires the "humbler tone" noted previously, which also creates a rhetorical effect of objectivity by placing emphasis more on *what* is being said rather than *who* is saying it, giving the poet's language a *transparency,* a greater compression and an effect of poetic distance, that allows him to sweep across time and space with fluidity (see chap. 4 for more on transparency and opacity).

The two most emotional moments in the poem, at the end of Parts 1 and 3, serve to vary the poet's tone and signal a shift in subject and perspective through a nonreferential *opacity* of expression, an increased rhetorical richness that adjusts our sense of poetic distance. The reader is pulled back to the expressive surface of the poem, to the poet's *pathos,* and focuses on the poet himself in his posture of humility. Thus, we see character and emotion, *ethos* and *pathos,* functioning together as subsidiary strategies to highlight the predominantly rational tone of the poem, enriching its variety and signaling a thematic transition.

Throughout his poetry, Pope places varying emphasis on rational argument, character, and emotion according to the implied purpose of his poem, which usually relies on some form of generic expectation. His various uses of these appeals, *logos, ethos,* and *pathos,* are central to his poetic invention and work inextricably with his poetic design and manner of expression to establish a particular relationship with his reader. This creative shaping of his poetry according to a purposive use of appeals reflects a cross-fertilization of rhetorical and poetical uses of language.

In Plato's "Phaedrus," Socrates declares that "the function of oratory is in fact to influence men's souls." The art of influencing men's souls, *psychagôgia*, relies on an orator's ability to know his audience, to comprehend what are the most effective means for persuading his listener. An orator must know "what type of man is susceptible to what kind of discourse."[25] In his *Rhetoric*, Aristotle provides a systematic account of "the faculty of discovering the possible means of persuasion in reference to any subject whatever." For Aristotle, the art of oratory and the art of poetry overlap in matters of style: "The poets, as was natural, were the first to give an impulse to style"; but each art remains essentially distinct: "for the style of prose is not the same as poetry."[26]

In Augustan Rome, the separation between oratory and poetry is diminished. With Horace's declaration, "Poets aim either to benefit, or to amuse, or to utter words at once both pleasing and helpful to life," poetry assumes a communicative responsibility akin to oratory. The influence of Horace's precept in the Renaissance reinforces the consanguinity of poetics and rhetoric;[27] and Horace, who "without Method *talks* us into Sense," provides a sanction for Pope to draw on oratorical method in creating his own *psychagôgia*.

Aristotle divides an orator's means of persuasion, his proofs, into two classes: inartificial and artificial. Inartificial proofs, existing outside of the orator's art, consist of "witnesses, tortures, contracts, and the like."[28] Artificial proofs, generally known as *ethos, pathos,* and *logos,* derive their power of persuasion from one of three sources, from either orator, audience, or rational argument: "The first [*ethos*] depends upon the moral character of the speaker, the second [*pathos*] upon putting the hearer into a certain frame of mind, the third [*logos*] upon the speech itself, in so far as it proves or seems to prove."[29] Whereas Aristotle's orator resorts to these proofs for persuasive argument, Pope employs these strategies as imaginative appeals, rather than proofs, for the aesthetic purpose of engaging his reader, for teaching, delighting, or merely impressing his ideas on him. Aristotle, in his primary concern with logical truth, emphasizes the intrinsic value of rational argument; but in the rhetorical world of probabilities, collateral to dialectic, he also understands that character and emotion are important but essentially subordinate sources for enforcing an argument.[30] In Pope's poetical world, *ethos, pathos,* and *logos* prove to be, as the occasion arises, equally valuable tools.

The literary use of appeals first appears in the speeches of the Homeric poems. Despite Aristotle's understatement of the contribution of poetry to oratory, a traditional use of appeals seems to have emerged by imitation among poets, as well as orators.[31] Furthermore, I will venture to speculate, Aristotle's proofs may have their origin in the alogical poetical performances of a primary orality frozen by transcription; it may be more than coincidental that the triad of orator, speech, and audience in a literate tradition relies on a fundamental, interactive psychodynamics similar to that found in the triad of poetic singer, song, and auditor in a preliterate tradition. Through the immediacy of an oral performance, a poet could enchant his listener with his physical presence, his voice and gesture, as well as his language. This physical immediacy, along with concomitant extralinguistic appeals, is unavailable to a literate poet but, in a manner, is regained through his formalization of language, his use of literary devices and rhetorical strategies.[32] In addition, the strategic function of a preliterate poet's visible attitude—his vocal tone and physical posturing—may be mirrored in literature through troping of words and figuring of thoughts as a corresponding means of moving the reader. Indeed, the rhetorical use of *pathos* relies especially on lively figures and tropes to affect a reader.

This is a much debated field of inquiry. Albert B. Lord does not see a continuity from orality to literacy occurring within "the creative brain of a single individual": "Once the oral technique is lost, it is never regained. The written technique, on the other hand, is not compatible with the oral technique, and the two could not possibly combine, to form another, a third, a 'transitional' technique." According to Lord, originally oral creations that have been inscribed can be distinguished from literate creations: "An *oral* text will yield a predominance of clearly demonstrable formulas, with the bulk of the remainder 'formulaic,' and a small number of nonformulaic expressions. A *literary* text will show a predominence of nonformulaic expressions, with some formulaic expressions, and very few clear formulas."[33] This suggests to him a corollary radical separation between oral and written tradition, since in a literate world "the formulaic" gives way to "the unique": "In a fully developed written tradition of literature the formulas are no longer present. They are not needed. There may be repeated phrases, but the proportion of them to the whole is small. Words are chosen for nontraditional effects and placed in patterns which are not those of tradition. Thus the basic patterns behind the formulas are changed. Lines are unique, and are intended as such."[34] Lord's underlying premise is that preliterate and literate minds are categorically different.[35]

Despite the strength of Lord's premise, there exist, I believe, discernible links between preliterate and subsequent literate traditions observable in part through rhetorical methods employed by a poet, and not only in transcriptions of oral poetry; links may even be seen in Homeric techniques transformed by Pope in his poetry. The *logos* of *An Essay on Criticism* and of *An Essay on Man*, with their extensive use of example and *enthymeme* (rhetorical syllogism), reflect poetically a syllogistic view of the world somewhere between a mythopoeic view of a preliterate culture and our modern logo-psychological view of a world resisting closure.[36] The rhetorical appeals of *ethos* and *pathos* found in Pope's poetry may be construed as poetic refinements of elements once existing in oral tradition, elements, as I have suggested, which gave suasive power to a poet singing before an audience, deriving not only from his song but from extra-linguistic resources—his authoritative presence as a poet, his vocal tone, gesturing, musical accompaniment, and so on. Furthermore, it would seem that the enchanting uniqueness of an oral performance could rely more on the singer than the song. Thus, in a literate tradition the loss of such resources perforce invites a surrogate in the uniqueness of written expression. The words *trope* and *figure* literally suggest a physical display mimetically transformed into expression. In such a way, a word or expressive configuration may seem to bend conceptually within the reader's mind in conformity to the apparent visual movement of print. To go a bit further, *ethos* and *pathos* in Pope's poetry could be viewed as establishing the synecdochic presence of speaker and reader.

Teaching "with Reason to Admire"

Putting his own advice into practice, Pope himself delights in teaching with a delicacy achieved through consummate technical control: "Men must be *taught* as if you taught them *not;* / And Things *unknown* propos'd as Things *forgot*" (574–75). Even when more than dabbling in philosophy as in *An Essay on Man*, he will not venture into the perilous waters of metaphysics. Rather he takes commonly comprehended wisdom, gives it a different, poetical light, and reposes confidently on its self-evident truth:

> *True Wit* is *Nature* to Advantage drest,
> What oft was *Thought*, but ne'er so well *Exprest,*

> *Something*, whose *Truth* convinc'd at *Sight* we find,
> That gives us back the *Image* of our *Mind*:
> As *Shades* more sweetly recommend the *Light*,
> So modest *Plainness* sets off sprightly *Wit*.
>
> (297–302)

When prophetically ironical, as in Book 4 of the *Dunciad* (see chap. 6), he shuns otherworldly speculation, envisioning rather the predictably natural consequences of the present.[37] To accomplish these ends, Pope often will employ empirically grounded forms of rational appeal.

An essential aspect of this empirical attitude lies in a recognition of the metaphysical limits of perception and of expression: "Launch not beyond your Depth, but be discreet, / And mark *that Point* where *Sense* and *Dulness meet*" (50–51). This attitude informs Pope's use of maxims and precepts as forms of *enthymeme* and examples. His reliance on shared wisdom becomes a mixture of inductive and deductive methods: "Those RULES of old *discover'd*, not *devis'd*, / Are *Nature* still, but *Nature Methodiz'd*" (88–89); and this poetical pattern of reasoning toward substantial truths of human nature can be found in Aristotle's *Rhetoric*; poets and critics "Receiv'd his Laws, and stood convinc'd 'twas fit / Who conquer'd *Nature*, shou'd preside o'er *Wit*" (651–52).

In the first sentence of his *Rhetoric*, Aristotle declares that rhetoric is the counterpart to dialectic, distinguishing them from other modes of reasoning. Dialectic deals not in logical certainties, but, like rhetoric, in probabilities—which includes the realm of human action. Rhetoric as a basis for knowledge, therefore, includes the language arts, giving esteem to the broader inventive domain of classical poetry. In comparison, we might reflect here on how modern poetry has diminished in authority and narrowed immensely in scope, relinquishing perforce much of its ground to specialized prose disciplines on the basis of authoritative knowledge. Hence, while Pope subscribes nostalgically to the former hegemony of poetry—and his plans for an "*opus magnum*" support this, he acknowledges the human limitations of such dominion:

> One *Science* only will one *Genius* fit;
> So *vast* is Art, so *narrow* Human Wit;
> Not only bounded to *peculiar Arts*,
> But oft in *those*, confin'd to *single Parts*.
>
> (60–63)

To supercede these personal limitations, according to Pope's hopeful poet, it is necessary to cull the best knowledge of the past.

Rational argument is the most effective source of appeal for Pope's deliberative purpose of impressing his older, more learned critic, and not surprisingly he turns to the quintessential logician, Aristotle, for his reasoning through probabilities, which relies on the use of the *exemplum:* "Examples are most suitable for deliberative speakers, for it is by examination of the past that we divine and judge the future."[38] Aristotle's remark concerning the use of examples suggests why they are so prevalent in *An Essay on Criticism*, as well as in the works of other concerned writers of the period who unabashedly revered and promoted ancient thought.

Aristotle describes two classes of examples, "one which consists in relating things that have happened before, and another in inventing them yourself. The latter are subdivided into comparisons or fables." Examples are a form of inductive proof and most usefully employed in conjunction with the *enthymeme*, a rhetorical syllogism that for its premises draws on maxims or precepts. Maxims have a particularly suasive appeal according to Aristotle: "Maxims are of great assistance to speakers, first, because of the vulgarity of the hearers, who are pleased if an orator, speaking generally, hits upon the opinions which they specially hold."[39] Throughout *An Essay on Criticism*, Pope joins the inductive method of example with the deductive method of *enthymeme*. In the same way that he merges Quintilian's deliberative and forensic paradigms in his rhetorical structure, Pope profitably combines Aristotle's recommended argumentation for each mode, examples for deliberation and enthymemes for forensic argument: "Enthymemes are most suitable for forensic speakers, because the past, by reason of its obscurity, above all lends itself to the investigation of causes and to demonstrative proof."[40] Pope hints at this mixing of method in the couplet: "Just *Precepts* thus from great *Examples* giv'n, / She drew from *them* what they derived from *Heav'n*" (98–99).

Now let us briefly examine one of several passages (19–25) that shows how Pope joins Aristotle's rhetorical equivalents of inductive and deductive methods and, thereby, follows his own advice on imitation of the ancients: "Thence [from Homer's works] form your Judgment, thence your Maxims bring, / And trace the Muses *upward* to their *Spring*" (126–27). He begins with his minor premise, a maxim,

> Yet if we look more closely, we shall find
> Most have the *Seeds* of Judgment in their Mind;

which follows from his major premise, another maxim,

> Nature affords at least a *glimm'ring Light;*
> The *Lines,* tho' touch'd but faintly, are drawn right.

He employs a comparative example, an analogical metaphor, to suggest the logical turn of the conclusion,

> But as the slightest Sketch, if justly trac'd,
> Is by ill *Colouring* but the more disgrac'd,

and ends his triplet with the conclusion that the seeds of good judgment must have received a false light because good sense should have resulted from the premises,

> So by *false Learning* is *good Sense* defac'd.
> (19–25)

Nature and the Passions

For Aristotle and other Greek rhetoricians, *pathos*—Greek for "experience; suffering; feeling"—was held to be separate from *ethos,* or character. Roman rhetoricians, however, blurred the distinction between *pathos* and *ethos,* viewing both as emotions differing in degree not kind. Kennedy explains: "Ethos, vigorously expressed, produces pathos, and both of these elements came more easily to the Roman character than did extensive or intricate logical argument."[41] For the Romans, *pathos* usually included the more violent emotions, while *ethos* the calmer ones.[42]

Pope's conceptualization of the human soul as being comprised of two sources of action—"Reason" and "the Passions"—corresponds to the concept of *logos* as the force of reason and to the Roman division of compelling emotions into *pathos* and *ethos.* In 1712 these ideas appear in Pope's *Spectator* essay (No. 408):

> The strange and absurd Variety that is so apparent in Mens Actions, shews plainly they can never proceed immediately from Reason; so pure a Fountain emits no such troubled Waters: They must

> necessarily arise from the Passions, which are to the Mind as the Winds to a Ship, they only can move it, and they too often destroy it; if fair and gentle they guide it into the Harbour; if contrary and furious they overset it in the Waves: In the same Manner is the Mind assisted or endangered by the Passions; Reason must then take the Place of the Pilot, and can never fail of securing her Charge if she be not wanting to her self: The Strength of the Passions will never be accepted as an Excuse for complying with them; they were designed for Subjection, and if a Man suffers them to get the upper Hand, he then betrays the Liberty of his own Soul [italics added].[43]

The gentler passions, like *ethos*, control the ship, a metaphor for human life, and can guide it safely into harbor. The "contrary and furious" passions, like *pathos*, can bring destruction if allowed free reign. Pope's metaphor in this passage emerges again in *An Essay on Man*:

> The rising tempest puts in act the soul,
> Parts it may ravage, but preserves the whole.
> On life's vast ocean diversely we sail,
> Reason the card, but Passion is the gale.
>
> (2.105–8)

The moral direction of reason in man becomes a reflection of Nature itself, which can calm its own tempestuous winds.

Pope's persona in *An Essay on Criticism* reflects an ideal balance of humility and poetic zeal as he reasons through the poem, exemplifying the ideal relation between poetry and nature.[44] The ordered rhetorical structure of the poem itself helps maintain this balance, bringing to mind Quintilian on the necessity of a natural order of argument:

> Nor can I regard as an error the assertion that order is essential to the existence of nature itself, for without order everything would go to wrack and ruin. Similarly if oratory lack this virtue, it cannot fail to be confused, but will be like a ship drifting without a helmsman, will lack cohesion, will fall into countless repetitions and omissions, and like a traveller who has lost his way in unfamiliar country, will be guided solely by chance without fixed purpose of the least idea either of starting point or goal.[45]

Besides providing beneficial inspiration for writing poetry, "Reason" and "the Passions" are effective sources for moving the reader. Here Pope describes the analogical interrelations of nature and mankind, nature and art, and art and mankind:

> Unerring Nature, . . .
> Life, Force, and Beauty, must to all impart,
> At once the *Source*, and *End*, and *Test* of Art.
> Art from that Fund each *just Supply* provides,
> Works *without Show*, and *without Pomp* presides:
> In some fair Body thus th' informing Soul
> With Spirits feeds, with Vigour fills the whole,
> Each Motion guides, and ev'ry Nerve sustains;
> *It self unseen*, but in th' *Effects*, remains.
>   (70–79)

By drawing on those "Spirits" from "th' informing Soul" of Nature, the poet not only invigorates but orders his work. Thus, Nature's vital force *("It self unseen")* emerges in the poet's own natural passions and, at another remove, likewise stimulates and guides his reader.

Pope's "Tours"

Pope divides his poetics into three processes, or "distinct tours": "the design, the language, and the versification (to which he afterwards seemed to add a fourth, the expression, or manner of painting the humours, characters, and things that fall in with your design)."[46] These elements overlap the main processes of classical rhetoric: invention *(inventio)*, arrangement of parts *(dispositio)*, and style *(elocutio)* [the other processes, memory and delivery, being strictly oratorical]. "Design" and "expression" comprise invention (topics and methods of appeal) and arrangement of parts (the ordering of verse paragraphs); "language" concerns matters of style (the use of tropes and figures and of poetic diction); and "versification" covers prosody and overlaps with stylistic concerns.[47] Pope describes these tours in *An Essay on Criticism*, prefacing their appearance with his precept: "A perfect Judge will *read each Work of Wit / With the same Spirit that its Author writ*" (233–34). Critical discussion of design and expression (235–304), of language (305–36), and of versification (337–83), covering Pope's own poetics, then follows.

Pope gives unflagging attention to the slightest differences in sound and sense insuring that proper words in proper places resonate at all levels of his poetry. This urges Pope's reader to discern fine distinctions in his style, to notice how his words function within a broader context of differentiation, and to relish discovering such connections. The incompetent poet "takes things in the lump" like Scriblerus's "great Genius" in *Peri Bathous*.[48] With surgical precision, Pope sutures together all of his poetic components—his "tours"—to make them work as a unified whole.

To complete this chapter, I would like to comment briefly on Pope's rhetorical use of representative meter: "The *Sound* must seem an *Eccho* to the *Sense*" (365), which belongs to his tour of versification, and suggest how it fits within his broader rhetorical intentions.

Probably the best known criticism of the limitations of representative meter are Samuel Johnson's observations. In his *Life of Cowley*, he states: "Verse can imitate only sound and motion"; and in his *Life of Pope*, he makes a mock substitution of William Broome's translation of the labor of Sisyphus in the *Odyssey*, Book 11, to show how the sound is unrelated to the sense. Johnson appears to have two objections in mind: first, he reacts to the "many wild conceits and imaginary beauties" that Pope's lines have inspired among lesser poets; second, he wishes to separate the intrinsic qualities in poetry from the reader's flights of imagination: "Beauties of this kind are commonly fancied; and when real are technical and nugatory, not to be rejected and not to be solicited."[49]

Regarding Johnson's first objection, Pope and Johnson really seem to be in agreement; in *An Essay on Criticism*, Pope attacks both those who judge and those who write solely "by *Numbers*" (337–59). In response to Johnson's second objection, Pope would agree that the beauties are technical, but not that they are nugatory. This divergence in opinion suggests a rift in their poetics.

Pope places a greater value on technical suggestiveness and a greater reliance on his reader's imagination. The key words are "must seem" ("The *Sound* must seem an *Eccho* to the *Sense*"). To put it another way, Pope is more rhetorical in his formalistic intentions, as we see in his evident concern with the effect of words on his reader:

> True *Wit* is *Nature* to Advantage drest,
> What oft was *Thought*, but ne'er so well *Exprest*,
> *Something*, whose Truth convinc'd at Sight we find,
> That gives us back the Image of our Mind.
>
> (297–300)

Pope's conception of representative verse has many precursors, and he mentions some of them in his digression on the progress of criticism (Part 3.E of the outline).⁵⁰ For one, Pope has modified a line of the Earl of Roscommon in his "An Essay on Translated Verse": "The *sound* is still a *Comment* to the *Sense*."⁵¹ In his letter to Henry Cromwell, 25 November 1710, he discusses representative meter, "a Style of Sound," and quotes examples from Vida; and in Vida's *De Arte Poetica,* we find the seed of Pope's advice in *An Essay on Criticism*: "But as you compose, let no force impel you to add empty material irrelevant to your plan for the sake of words alone; but rather compel your words without exception to subserve your subject matter, weighing with care every sonorous section of your verse."⁵² Pope also knew that these writers were indebted to Dionysius of Halicarnassus, whose words best express Pope's sense of the integral function of representative meter:

> When the same men in the same state of mind report occurrences which they have actually witnessed, they do not use a similar style in describing all of them, but in their very way of putting their words together imitate the things they report, not purposely, but carried away by a natural impulse. Keeping an eye on this principle, the good poet and orator should be ready to imitate the things of which he is giving a verbal description, and to imitate them not only in the choice of words but also in the composition.⁵³

Thus, we can see how knowledgeable Pope was of the historical connections between poets and rhetoricians of the past. In the next chapter, Pope's rhetorical debt to Dionysius of Halicarnassus will be seen to extend much beyond the stylistic issue of representative meter.

3
Design in *Windsor-Forest*

Readers often view the poetic design of *Windsor-Forest* as capricious—and not only readers unfamiliar with conventions of occasional poetry or depreciative of encomium. Moreover, sympathetic critics have found generic identification of the poem troublesome and often its poetic design inexplicable. Some have pointed to family resemblances with Virgilian georgic;[1] while others have viewed the poem as a distinctly eighteenth-century creation. Its obvious departure from the georgic has led some critics to declare the poem one of a new poetic kind—topographical poetry, first seen in John Denham's *Cooper's Hill* (1642); surely, *Windsor-Forest* has many thematic affinities with Denham's poem, as Earl R. Wasserman has shown by way of defining the poem anew—as a cosmological poem.[2] Such resourceful attempts at generic identification, however, have mistaken *Windsor-Forest's* "different dress" for something entirely new and overlooked encomiastic strategies and formal qualities characteristic of the Pindaric ode, a form inviting creative innovation in Pope's time. In exploring the Pindaric nature of the poem, I have discovered that *Windsor-Forest* closely resembles a paradigm for a festival panegyric found in an "Art of Rhetoric" once believed a work of Dionysius of Halicarnassus, a Homeric critic and rhetorician who, as we know, was revered by Pope.

Pope constantly sought in his poetry to take the old and make it better and, in so doing, often metamorphosed generic forms. In this poetic role, John Dryden was one of his great mentors. Dryden's remarks in his preface to *Eleonora* (1692) show how he had experimented generically in a way similar to that of Pope in *Windsor-Forest*: "For the whole poem, though written in that which they call Heroique Verse, is of the Pindarique nature, as well in the Thought as the Expression; and as such, requires the same grains of allowance for it."[3] In this chapter, I will compare *Windsor-Forest* with the pseudo-Dionysian festival panegyric and its poetical kin, the English Pindaric ode.

Poetic Kind

Pope often relies on the literary convention of "poetic kind" as a starting point for the formal construction of an original poem. A poetic kind has a prescribed scope and function and serves as a public declaration of an author's intention; and recognition of a kind ushers in certain expectations of subject matter, arrangement, and manner of expression, enabling Pope to rhetorically engage his reader. The design of *Windsor-Forest* functions on such generic premises.

Though generic expectations restrict the range of a work, they enable an author to employ his rhetorical skills to vary a prescribed formula. When Pope declares in *An Essay on Criticism:* "In ev'ry Work regard the *Writer's End,* / Since none can compass more than they *Intend*" (255–56), he warns his critic not to overlook the implications of poetic kind and to judge an author on what he has done within its restrictions. This is another way of asking a critic to view his poems first as a reader.

The eighteenth-century reader understood that the possibilities of a genre were limited by traditional restraints; and we find this shared understanding generally true of other literary periods: "When an author chooses to write in a given genre, he is not merely responding to the achievements and the pronouncements of others; he himself is issuing certain statements about his art and about art in general. The very act of adopting a literary form, especially a well-established one, implies a respect for the past, or at least for one particular period or school within it."[4] The mere choice of a genre establishes provisionally the poetic shape and extent of a work, calling forth comparison and contrast with other works within its tradition. The critical eye must range not only on the work itself but also on its generic terrain. For without a proper identification of a genre and a familiarity with its tradition, conventional and creatively paradigmatic qualities of a poem are unappreciated, misunderstood as faults, or simply overlooked.

In *A Parallel of Poetry and Painting* (1695), Dryden describes how rhetorical components of poetic design—invention and disposition—must conform to generic conventions within a literate culture:

> Under this head of *Invention* is placed the disposition of the work; to put all things in a beautiful order and harmony, that the whole may be of a piece. The compositions of the painter should be conformable

to the text of ancient authors, to the customs, and the times. And this is exactly the same in Poetry; Homer and Virgil are to be our guides in the Epic; Sophocles and Euripides in Tragedy: in all things we are to imitate the customs and the times of those persons and things which we represent. . . . if the story which we treat be modern, we are to vary the customs, according to the time and the country where the scene of action lies; for this is still to imitate Nature, which is always the same, *though in a different dress* [italics added].⁵

The reader stands on common ground with the poet by recognizing a conventional form in "different dress." Pope does not want his critic to forget this and incur a myopia from close reading:

> Most Criticks, fond of some subservient Art,
> Still make the *Whole* depend upon a *Part*,
> They talk of *Principles*, but Notions prize,
> And All to one lov'd Folly Sacrifice.
>
> (*Essay on Criticism*, 263–66)

The design of a poem is determined by its *whole* rather than its *parts*, by the general rather than the individual. The whole of a poem is, therefore, more than a sum of its parts, which includes an intertextuality shaped by the literary tradition of its *kind* and the context of its cultural moment.

The Reader's Perception

Critics generally have considered the formal design of *Windsor-Forest* its major weakness. Readers, more often, fail to see a design at all, and a reader's blindness to any cohering framework in *Windsor-Forest*, we should readily see, results in a vitiated and idiosyncratic reading. When distinguishing aspects of poetic design become invisible, the reader soon expects that the poem will accomplish what was never its purpose. Its panoramic scenes, shifting rapidly through time and space, might seem only a kaleidoscopic sequence of poetic images, and its poetic voice, rising with sudden crescendos of emotion, might sound terribly erratic and hollow.⁶ Such consequences following a failure to perceive a design in the poem often arise from a neglect of generic tradition and of historical context.

Historically, the poetic design of *Windsor-Forest* has been a favorite target of critics. John Dennis called it "a wretched Rhapsody, not worthy the Observation of a Man of Sense"; according to Johnson's *Dictionary* (1755), a "rhapsody" is "any number of parts joined together, without necessary dependence or natural connection."⁷ In such a way Dennis unmercifully considered the poem a hodge-podge, further asserting in "Observations Upon *Windsor-Forest*" (1717) that it lacked "any Artful and Beautiful Disposition of Parts."⁸ Particularly interesting here, Dennis's criticism reveals his rhetorical training, evident throughout his writings, and exemplifies a Renaissance habit of merging poetics with rhetoric, as "Disposition of Parts" certainly refers to the second part of classical oratory, disposition *(dispositio)*, or arrangement of parts. In his *Life of Pope*, Johnson agreed with Dennis's criticism: "There is this want in most descriptive poems, because as the scenes, which they must exhibit successively, are all subsisting at the same time, the order in which they are shown must by necessity be arbitrary, and more is not to be expected from the last than from the first."⁹

Windsor-Forest would appear a brilliant patchwork to those perceiving a disruption between form and content. The juxtaposition of historical, legendary, and mythical scenes with contemporary sketches of nature begs a bedazzled reader to ferret out analogical correspondences—to perceive unity in multeity, hardly possible when the poem is viewed in textual isolation. It is not surprising, therefore, that the formal design of *Windsor-Forest* remains an inkblot test for modern critics; as Pope tells us, " 'Tis with our *Judgments* as our *Watches*, none / Go just *alike*, yet each believes his own" (*Essay on Criticism*, 9–10). A different poem is seen, depending on where a critic has fixed an eye. Thus, its thematic and topographical alliances with John Denham's *Cooper's Hill* might suggest a loco-descriptive poem; its country setting, hunting tableaux, and Virgilian ending might constitute a georgic; while an unrelenting focus on a theme of *discordia concors* might yield a cosmological poem.¹⁰

On closer examination, however, *Windsor-Forest* resists each of these classifications. Not descriptive enough for a loco-descriptive poem, nor sufficiently instructive for a georgic, and too emotional for the somber reasoning of a cosmological poem, *Windsor-Forest* has acquired a protean aspect which may be more a product of a hermeneutic circle than of true generic intractability.¹¹ Though readings in each of these putative categories are forceful, enlightening, and for the most part compatible, a critical standoff has occurred, and none of these diverging interpretations has emerged as overwhelmingly convincing. The perceptual bias of each approach, as it turns out, is grounded on a generic premise.

The murky compositional history of *Windsor-Forest* might partially account for such critical uncertainty about its design; and, perhaps, Pope's free use of fragments in different poems might subvert a reader's confidence in the structural integrity of the poem.[12] Whatever be the case, an examination of how *Windsor-Forest* operates on the level of discourse—as a rhetorical presentation—would support a view that poetic composition for Pope proceeds deliberately from, not intuitively toward, a controlling design.

The controlling design of the poem derives from an initial choice of genre; and the poem becomes a matter of conscious planning and consideration of form, method, and function. Generic examination of *Windsor-Forest* enables us to delineate an overlooked domain of poetic craftsmanship that includes Pope's rhetorical art. His kind of discourse, emerging from an initial choice of genre, and his method of composition, proceeding according to a controlling design, ultimately determine both form and content. That is, rhetorical concerns direct Pope's poetic hammer. A rhetorical perspective sets the poem in a context that enables us to examine, more fruitfully, Pope's poetic technique.

Festival Panegyric

The descriptive, didactic, and philosophical strains in *Windsor-Forest*, though important and seductive in their prominence, are secondary to the explicit purpose of the poem, which is public praise of the recent achievements of George Granville, Baron Lansdowne, dedicatee of the poem.[13] As we shall see, *Windsor-Forest* has the encomiastic intentions of a panegyric in the Pindaric tradition.

In a panegyrical ode, exuberant lavishings of praise are expected, requiring the reader's recognition and acceptance of them for successful appreciation and understanding. In his preface to *Miscellanies in Verse and Prose* (1693), Dennis writes:

> How I have succeeded I must leave to the Readers to judge; yet not to every Reader. For the Pindarick way, if you'l give credit to a great Master, is dangerous both to Writer and Reader. The first must have

some qualities at the time of writing, which are rarely to be found together, as Precipitation and Address, Boldness and Decency, Sublimeness and Clearness, Fury and Sense; the last must have Fancy to see his flights, and Skill to judge of their Art.[14]

Certainly, many in Pope's audience were averse to the encomiastic posture of panegyric and, jaded by a constant barrage of mediocre panegyric, would have been blinded or dulled to Pope's ingenious use of encomiastic method in *Windsor-Forest*. His poem faced a severe test in attempting a kind of poetry particularly attractive to poetasters of his time. Public acceptance of the poem was further complicated by controversy over the peace treaty itself, unfortunately subjecting the poem to praise or censure on factional grounds: "The Peace became the political test of the hour, and every artifice of prose and verse was employed to appease public opinion."[15]

Pope had high hopes for *Windsor-Forest*. "I might then hope," he writes to Lord Lansdowne in a letter of 10 January 1712/13, "that many years hence the world might read, in conjunction with your name, that of [my own]."[16] The death of Queen Anne, ending the Stuart reign, quelled his political hopes; and the mixed public reception of *Windsor-Forest* might explain why he never again composed a poem "of a Pindarique nature."[17] He did not abandon panegyrical techniques completely, however, as we find him inverting them for censure in his later satires; but Pope's revised attitude toward encomiastic poetry is evident in *Peri Bathous* (1727): "Of all our Productions none is so short-liv'd as the *Dedication* and *Panegyric*, which are often but the *Praise of a Day*, and become by the next, utterly useless, improper, indecent, and false."[18] Perhaps his disappointment with the success of *Windsor-Forest* accounts for the bittersweet tone of these words.

In 1704 a Latin translation by John Hudson of an *Art of Rhetoric* was published in London and, as was usual then, mistakenly included among the writings of Dionysius of Halicarnassus (an erroneous attribution of authorship continued even into this century). Whether this edition, or an earlier Greek text, was available to Pope between 1704 and 1713, the gestation period for *Windsor-Forest*, I have not been able to confirm. The contemporary importance, however, of the Dionysius rhetoric and of another rhetoric by Menander of Laodicea to the theory of panegyric has been noted by James D. Garrison: "Although these two authorities often appear side by side in Renaissance discussions of panegyric, the Dionysius rhetoric was probably the more influential, at least in England."[19] We do know that Dionysius of Halicarnassus found a place among Pope's list of esteemed writers in *An Essay on Criticism;* also, in his preface to *The Iliad,* Pope praises "his treatise of the *Composition of Words*" and cites the author throughout his translation.[20]

We might assume that Pope would have considered the Dionysius rhetoric genuine. Therefore, it appears more than coincidental that the topics and order of *Windsor-Forest* closely resemble a paradigm for a festival panegyric in the Dionysius rhetoric, described in detail in chapter 1 of the work. George Kennedy has outlined this paradigm for us:

> The panegyric, for example, is to begin with praise of the god who presides over the festival, listing his attributes. Then comes praise of the city where the festival is located: its location, origin, founder, history, size, beauty, power, public buildings, rivers, legends, and history. Other festivals may be compared unfavorably. Then comes the program of the festival which includes music and literature and one which is purely athletic. The prize is then described and praised and can also be compared with other prizes. Finally there is to be praise of the emperor or king or others in charge.[21]

It is possible that Pope drew his design for the poem from this paradigm, converting its Greek city into the English countryside of Windsor Forest. A similar conversion already had been made in a letter to him from William Wycherly (5 November 1705):

> But I know your Charity always exceeds your Revenge, so that I will not despair of seeing you, who, in return to your inviting me to your Forest, invite you to my Forest, the Town; where the Beasts that inhabit, tame or wild, of long Ears or Horns, pursue one another either out of Love or Hatred. You may have the Pleasure to see one Pack of Bloodhounds pursue another Herd of Brutes, to bring each other to their Fall, which is their whole Sport: Or, affect a less bloody Chace, you may see a Pack of Spaniels, called *Lovers,* in hot pursuit of a two-legg'd *Vixen,* who only flies the whole low'd Pack to be singled out by one Dog, who runs mute to catch her up sooner from the rest, as they are making Noise, to the Loss of their Game. In fine, this is the Time for all sorts of Sport in the Town, when those of the Country cease; therefore leave your Forest of Beasts, for ours of Brutes, call'd Men, who now in full Cry, (pack'd by the Court or County) run down in the House of Commons, a deserted horned Beast of the Court, to the satisfaction of their Spectators.[22]

Wycherly metaphorically condemns London at the expense of the country. In *Windsor-Forest,* Pope inverts Wycherly's playful condemnation, proclaiming the merits of Windsor Forest by association to its equally esteemed metropolitan counterpart. Thus, the celebration of peace after the Treaty of Utrecht, in which Granville played a substantial role, is the festive occasion for *Windsor-Forest*; and Windsor Forest becomes a sacred arena for ritual contests, historical, mythic, legendary, and contemporary.

A detailed comparison of *Windsor-Forest* with the paradigm for the festival panegyric described in the Dionysius rhetoric reveals striking similarities. I shall follow Kennedy's outline of the paradigm [in brackets] in making this comparison:[23]

I. ["The panegyric . . . is to begin with praise of the god who presides over the festival, listing his attributes."] The poem opens with an invocation to the muses of Windsor Forest on behalf of Granville, the presiding judge (1–6):

> Unlock your Springs, and open all your Shades.
> *Granville* commands: Your Aid O Muses bring!
> (4–5)

II. ["Then comes praise of the city where the festival is located:"] A simile compares Windsor Forest to Eden (7–10).[24]

    A. ["its location,"] We are given an extended pictorial and mythic description of the Windsor countryside (11–42):

> Here Hills and Vales, the Woodland and the Plain,
> Here Earth and Water seem to strive again.
> (11–12)

    B. ["origin, founder, history,"] Windsor is described historically as a wasteland under William I and his heirs (43–84) and seen in its subsequent development to its present state (85–92):

> Succeeding Monarchs heard the Subjects Cries,
> Nor saw displeas'd the peaceful Cottage rise.
> (85–86)

    C. ["size, beauty, power,"] These elements are displayed in picturesque hunting and fishing tableaux within which are interposed wartime analogues. A mythic contexture further enhances these activites as triumphal games, with a reference to Queen Anne as Diana's worldly equal (93–170):

> Nor envy *Windsor!* since thy Shades have seen
> As bright a Goddess, and as chast a Queen;
> Whose Care, like hers, protects the Sylvan Reign,
> The Earth's fair Light, and Empress of the Main.
>
> (161–64)

D. ["public buildings, rivers, legends, and history."] The Ovidian episode of Lodona (171–218) functions as an emotional prologue to praise of the Thames, "great Father of the *British* Floods" (219–34).

E. ["Other festivals may be compared unfavorably."] While *Windsor-Forest* celebrates the occasion of the Treaty of Utrecht, in which Granville achieved his glory, there have been other similar occasions for praise, in which "happy" men, such as Scipio Africanus, Titus Pomponius (Atticus), and Sir William Trumball, have succeeded their political triumph with country retirement (235–58):

> Such was the Life great *Scipio* once admir'd,
> Thus *Atticus*, and *Trumbal* thus retir'd.[25]
>
> (257–58)

III. ["Then comes the program of the festival which includes music and literature"] The achievements of Cowley and Denham, as former poets of Windsor Forest, are heralded as models for Granville (259–90):

> Who now shall charm the Shades where *Cowley* strung
> His living Harp, and lofty *Denham* sung?
> But hark! the Groves rejoice, the Forest rings!
> Are these reviv'd? or is it *Granville* sings?
>
> (279–82)

["and one which is purely athletic."] Surrey is portrayed as a jousting knight (291–98):

> Here noble *Surrey* felt the sacred Rage,
> *Surrey*, the *Granville* of a former Age:
> Matchless his Pen, victorious was his Lance;
> Bold in the Lists, and graceful in the Dance.
>
> (291–94)

IV. ["The prize is then described and praised and can also be compared with other prizes."] The peaceful reign of Queen Anne, the symbolic prize, is compared with the less fortunate reigns of Edward III, Henry VI, and Charles I, monarchs associated with Windsor Forest (299–328).[26] "Old Father Thames" then enters and personifies other rivers that have not experienced such splendorous peace. His speech attains the highest emotional level of the poem with its visionary praise of the British realm (329–422):

> Hail Sacred *Peace!* hail long-expected Days,
> That *Thames's* Glory to the Stars shall raise!
>
> (355–56)

> The Time shall come, when free as Seas or Wind
> Unbounded *Thames* shall flow for all Mankind,
> Whole Nations enter with each swelling Tyde,
> And Seas but join the Regions they divide.
>
> (397–400)

V. ["Finally there is to be praise of the emperor or king or others in charge."] The poem concludes as briefly as it began, with praise of Granville, presiding over the festival, and a personal coda by the poet, echoing Virgil at the end of his *Georgics* (423–34):[27]

> Here cease thy Flight, nor with unhallow'd Lays
> Touch the fair Fame of *Albion's* Golden Days.
> The Thoughts of Gods let *Granville's* Verse recite,
> And bring the Scenes of opening Fate to Light.
>
> (423–26)

The significance of this comparison is threefold: (1) that this standard model for a festival panegyric was widely known, and that this model or one like it was probably known to Pope; (2) that *Windsor-Forest* conforms closely to the paradigm of the Dionysius rhetoric; and (3) that the design of *Windsor-Forest*, in possessing such a rhetorical character, therefore, must rely as much on convention as internal coherence for overall unity. Furthermore, such a reliance on convention begs that critical attention be shifted to Pope's manipulation of voice and argument as the imaginative center of the poem.

The English Pindaric

The panegyric described in the Dionysius rhetoric challenges the technical skills of an orator. Through fluctuations of emotion and shifts in traditional topics, he must engage his listener, hold his attention, and anticipate when his listener's attention will flag. The emotional character and topical movement of this paradigm also resembles the design of Pindaric odes in the late seventeenth and early eighteenth centuries, which were poetical forms of panegyric. This is not surprising, since the Dionysius rhetoric and the later English Pindaric ode have a common origin: "These topics [of the Dionysius rhetoric] are found in various odes of Pindar, which are general models for the type."[28]

In the early eighteenth century, Pindar was associated with the greater ode, which was considered to be a major literary form alongside tragedy and epic. As generic forms, tragedy and epic already had well-established identities, and critics attempted to do the same for the more nebulous character of the greater ode. In his preface to *The Court of Death* (1695), Dennis distinguishes between the greater ode and heroic poetry:

> The Design of the Ode (I mean upon great occasions) is, like that of Heroic Poetry, to move the Reader, and cause in him admiration. Now by Heroic Poetry, the readers mind is exalted gradually, with a more sedate and compos'd Majesty; but the Ode, by reason of the shortness of its compass, is oblig'd to fly into transport at first, and to make use immediately of all its fury, and its most violent efforts, or else it would want time to work its effect.[29]

In his *Dictionary*, Johnson recognizes a commonly held distinction between the greater and the lesser ode: "The ode is either of the greater or the less kind. The less is characterized by sweetness and ease; the greater by sublimity, rapture, and quickness of transition." Pindar was highly esteemed by Pope, as well as by two of Pope's favorite authors, Horace and Quintilian.[30] Pope manages to incorporate the emotional verve and sweeping thematic range of the greater ode into *Windsor-Forest*, with a *pathos* similar to that which Longinus sees in Pindar and Sophocles, who with "Impetuosity . . . like a devouring Flame seize and set on Fire whatever comes in [their] way."[31]

As seen in our comparison above, the topical structure of *Windsor-Forest* conforms closely to a festival panegyric, even granting the unique, imaginative texture that Pope gives it. Pope never attempted a greater ode, but was conscious of the rich poetic material that it could provide him for his original poems. He was also very aware of the protean nature of the form and of the many experiments with it that his predecessors and contemporaries had attempted. By the early eighteenth century, the ode had acquired certain formal characteristics of either irregular measure or stanzaic pattern. Though the pentameter couplets and verse paragraphs of *Windsor-Forest* seem far removed from the more lyrical, irregular stanzaic patterns of English odes based on Pindaric models, as we shall see later in this chapter, Pope employs the rhetorical strategies of English Pindaric odes in his poem.

In the early eighteenth century, there was still no consensus about what an English Pindaric ode should be. In fact, the nature of the ode remained a part of a greater rhetorical controversy throughout Europe. The "lucidity" of direct expression was preferred by many over the "turgidity" of the irregular ode.[32] Despite conflicting rhetorical attitudes, it was generally accepted that Pindaric measures could not be successfully written in English and that the spirit of Pindar could not be achieved through a slavish imitation of his metrics, as Robert Shafer remarks: "For an essential element of Pindar—his complex and conscious art—will be quite lost if any attempt is made to achieve merely his 'spirit' in free or irregular verse. Indeed, fundamental to Pindar's quality is the achievement of his lyric enthusiasm within the restraining limits of a difficult and complicated verse form."[33] Pope's early fidelity to the rhetorical views of his Greek and Roman masters probably had much to do with his never attempting the excessive ornamentation of Pindaric forms then in vogue.

Indecisiveness over Pindaric form becomes even more apparent into the 1720s in the example of John Dyer, who published *Grongar Hill* "in at least three different miscellanies, with differing texts," the first two in tetrameter couplets and the last in Pindaric form.[34] Whatever consensus of form the irregular Pindaric ode had acquired in the previous decades was now waning: "Dyer's revision indicates the extent to which the traditional Pindarick had lost caste."[35] According to Geoffrey Tillotson, Pope never suffered from equivocation over his measures: "When poets like Thomson, Young, Dyer, and to a less extent John Phillips, wanted to describe landscape or skyscape more often than their fellows, they were wise to break away from the couplet into blank verse. In any case they could not have used the couplet as Pope used it. Pope was never tempted to break away from the couplet for any major work because he could make it do all that he wanted."[36] It appears, however, that in the writing of *Windsor-Forest*, Pope was tempted to meddle with his couplet form.

A comparison of the 1712 holograph of *Windsor-Forest* with the version published a year later indicates a great amount of revision, suggesting that the youthful Pope may have experienced some of the equivocation that Dyer later did in composing *Grongar Hill*.[37] There are hints in the 1712 holograph that earlier versions of the poem may have appeared even more different from the published version. The 1712 holograph contains three triplets and four alexandrines. Except for the triplet interlined in the 1712 holograph, triplets are placed at the end of verse paragraphs. Also, as Schmitz remarks: "Each of these alexandrines is the terminal verse in a poetical paragraph, a device drawn directly from Dryden's practice."[38] But such placement of the alexandrine was also customary in English Pindaric odes, where the occurrence of an alexandrine or triplet often matched a crescendo of emotion and signaled a change of theme, time, or place. In his published version of *Windsor-Forest*, Pope regularized his verse, eliminating all but one alexandrine (218).

Efforts toward regularization also may be seen among earlier writers attempting odes in a Pindaric vein. In his preface to the *Sylvae*, John Dryden benignly criticizes the verse irregularities of Abraham Cowley's Pindaric imitations:

> But if I may be allowed to speak my mind modestly, and without injury to his sacred ashes, somewhat of the purity of English, somewhat of more equal thoughts, somewhat of sweetness in the numbers, in one word, somewhat of a finer turn and more lyrical verse is yet wanting. . . . Since Pindar was the prince of lyric poets; let me have leave to say, that, in imitating him, our numbers should for the most part be lyrical: for variety, or rather where the majesty of the thought requires it, they may be stretched to the English heroic of five feet, and to the French Alexandrine of six.[39]

More balance and "sweetness," urges Dryden, the very qualities for which Waller is praised in Dryden and Sir William Soames's translation of Boileau's *The Art of Poetry*.[40] Dryden's discontent with Cowley's lyrics reflects a deepening faith in the heroic couplet as a more adequate vehicle to achieve Pindaric effects. In his *Epistle Dedicatory of the Rival Ladies*, Dryden suggests the avenue to be taken: "This sweetness of Mr. Waller's lyric poesy was afterwards followed in the epic by Sir John Denham, in his *Cooper's Hill*, a poem which your Lordship knows for the majesty of style."[41] Dryden's comment is echoed in Pope's couplet in *An Essay on Criticism:* "And praise the *Easie Vigor* of a Line / Where *Denham's* Strength, and *Waller's* Sweetness join" (360–61). In *Windsor-Forest*, Pope completes the circle by joining Cowley and Denham, who each had found Windsor Forest a common ground for his own lyrical inspiration.

Thus, in his preface to the *Sylvae*, Dryden disdains the artificially abrupt transitions of Cowley's odes. What Dryden himself seeks is "a finer turn" where "the sound of the former must slide gently into that which follows; without leaping from one extream into another . . . like the shadowings of a Picture, which fall by degrees into a darker colour."[42] How to accomplish such "shadowings" remains a prosodic experiment for Dryden. His four Horatian lyrics in the *Sylvae* are rendered in four distinct ways.[43] His longer ode, *Threnodia Augustalis: A Funeral-Pindarique Poem Sacred to the Happy Memory of King Charles II*, employs an irregular Pindaric form, with lines ranging from two to six feet. The vatic entrance of the river Thames in *Windsor-Forest:* "In that blest Moment, from his Oozy Bed / Old Father Thames advanc'd his rev'rend Head" (329–30) owes a specific debt to a similar application of the classical trope in Dryden's poem: "While starting from his Oozy Bed, / Th'asserted Ocean rears his reverend Head."[44] Another irregular Pindaric ode included in the *Sylvae*, *To the Pious Memory of the Accomplisht Young Lady Mrs Anne Killegrew*, features common topics of panegyric: an invocation to an apotheosized laudandus; her origins; her ancestry; a praise of attributes, legends, and history.[45] Though conforming in their topical character to traditional panegyric, Dryden's Pindaric odes reveal a great amount of prosodic experimentation.

Another effort promoting neoclassical regularity occurs in Edward Bysshe's *Art of English Poetry*, published in 1702, in which he limits the use of alexandrines. He allows them only when they conclude "an Episode in an Heroick Poem," "a Triplet and full Sence together," or "the Stanzas of Lyrick or Pindarick Odes; Examples of which are frequently seen in Dryden and others."[46] According to A. Dwight Culler, "Pope knew and used" Bysshe's "bedside" book, which was reprinted three times by 1710.[47] In his letter to Walsh of 22 October 1706, Pope declares his objection to any but the strictest use of alexandrines: "I would also object to the Irruption of *Alexandrine* Verses of twelve syllables, which I think should never be allow'd but when some remarkable Beauty or Propriety in them attones for the Liberty: Mr. *Dryden* has been too free of these, especially in his latter Works. I am of the same opinion as to *Triple Rhimes*."[48]

In 1706 William Congreve published his *Discourse on the Pindarique Odes,* in the same year that he read a manuscript of Pope's *Pastorals*.[49] In his *Discourse,* Congreve disavows the myth of Pindar's irregularity and appeals for internal coherence in Pindaric imitations: "There is nothing more regular than the Odes of Pindar, both as to the exact observation of the Measures and Numbers of his Stanzas and Verses, and the perpetual Coherence of his Thoughts. For tho' his Digressions are frequent, and his Transitions sudden, yet there is ever some secret Connexion, which tho' not always appearing to the Eye, never fails to communicate itself to the Understanding of the Reader."[50] In refuting the artificial, lyrical abandon of Cowley, the reigning poet of only a generation before, Congreve affords a bold, new prospect for Pope, then in the early stages of composing *Windsor-Forest.*

Congreve's *A Pindarique Ode Humbly offer'd to the QUEEN On the Victorious Progress of HER MAJESTY's Arms, under the Conduct of the DUKE OF MARLBOROUGH* bears a thematic likeness to *Windsor-Forest,* as hinted in its sententious title. The poem has a triadic structure of strophe, antistrophe, and epode, with lines from three to six feet in reflexive and in irregular rhyme patterns. Overlooking metrical differences with *Windsor-Forest,* we might still compare Pope's lines: "Rich Industry sits smiling on the Plains, / And Peace and Plenty tell, a STUART reigns" (41–42) with those of Congreve, which also depict an end to tyranny by royal ascendency:

> For now is come the promis'd Hour,
> When Justice shall have Pow'r;
> Justice to Earth restor'd!
> Again *Astrea* Reigns![51]

Despite his own example of Pindaric verse, Congreve allows for further revision of the ode form, as he remarks in his *Discourse*: "I hope I shall not be so misunderstood, as to have it thought that I pretend to give an exact Copy of Pindar in this ensuing Ode; or that I look upon it as a Pattern for his Imitators for the future: Far from such Thoughts, I have only given an Instance of what is practicible, and am sensible that I am as distant from the Force and Elevation of Pindar, as others have hitherto been from the Harmony and Regularity of his Numbers."[52] Interestingly, Congreve reflects here a confused conception of Pindar arising primarily from the influence of Cowley's imitations.[53] The choric structure of Pindar's poems had been recognized long before by Dionysius of Halicarnassus; and even as recently as the publishing date of 1640, Ben Jonson had employed a strophic form in *To the Immortal Memory and Friendship of That Noble Pair, Sir Lucius Cary and Sir H. Morison*.[54]

You may recall Dryden's prefatory remarks to his *Eleonora*, quoted at the beginning of this chapter, declaring his heroic verse poem written in the spirit but not the form of Pindar. English Pindaric odes had also been attempted in heroic couplets. The poems of Richard Crashaw, Cowley's fellow poet, had already set a precedent for composing odes in pentameter couplets.[55] In a letter to Henry Cromwell dated 17 December 1710, Pope lists a number of favorite poems found in Crashaw's *Delights of the Muses*. About these poems, he writes: "To speak of his *Numbers* is a little difficult, they are so various and irregular, and mostly Pindarick: 'tis evident his heroic Verse . . . is carelessly made up; but one may imagine from what it now is, that had he taken more care, it had been musical and pleasing enough, not extreamly majestic, but sweet."[56] Among secular poems found in this same collection are several odes written in pentameter couplets. Of these couplet odes, *In the praise of the Spring*, based on Virgil's *Georgics*, anticipates a few of the topics in *Windsor-Forest*.[57]

Thus, Pope must have realized that English attempts at the Pindaric ode left much to be improved on. For Pope, this period of rediscovery and re-creation of the English Pindaric ode offered him an invitation to experiment with its generic intentions in *Windsor-Forest*. Though he reveals a conventional attitude toward Pindar in his *Temple of Fame*, calling him "some furious Prophet . . . Irregularly great," Pope had great admiration for him, telling Spence in 1736: "The works of Pindar that remain to us are by no means equal to his great character. His Dithyrambics, which were his best things, are lost, and all that is left of his works, being on the same subject, is the more apt to be tiresome."[58] For a young poet eager to establish himself by first attempting and succeeding with classical models, *Windsor-Forest* might stand as his unacknowledged tribute to Pindar: "I had once a design of giving a taste of all the most celebrated Greek poets by translating one of their best short pieces, at least from each of them: a hymn of Homer, another of Callimachus, an ode or two from Pindar, and so on. And [I] should have done so had not I engaged in the translation of the *Iliad*."⁵⁹ Though unlike Pindar's "best short pieces," *Windsor-Forest* possesses many rhetorical qualities "of the Pindarique nature," as we shall now see.

Rhetorical Design

As with Pindaric odes, *Windsor-Forest* has "a distinguishable beginning, middle, and end."⁶⁰ Returning to our outline comparison of Pope's poem with the festival panegyric of the Dionysius rhetoric, we see that *Windsor-Forest* has a distinctive opening (Part I) and closing (Part V). The middle parts function as explicative praise of the glory of Windsor Forest (Part II), of Lord Granville (Part III), and of Queen Anne's reign (Part IV).

The structure of the poem may be further elaborated with a comparison to that of the epideictic mode found in *Rhetorica Ad Herennium*. The *Ad Herennium* author describes three parts in this mode, which conform with the topical arrangement of *Windsor-Forest*: the Introduction (Part I), the Division (Parts II, III, and IV), and the Conclusion (Part V).⁶¹ He establishes the topical order of the Division as follows:

> We shall set forth the things we intend to praise or censure; then recount the events, observing their precise sequence and chronology, so that one may understand what the person under discussion did and with what prudence and caution. But it will first be necessary to set forth his virtues or faults of character, and then to explain how, such being his character, he has used the advantages or disadvantages, physical or of external circumstances.⁶²

The order and topics of praise are next, which "we must keep when portraying a life"; first to be shown are (1) external circumstances: "the ancestors of whom he is sprung"; next, (2) physical advantages, such as "impressiveness and beauty . . . exceptional strength and agility . . . continual good health"; and then, again, other (3) external circumstances, such as his uses of wealth, power, and "titles to fame," his feuds, and his friendships.⁶³

Reviewing Part II of our outline which contains explicative praise for Windsor Forest (7–258), we now can see how Pope has combined the topical order of both the Dionysius rhetoric and the *Ad Herennium* models: first described are (1) external circumstances: (A) location and (B) origin, founder, and history;

next (2) physical advantages: (C) size, beauty, and power; and then again, other (3) external circumstances: (D) rivers, legends, and history and (E) other festivals.

Proceeding as a celebration, the poem relies primarily on emotional appeal *(pathos)* for reader engagement, whereas appeals through logic *(logos)* and character *(ethos)* play secondary roles; we see the poet's character and rational appeals are subsumed by his projected emotional attitudes. Moreover, even though praise often entails a gnomic element of advice and caution, didactic purpose does not drive the poem.[64] Though critics have emphasized its didactic function, *Windsor-Forest* does not make a serious effort to persuade its audience. The occasion of national victory has polarized many of its British readers and prepared them to receive a public display sympathetically. In part, the success of encomiastic poetry must rely on the predilection of its audience, which can be precariously capricious. If the occasion for praise is not sufficiently compelling, as was the case for Whig readers opposing the treaty, the poem fails on its own terms. In addition, if a later reader detaches it from its historical context, that reader will lose sight of its encomiastic purpose, for it is emotional appeal that often informs Pope's choice of language and imagery. We might describe elements of the poem as cohering histrionically in a dramatic and a ceremonial way, striving to be a synchronic and diachronic convergence of occasion and convention, comparable, for example, to a particular performance of a masque or a ballet.

The opening of *Windsor-Forest* has two immediate purposes: first, to dispose its reader for what is to follow, striking an emotional chord on which the poem will move; and second, to declare its subject matter. Brevity characterizes the opening (Part I) as well as the closing (Part V) of the poem. By employing recognizable associations of subject matter, the opening seeks to evoke an appropriate emotional response from its reader, which sets the stage for the lyrical narrative that follows. Finally, the poem concludes by referring back to the original subject, so that a reader may place in perspective the particular emotional state that induced the poet to poetry, thus amplifying the significance of the occasion.

In the Dionysius rhetoric, we are told the opening should begin with praise of the god of the festival, enumerating his attributes (Part I). The muses of Windsor Forest invoked within the first six lines comprise this element of praise, though specific mention of their attributes are missing:

> Thy Forests, *Windsor!* and thy green Retreats,
> At once the Monarch's and the Muse's Seats,
> Invite my Lays. Be present, Sylvan Maids!
> Unlock your Springs, and open all your Shades.
> *Granville* commands: Your Aid O Muses bring!
> What Muse for *Granville* can refuse to sing?
>
> (1–6)

The 1712 holograph, however, does list each deity and place of power:

> Chast Goddess of the Woods,
> Nymphs of the Vales, and Naiads of the Floods,
> Lead me, oh lead me thro' the Bow'rs and Glades.[65]

In the published version, these lines have been compressed into the invocation: "Be present, Sylvan Maids!" (3). Pope's abbreviation succeeds in accomplishing three tasks: first, it reduces the classical character of the local deities and further nationalizes them; second, it suppresses the effusiveness of the poet importuning the deities to "Lead me, oh lead me"; and third, it simplifies and domesticates a hierarchy of power by compression. Commanded by Granville, the poet more confidently summons the Sylvan Maids to duty, "Unlock your Springs, and open all your Shades" (4), and signals his audience to a successive flooding of emotion and expansion of imagery.

In addition, the poet establishes his role as mediator between Granville and the Windsor muses, as well as between the people of England and the regal and the mythic powers of the sacred ground of Windsor Forest, seeking to protect the forest from the temporary hubbub of England on a dual level of monarch and muse. The poetical relations binding the poem from within (Granville, Windsor muses, and Windsor Forest) and the rhetorical relations binding it from without (laudator and listener) resonate with the ambiguous symbolism of Windsor Forest, which serves as a residential mansion, on a metaphorical level as the "seat" of the muses and on a literal level as the "retreat" of the monarch. In describing the forest as "at once the Monarch's and the Muse's Seats," Pope accomplishes an effective synthesis.

Our laudator employs the first of two subjective rhetorical foils in elevating his own abilities to match the subject matter.[66] The words "*Granville* commands" (5) both subordinate the poet and summon him to speak. Delegated by authority, he can sing Granville's praise and all that it entails.[67] Given sanction to uplift himself into an emotional level of exaltation, the laudator can petition the power of the Windsor muses, proclaim the various achievements of England's heroes and deities, and essay the splendor of Windsor Forest. In effect, Granville has been apotheosized into power, uniting political with poetical authority. By naming him prominently twice, the poet provides a concrete climax with a *name cap* for these lines.[68] The opening also culminates with a rhetorical question *(ratiocinatio)*[69] to emphasize further the poet's subservience: "What Muse for *Granville* can refuse to sing?" (6). Such a figure signals a shift of theme, while at the same time inducing from the audience sympathy for the laudator's difficult task. Thus, the opening of the poem foreshadows the subjects of praise and the topical order of the Division of *Windsor-Forest*: Windsor Forest (Part II), Lord Granville (Part III), and Queen Anne (Part IV).

Praise directed at Windsor Forest, the location of Pope's imaginative festival (Part II.A), follows in the second paragraph, and a definite change in tone signals the beginning of the Division. The first couplet resembles the tone and syntax of familiar speech, providing a relaxation calculated to contrast with the emphatic opening lines:

> The Groves of *Eden*, vanish'd now so long,
> Live in Description, and look green in Song.
>
> (7–8)

The name cap "*Eden*" clues a reader to subsequent thematic play. The entire paragraph functions as a *priamel*, or *praeambulum:* "a focusing or selecting device in which one or more terms serve as a foil for the point of particular interest."[70] The poet, therefore, consciously maneuvers his audience with this opening device.

The city of the Dionysius rhetoric has been transformed into the countryside of Windsor Forest, yet a subtle association remains between city, as a symbol of political power, and country, as a symbol of poetical power. The poet achieves this association, in Congreve's words, through "some secret Connexion, which tho' not always appearing to the Eye, never fails to communicate itself to the Understanding of the Reader."[71] The alliteration of "*Granville*" with "Groves of Eden" links the first with the second paragraph. The name *Granville* implicitly bears an etymological, Norman association to place in the French *grand ville*, meaning a great town. This allows the poet a denotative transition through a connotative channel of meaning.[72] Thus, as Dryden urges, "like the shadowings of a Picture, which fall by degrees into a darker colour," *Eden* as a place name related both in sound and sense to *Granville* becomes a *name foil* for Windsor Forest.[73]

At the beginning of the second verse paragraph (Part II), the laudator introduces a second type of subjective rhetorical foil through recognition of his own limitations: "were my Breast inspir'd with equal Flame" (9).[74] Windsor Forest, he argues, matches the beauty of Eden, which a sufficiently pious and sympathetically patriotic reader would readily understand as impossible to express. The poet must do his duty, however. Therefore, the second paragraph (7–42) focuses on the location itself, attempting to describe the majesty, industry, peace, and plenty of Windsor Forest. Name foils of places *(Eden, India,* and *Olympus)* and of deities *(Pan, Pomona, Flora,* and *Ceres,* who also bless the landscape of Windsor) enable the poet to amplify the local harmony of the forest into a universal emblem: "as the World, harmoniously confus'd" (14). The chauvinistic zeal of the lines also marks an emotional crescendo, appropriately capped with "a STUART reigns" (42), signaling a strophic shift in the next paragraph and again, of course, referring to Queen Anne.

The origin of the festival, its founder, and its history follow in the Dionysius panegyric (Part II.B); similarly, Pope imaginatively incorporates the New Forest of Hampshire into the *mythos* of Windsor.[75] The third verse paragraph (43–92) begins with a diminuendo achieved by an abrupt movement into the past: "Not thus the Land appear'd in Ages past" (43). The New Forest of Hampshire, serving as a well known historical example, in effect functions as a gnome and, therefore, becomes a foil for further praise of present day Windsor Forest.[76] The land was originally a gloomy waste, lawless and unproductive. The founder "Our haughty *Norman*" (63), being a subtle foil to the Norman name *Granville* and an obvious one to his legendary archetype "Proud *Nimrod*" (61), functions primarily as a foil to Queen Anne, mentioned in the final line of the preceding verse paragraph, "And Peace and Plenty tell, a STUART reigns" (42), and alluded to in the subsequent lines ending this verse paragraph, "Fair *Liberty, Britannia's* Goddess, rears / Her Chearful Head, and leads the golden Years" (91–92). Thus, in this verse paragraph, we see a triadic movement build gradually toward another emotional crescendo by introducing diachronically a mythic pattern of falling and rising, which will be repeated in the seasonal regeneration that follows in the next five paragraphs (93–164); from the tableau of a desolated waste in "a Despotick Reign" (43–84), the topic turns to those "Succeeding Monarchs" who nurtured a regeneration (85–90), and then stands with an epodic crescendo of Windsor Forest's present prosperity (91–92).

In the 1712 holograph, the third verse paragraph (43–92) ended with a patriotic flourish which demanded revision in the published version. The penultimate couplet of this paragraph in the holograph was deleted in 1713, probably for its ambiguous references to William III and to incumbent George I, England's two "foreign masters":

> Oh may no more a foreign Master's Rage
> With Wrongs yet Legal, curse a future Age!
> Still Spread, fair Liberty! thy heav'nly Wings,
> Breathe Plenty on the Fields, and Fragrance on the Springs.[77]

Pope succeeds in maintaining his nationalistic pitch, nevertheless, by deleting the final alexandrine of the 1712 holograph and personifying the familiar symbol "Liberty," whose gender now brings to mind Queen Anne:

> Fair *Liberty, Britannia's* Goddess, rears
> Her chearful Head, and leads the golden Years.
> (91–92)

The lament and gnomic climax of the deleted couplet, "Oh may no more a foreign Master's Rage / With wrongs yet Legal, curse a future Age!" frustrated the swelling crescendo of emotion rising into the next verse paragraph (93–110). By deleting the alexandrine and gnomic couplet and including a name cap—"Fair *Liberty, Britannia's* Goddess"—Pope sustains the emotional pitch and signals another movement.

Moreover, Pope's patriotic personification of *Liberty* (91–92) enhances the published version with greater relevance for its royal and public audience. Indeed, the rhetorical strategy purposefully employs two common themes of restoration and of limitation frequently found in panegyric.[78] In *Windsor-Forest* the theme of restoration addresses the English audience by eliciting pride in the glory of Windsor Forest, representing for them the British nation and its beneficent majesty. The theme of limitation reminds the monarch of the dangers of tyrannical excess.

In the occupational list that follows, the endeavors of fowler, shooter, fisherman, and deerhunter act as foils to recent military victories and to the blights of the past:

> The Youth rush eager to the Sylvan War;
> Swarm o'er the Lawns, the Forest Walks surround,
> Rowze the fleet Hart, and chear the opening Hound.
>
> (148–50)

The visual concreteness of these images embellishes the present glory of Windsor Forest and, in turn, more forcefully shows what the deleted gnomic couplet only told.

In these five paragraphs (93–164), themes of size, beauty, and power are elaborated through a close description of the triumphal games of Windsor Forest (Part II.C). A sense of physical proximity is required to match the poet's thematic purpose. In the preceding paragraphs, a rhetorical transparency allowed the poet a compressed historical overview, and a fluctuation between emotional tension and relaxation engaged his reader through these paragraphs. To achieve the visualization of the succeeding paragraphs, the rhetorical opacity of expression increases, vivifying by contrast the scenes for the reader. Furthermore, the poetic voice shifts from narrative to direct speech, creating an effect of the poet stepping forward, along with his reader, to view scenes immediately before him.[79]

In the verse paragraph beginning with "Ye vig'rous Swains!" (93–110), an analogy is set up between snaring partridges with a "waving Net" (96) and besieging a town with English forces. The hunt in the sacred world of Windsor Forest is juxtaposed with an English battle in the secular world of Europe: "Some thoughtless Town, with Ease and Plenty blest, / Near, and more near, the closing Lines invest" (107–8). The partridge must provide the feast in this forest world of "vig'rous Swains." Similarly, the foreign enemy acts as unwitting prey in the outer world of Albion's "eager Sons" (106). Familiar with such hunting scenes, Pope's contemporary reader can compare the successful hunt to a patriotically pleasing military victory, perhaps recalling the capture of Gibraltar in 1704.[80] In fact, the sweeping play of images in the mind's eye, across (the net) and up (the flight of the partridges), parallels the seizure of the town and raising of the victory banner; it also prepares the reader for a similar movement in the next paragraph.

The poetic description in the next verse paragraph (111–18) possesses the greatest formal realism of the poem. The spectacle of the wounded pheasant is framed dramatically, and the fowler's presence is only implicit. The pheasant, royally bright and colorful, seems to rise before our eyes, as if before our fowling-piece.

Also, the movement from the siege at the end of the last paragraph to this scene is carried symbolically into these lines through the "heraldric" colors of the bird and its bloody death. Recall Pope's satiric description of the use of colors in *Peri Bathous:* "As to what are commonly call'd the *Colours* of *Honourable* and *Dishonourable*, they are various in different Countries: In this they are *Blue, Green*, and *Red*."[81]

These occupational foils form concentric rings of association. The iconic descriptions of domestic conquest ripple outward synchronically with associations of imperial conquest and diachronically across mythic time. The pattern of rising and falling complements the cyclic pattern of the scenes themselves, which begins in late summer, just before "milder Autumn Summer's Heat succeeds" (97), and ends in summer, "Now *Cancer* glows with *Phœbus'* fiery Car" (147).[82] This mythic contexture also prepares the reader for the succeeding verse paragraph (165–70) and the Ovidian episode of Lodona (171–218; Part II.D).

The name foils appearing immediately after the hart chase, *Arcadia* and *Windsor,* also indicate that the poet is about to shift his topic:

> Let old *Arcadia* boast her ample Plain,
> Th' Immortal Huntress, and her Virgin Train;
> Nor envy *Windsor!* since thy Shades have seen
> As bright a Goddess, and as chast a Queen;
> Whose Care, like hers, protects the Sylvan Reign,
> The Earth's fair Light, and Empress of the Main.
>
> (159–64)

The next paragraph (165–70) contains two other foils, "old *Diana*" (165) and "*Cynthus'* Top" (166), and serves as a *priamel* signaling the major emotional and thematic turn of the *Lodona* episode. Indeed, the topical movement finally comes to a stand after this *priamel* with the poet's apostrophe: "Above the rest a rural Nymph was fam'd, / Thy Offspring, *Thames!* the fair *Lodona* nam'd" (171–72).

The poet's praise of the personified *Thames,* an emblem of English royal power and commerce, follows (219–34), foreshadowing the river god's later entrance in the poem (329–422). Through *prosopopoeia,* the poet's *ethos* will later be transformed into a national *ethos* through *Thames's* direct speech (Part IV). Praise from England's mighty river god possesses a greater dignity than that of our humble poet. This strategy allows Pope to overcome the limits of humility imposed on his *persona* and elevate the level of poetic praise even further. Given the laudator's posture of humility, Pope resorts to *prosopopoeia* so that the national *ethos* of *Thames*, the river god, can appropriately match the import of his majestic visionary speech, crowning the praise of Windsor Forest. Thus, Pope will achieve the greatest encomiastic height of the poem.

There is no need to explore in more detail what has already been sketched out in the festival panegyric outline above. *Windsor-Forest* continues in the same predictable pattern of emotional tension and relaxation. The frequent use of name foils continue to add lustre to the poet's praise of Windsor Forest, Lord Granville, and Queen Anne and function as transitional signals within selecting devices to introduce new topics.

What I have sought to show is that *Windsor-Forest* has a definite rhetorical structure and that its design has been unjustly maligned. In addition, the rhetorical strategies that I have described give Pope's great generic experiment *Windsor-Forest* the "sublimity, rapture, and quickness of transition" that, according to Johnson, defined the greater ode.

4
Persona, Drama, and Epic in *The Rape of the Lock*

In *The Rape of the Lock*, Pope satirizes through dramatic irony, and the tainted vision of Belinda's world provided by her poet—Pope's *persona*—itself becomes a subject of ridicule. Since Pope never allows his poet to drop his mask, we cannot help but view him as a member of her logically fractured world and, therefore, as an object of Pope's humor. In this way, both the poet and his poem are put on display, and the reader perceives *The Rape of the Lock* as a self-enclosed world of superficial reality; and at the center of this world is Belinda, whose "heav'nly Image" becomes "the stuff dreams are made on."

Pope evokes wonder in his reader through epic description, but a wonder of microscopic, rather than macroscopic, proportions. As a mock *épos* (an utterance) aggrandizing the individual rather than the species, *The Rape of the Lock* becomes a gloss for "Self-Love," in which "one master Passion in the breast, / Like Aaron's serpent, swallows up the rest" (*Essay on Man*, 2.131–32). Pope's poem becomes a highly stylized dance between playful and purposive expression, portraying a fragile and painless world of transformation, charming us into visualization with its vivid imagery, and captivating us like time-lapse photography, where form and motion dominate. The poem parodies "customs and manners" of Pope's milieu, and yet, through epic allusion, it also invites us by contrast to compare the mythology of the present with that of the past. In possessing such vitality, *The Rape of the Lock* appeals to a timeless audience, despite an undeniable Augustan stamp; and as a rhetorical performance, it succeeds in the best sense of being seductively artificial, pictorial, and literary.

In his *Poetics*, Aristotle describes our pleasure in seeing representations that if real would be distasteful: "And then there is the enjoyment people always get from representations. What happens in actual experience proves this, for we enjoy looking at accurate likenesses of things which are themselves painful to see, obscene beasts, for instance, and corpses."[1] And there is something "obscene" in the mannequin world of Belinda—a world of phatic gesture, pure affectation, and a plenitude of bloodless corpses—that haunts us only after leaving that world: "And now a bubble burst, and now a world" (*Essay on Man*, 1.90). Through the alembic of afterthought, we ultimately experience a psychological *peripeteia* by which Pope's illusive magic reveals itself as disguised censure, a reversal anticipated by Belinda's own transformation from sweet to sour, seen in the usurpation of her sylphan reign by gnomish anarchy. Pope completely frames a vision of enchanting detail and frivolity and manages through rhetorical indirection to present us with a bewitchingly complex, yet tough-minded, moral condemnation of egocentricity.

It is well known that the poem was inspired by an actual theft of a lock, rupturing the relations between the families of Arabella Fermor and of Robert, Lord Petre, the historical shadows of Belinda and the love-struck lord. The purpose of the poem in its two-canto version of 1711 was to laugh the families back together; as Pope writes in his dedicatory letter to Arabella Fermor (1714), he "intended only to divert a few young Ladies, who have good Sense and good Humour enough, to laugh not only at their Sex's little unguarded Follies, but at their own."[2] But that seed of reality, of injured vanity and social disruption, which inspired Pope's composition has fructified imaginatively into a purely poetic creation that functions both as an *objet d'art* and a vehicle for moral censure. Belinda's poet, Pope's *persona*, possesses an insularity that sets him apart, as it does the *Dunciad* poet, from Pope's satirical *personae*. Through his hermetic narrator and his fusion of epic and dramatic methods, Pope creates an empirical effect of seeing Belinda's world encased "Pretty! in Amber to observe the forms" (*Epistle to Dr. Arbuthnot*, 169).

The Insular *Persona*

With the exception of *Eloisa to Abelard*, in each of Pope's poems a putative outside voice, a poet *persona*, guides the reader toward a particular attitude and mode of reception.[3] Pope's rhetorical pose enables him to create an informing intelligence with a unique angle of perception and an *ethos* appropriate to his topics. His reader, that eighteenth-century Englishman or English woman, rhetorically literate, socially stratified, and morally committed, is expected to scrutinize that poetic *ethos* for the validity of his thoughts. A *persona* is a deeply rooted literary convention, not a defensive barrier seeking to dissociate the author from the poem by a dissimulation; and to an empirically minded eighteenth-century audience, a poet's muse serves as a bridge toward a publically accessible, objectively perceived world. Pope shares with his reader a *sensus communis* that liberates him to create an ethical, logical, or emotional perspective to which his reader can respond through commonly understood tokens for attraction, repulsion, or wonder. As previously stated, Pope's rhetorical energies are directed toward engaging his reader, whether it be through the resonation of shared values or through the *agon* of a controversial wit. His poetry reflects a stern awareness of the factional spirit of his time, and consequently, his *personae* make a clear commitment to values that are subject to praise or censure, acceptance or rejection. Forcefulness and skill in a speaker are suasive requisites in an age of declamation, where imaginative novelty and subjective self-interest are considered foreign and suspicious; and, for Pope's contemporary audience, the magisterial effect of purposive expression can be equally instructive and delightful. Stirring an audience, therefore, is not an empty metaphor for a public poet like Pope.

Johnson tells Boswell: "Are we to think Pope happy, because he says so in his writings? We see in his writings what he wished the state of his mind to appear."[4] Just so, Pope requires that his reader be able to separate the wheat from the chaff and perceive the deliberate artfulness of his protean postures, the "state of his mind [he wishes] to appear." This effort of sorting becomes quite complex with the *personae* of his later satires, in which Pope mischievously mixes personal denunciation with that of his speakers.[5] Pope's use of a *persona* is an invitation to a reader to evaluate the artfulness of his poetic voice, challenge its authority, and judge its validity. Pope enjoys his own artifice and wishes us to appreciate his mastery of technique made visible through an obvious imposture. For Pope, his poem reposes on "the stability of truth" only after being compared to the reader's world. It is no accident that, perhaps, the century's best critical reader, Samuel Johnson, constantly relies on the act of comparison. In his preface to *Shakespeare*, he writes: "What mankind have long possessed they have often examined and compared, and if they persist to value the possession, it is because frequent comparisons have confirmed opinion in its favour."[6] Thus, Pope expects his reader to evaluate his art by comparing it to an outside reality.

The poet envisioning Belinda's world startles and humors us with his profound eccentricity, reminding us of the otherworldliness of the *Dunciad* poet. Though radically different, the worlds of Belinda and the Dunces have this in common: they are not like the reader's. Both poems are fundamentally intellectual in their comic spirit, with a *logos* poisoned by an irrationality that accounts for their comic appeal. Patently false, these two intellectual universes require a disciplined clarity and charm for success; as Quintilian shrewdly warns: "For with things which are false and incredible by nature there are but two alternatives: either they will move our hearers with exceptional force because they are beyond the truth, or they will be regarded as empty nothings because they are not the truth."[7] *The Rape of the Lock* and *The Dunciad* are apocalyptic visions obscured by either a surreal radiance or a dullness, though "beyond the truth," still within the realm of human conception.

In the title of the poem, we are given a clue to Pope's ironic intention and the function of his *persona*. His titles are usually generic, less often thematic, and serve to frame his poems. As do his prefaces, dedications, advertisements, and arguments, his titles work to establish generic expectations within the reader's mind. They are wholly functional in nature, terse and businesslike. Rhetorically keen, Pope is a psychological master of suspense, knowing best when to let the cat out of the bag, and if his titles tell us something, it is for a reason. While his generic titles promote in the reader general stances or postures from which to experience his poetry, his thematic titles work in a more specific fashion, suggesting the posture of its *persona*, such as piousness in *Messiah* and *The Universal Prayer*, the laudatory dream state of *The Temple of Fame*, and praise associated with a national symbol in *Windsor-Forest*. Pope's ironic titles *The Rape of the Lock* and *The Dunciad* point to the function of their particular *persona*.

In *A Rhetoric of Irony*, Wayne C. Booth describes how a title can be a rhetorical signal that irony is at hand: "Occasionally an author will use a direct epithet in his title to describe one of the qualities of his speaker." Like "nudges of the elbow and winks of the eye," Booth tells us, a title can be a warning to impending jest. Ironic titles, however, are "Straightforward warnings in the author's own voice." Indeed, an ironic title is often a linchpin between an author and his ironic voice, and Booth's examples of

Ring Lardner's "Gullible's Travels," Bruce Bliven's "Diary of a Worrier," and T. S. Eliot's "The Hollow Men" reveal an author's supervening lucidity.[8] Even so, ironic titles are not always so straightforward, as with two titles Booth also mentions, *The Dunciad* and "Memoirs of Martinus Scriblerus." Perceiving these titles as "in the author's own voice" overlooks how completely Pope has realized his *personae*.

The *Dunciad* poet is as good a poet as Pope could make him, given that darkness not light, dullness not understanding, is his shibboleth; hence, Pope creates a poet *persona* with a skewed mind and an obscured vision, making possible his epic praise of dunces. Furthermore, I would argue, it is the *Dunciad* poet who has supposedly entitled his own creation, and Pope later reinforces this interpretation by placing the poem within extrapoetic frames of Scriblerian apparatus; likewise, the prolific Martinus Scriblerus, whose name itself proclaims his obsessive urge for scribbling, we would suppose entitled his own memoirs. In this way, the title *The Rape of the Lock*, being an allusion to Shakespeare's *The Rape of Lucrece*, is dramatically ironical. Belinda's poet, though an exceptionally good one, possesses an incorrigible myopia, as well as a too obvious veneration for Belinda's lock; and his title fits within the totality of his defective vision and wrong-headed morality. His title not only announces the main action of the poem, it carries with it a double-entendre that he is incapable of recognizing; and the unwitting irony of the *persona*'s naively composed title prepares the reader for the spirit of the poem.[9]

Transparency and Opacity

The Rape of the Lock is the most pictorial of Pope's poems; and this is not surprising, in light of its being a complete artifice. It is a display piece to be viewed emotionally and intellectually from beyond its self-contained universe, and demands a psychologically different kind of reader engagement from that sought in poems like *Elegy to the Memory of an Unfortunate Lady* and *Eloisa to Abelard* (see chap. 5). In the spirit of Horace's *ut pictura poesis*, the poem may be viewed as a verbal painting, characterized by poetic corollaries to canvas size, perspective, line, color, brush stroke, and so on; that is, there is a visual proportioning, a pictorialization, accomplished through language that focuses our mind's eye at a particular distance from the poem.[10]

Richness of expression varying within these particular perspectives further contributes to this pictorial quality.

Pope's precise control of language achieves pictorial effects that are essential to his rhetorical practice. I borrow the terms *transparency* and *opacity* from Richard A. Lanham's theory of style in order to describe Pope's calculated variations of expression.[11] Through these variations, he adjusts his poetic frames to create different senses of distance and shift our perspective from one frame to another by careful shadowings of stylistic richness. Also by modulating the tone of his poetic voice, Pope can move his *persona* in or out of the frame at will. Lanham describes a similar effect in Chaucer:

> [In the Chaucerian situation] Do we see a *neutral*, transparent, literal description of an odd literary reality or a literary, conventionalized picture of a normative reality? Chaucer is continually playing variations on this dilemma. He creates as narrator a "walking literal" who offers a "transparent window" invitation. But he is too obviously a literal, and so Chaucer the poet reenters and the transparent window becomes—another possibility—opaque.[12]

Lanham further describes the "opaque style":

> I am going to call such self-conscious rhetoric, in a generic singular, the Opaque Style. What we must first notice about the Opaque Style is that it works like a simple *At/Through* switch. Verbal patterns can vary in small increments, but our attention does not seem to. Either we notice an opaque style *as a style* (i.e., we look *at* it) or we do not (i.e., we look *through* it to a fictive reality beyond). We see either a compulsive compound syntax or a weary Hemingway hero home from the wars. Our gaze snaps from one discrete attitude to another, as in those multistable illusions in which a vase becomes two facing profiles or an old crone changes into a young girl.[13]

In such a way, Pope varies his own style, either with an opacity that draws us to the surface of his expression or to the speaker himself; or with a transparency that allows us to see through his language at what is described. Increasing figurative richness or elevating emotion are two ways he accomplishes an opacity of expression; and minimizing either figurative richness or emotional elevation works toward a transparency of expression. Pope's expressive variations through linguistic transparency or opacity derive from Homer's technique of distancing through "light" or "shadow," which he further developed in his Homeric translations.

Deft control of the relationship between style and subject matter is crucial for poetic pictorialization. In *An Essay on Criticism*, Pope describes how Homer's stylistic variations are intended to vary the reader's distance from a poetic scene and how a reader should be attentive to them:

> I know there are, to whose presumptuous Thoughts
> Those *Freer Beauties*, ev'n in *Them*, seem Faults:
> Some Figures *monstrous* and *mis-shap'd* appear,
> Consider'd *singly*, or beheld too *near*,
> Which, but *proportion'd* to their *Light*, or *Place*,
> Due Distance *reconciles* to Form and Grace.
> A prudent Chief not always must display
> His Pow'rs in *equal Ranks*, and *fair Array*,
> But with th' *Occasion* and the *Place* comply,
> *Conceal* his Force, nay seem sometimes to *Fly*.
> Those oft are *Stratagems* which *Errors* seem,
> Nor is it *Homer Nods*, but *We* that *Dream*.
>
> (169–80)

Steven Shankman has observed how the "due distance" described in this passage informs Pope's treatment of subject matter and style in his Homeric translations, which accounts for Pope's sympathy with the "unmannered boldness" of Homer's epic style.[14]

The importance of light and shadow in the Homeric poems for creating a sense of distance was commonly appreciated in the eighteenth century. Madame Dacier, a French contemporary who also translated the *Iliad*, criticized Pope for his inability to capture Homer's skill in his own translation; and John Dennis insured that Pope's English audience did not overlook her criticism by translating her at length in his "*REMARKS upon Mr. POPE's DUNCIAD*" (1729). Madame Dacier disagrees vehemently with Pope's statement in his preface that the *Iliad* is "a wild paradise," and in doing so describes Homer's technique of distancing through light and shadow:

> Every thing that is in them [the Homeric poems], is not only in the Place in which it ought justly to be, but every thing is formed on Purpose for the Place it possesses. He presents you at first with that which ought first to be seen; he places in the Middle what ought to be only there; and what would be improper either at the Beginning or End; and he places Things at a greater Distance, which ought to be so dispos'd, in order to create a greater and a more agreeable Surprize; and to make use of a Comparison drawn from Painting, He disposes that in the greatest Light, which cannot be too visible; and sinks and

hides in the Obscurity of the Shadows, what does not require to be expos'd so fully to Sight. So that we may say, that *Homer* was the Painter who best knew how to employ the Lights and the Shadows. And it was this beauteous and admirable Order, which *Horace* admir'd in his Poems, and upon which he founded his Rules for perfecting the Art of Poetry.[15]

Dacier and Dennis, we well know, were not disinterested in their criticism of Pope, nor were they correct; a sensitive reading of Pope's poetry reveals him a master of pictorialization, of light and shadow, and of transparent and opaque styles. In *The Rape of the Lock*, we find what Shankman calls a "precious style of the picture" courting the shade (in referring to Pope's *Iliad*), where person and object are "*proportioned* to their *Light*, or *Place* [and] / Due Distance reconciles to Form and Grace."

In Pope's pictorialization, we see an instrumental connection between the rhetorical quality of his language and its referential content determining how he employs epic style. As with Homer, Pope contours his poetry with light and shadow by oscillating the magnitude of conception with a changing transparency (or opaqueness) of expression. A grander scale of action requires a reader be placed at a more distant perspective by giving it greater light, by subduing or compressing the language in the interest of achieving greater scope; and by increasing the richness of figurative description or level of emotion, Pope decreases his pictorial range, drawing his reader's attention away from the conceptual action back to the linguistic strokes describing it. In this sense, language can obscure pictorial clarity or perspective and become opaque or shadowed.

To illustrate further, let us take an example from Pope's *Iliad*, the majestic entrance of Sarpedon into the battle plain below:

> So press'd with Hunger, from the Mountain's Brow
> Descends a Lion on the Flocks below;
> So stalks the lordly Savage o'er the Plain,
> In sullen Majesty, and stern Disdain:
> In vain loud Mastives bay him from afar,
> And Shepherds gaul him with an Iron War;
> Regardless, furious, he pursues his Way;
> He foams, he roars, he rends the panting Prey.
>
> (Book 12:357–64)

The approach of Sarpedon to the scene of battle parallels the reader's. We follow Sarpedon, from his detached point of observation, as he descends from the mountain slope to participate in the fray below. The scale of perspective is rapidly diminishing, and we find his configuration of language increasing. Personification ("Mountain's Brow"), simile ("a Lion on the Flocks below"), and epithet ("lordly Savage"; "Iron War"; "panting Prey"), while obscuring the individual action, succeed in telescoping the scale of action to allow finally the mimetic isomorphism of asyndeton ("He foams, he roars, he rends"), focusing at close range on Sarpedon's battle hunger. Thus, we see that, as the field of action decreases, expression becomes more prominent and the opacity of that expression increases. This then establishes a new perspective and a new scale of relative transparency and opacity from which Pope's expression can further fluctuate. In *The Rape of the Lock*, Pope's opacity is often at work scaling and shifting his poetic frames in order to keep our mind's eye on its reduced world, whether on a human scale or on that of sylphs or gnomes. There are, however, significant moments when the scope of action suddenly enlarges, and we are allowed to peer out of Belinda's immediate universe. Let us observe when these moments of increased transparency occur.

In the *exordia* of the first three cantos, a sun metaphor, a trope for exalting Belinda's beauty, is used, establishing a highly controlled transparency and granting us a fleeting glance at a larger world beyond the local field of action. The position of the sun has a two-fold purpose, mimetically marking the time of day and serving metaphorically as a foil to Belinda's luminescence; as in canto 1: "*Sol* thro' white Curtains shot a tim'rous Ray, / And op'd those Eyes that must eclipse the Day" (1.13–14). In canto 2, mimesis and metaphor again combine, and the rising sun becomes a foil to Belinda as she embarks on "the painted Vessel":

> Not with more Glories, in th' Etherial Plain,
> The Sun first rises o'er the purpled Main,
> Than issuing forth, the Rival of his Beams
> Lanch'd on the Bosom of the Silver *Thames*.
>
> (2.1–4)

In canto 3, Belinda arrives at Hampton Court, where she achieves the height of her radiance; and though neither she nor the sun are visible during the social interlude of the second paragraph, we know that it is around midday. This becomes evident in the first couplet of the third paragraph, which foreshadows Belinda's fate: "Mean while declining from the Noon of Day, / The Sun obliquely shoots his burning Ray" (3.19–20). The lifegiving light of the sun elevates the egocentric power of Belinda's face, couching Scriblerian purpose in an "approved" use of metaphor; as Johnson tells us in his *Life of Gray:* "An epithet or metaphor drawn from Nature ennobles Art."[16]

Pope's use of a rising and a setting sun to mark the changes in Belinda's radiant power emerges at the end of the poem as performing an even greater function. As a temporal infrastructure, the waning of light marked by the movement of the sun gives to the culminating transformation of her lock a climactic inevitability. Transforming her lock solely on the strength of mythopoeic fiat or of literary parallel (as in the stellar transformations of Julius Caesar at the end of Ovid's *Metamorphoses* and Berenice's lock in Catullus's translation) would have been too much like the unintentional sinking he describes in his "A Receipt to make an Epic Poem": "When you cannot extricate your Hero by any human means, or yourself by your own wit, seek relief from Heaven, and the Gods will do your business very readily."[17] The reappearance of her lock as a star achieves an effect of a natural resolution in a world gone dark; though for Belinda's poet it is a divine miracle, for Pope's reader it is a product of poetic logic.

The first three paragraphs of canto 3 give us our hardest look at a world beyond Belinda's sphere of influence. Though in isolation these lines may seem an intrusive projection of Pope's own voice, they belong to the poet in the poem. In using the greater world to exalt Belinda's world, our poet remains faithful to his bathetic muse. We observe that canto 3 begins with the wider scope of serious epic narrative:

> Close by those Meads for ever crown'd with Flow'rs,
> Where *Thames* with Pride surveys his rising Tow'rs,
> There stands a Structure of Majestick Frame,
> Which from the neighb'ring *Hampton* takes its Name.
>
> (3.1–4)

Thames and *Hampton*, acting as name foils for "Great *Anna*" (7), create an elevation necessary for the rapid fall into *bathos*, which is mirrored by the prophetic fickleness of "*Britain's* Statesmen":

> Here *Britain's* Statesmen oft the Fall foredoom
> Of Foreign Tyrants, and of Nymphs at home;
> Here Thou, Great *Anna!* whom three Realms obey,
> Dost sometimes Counsel take—and sometimes *Tea*.
>
> (3.5–8)

Belinda's poet, artful in his use of zeugma ("Dost sometimes Counsel take—and sometimes *Tea*"), commits the same philosophical error of his characters, blindly yoking together the consequential with the inconsequential; and the poet's continual falling into *bathos* resonates with the greater thematic fall of Belinda. In Pope's poetic worlds, all levels of expression and meaning fit together into one intricate mosaic, just as in his natural world "harmoniously confus'd: / Where Order in Variety we see, / And where, tho' all things differ, all agree" (*Windsor-Forest*, 14–16). Thus, the rhetorical infrastructure of bathetic falling underscores the naïveté of Pope's poet, and the satirical thrust of his words is a product of dramatic irony.

This texture of unwitting worldly wit continues through the second paragraph, where: "One speaks the Glory of the *British Queen*, / And one describes a charming *Indian Screen*" (13–14). But in the third paragraph, when the poet focuses on Belinda immediately prior to her game of Ombre, the tone is disrupted by unexpected gallows humor:

> Mean while declining from the Noon of Day,
> The Sun obliquely shoots his burning Ray;
> The hungry Judges soon the Sentence sign,
> And Wretches hang that Jury-men may Dine;
> The Merchant from th' *Exchange* returns in Peace,
> And the long Labours of the *Toilette* cease.
>
> (3.19–24)

Pope's thinly disguised scorn against "The hungry Judges" and, through juxtaposition, "The Merchant" calls to mind Samuel Garth's couplet in *The Dispensary*: "Where little Villains must submit to Fate, / That great Ones may enjoy the World in State"; however, unlike Garth, Pope has by this time established a consistent poet *persona* and can afford for a moment to threaten his authorial detachment.[18] Since our bathetic poet has been unaware throughout the poem of his indiscriminate leveling, it remains consistent to view his words as unintentionally ironical.

This abrupt oscillation to an expressive transparency, contrasting so much with the rest of the poem, would still appear to challenge the argument for an insular *persona*, if not for other evidence. In a note to a line in *The Dunciad Variorum* (*Dunciad A*, 2.258), we find Pope's explanation for a similar epic use of marking time:

> It is between eleven and twelve in the morning, after church service, that criminals are whipp'd in *Bridewell*. . . . This is to mark punctually the Time of the day: *Homer* does it by the circumstance of the Judges rising from court, or of the Labourer's dinner.[19]

Thus, we find that the seemingly pointed satire toward "The hungry Judges" functions as epic allusion and continues to operate within the insularity of the poem. Though for their poetic merit Pope must have admired these lines, they would not have survived his expansion of the poem unless they subserved his ends: "I would not be like those Authors, who forgive themselves some particular lines for the sake of a whole Poem, and *vice versa* a whole Poem for the sake of some particular lines."[20] What these lines disclose, according to the internal logic of the poem, is Pope's most serious target, namely, what can be the worst consequences of egocentricity. Despite their humorous frivolity and apparent innocuousness, Belinda's companions at Hampton Court are really no different than these modern-day Neros who value food over human life. Hence, the didactic thrust of *The Rape of the Lock* lies in an extrapolation of a system of false values, extending from a harmless broil at an afternoon card game outward to selfish cruelty in the halls of justice. Belinda's poet, then, has disclosed himself ironically as a philosophical companion of his characters; and we find in this momentary glimpse of London life, not in the red herring of Clarissa's speech, the most emphatic moral comment in the poem.[21]

Dramatic Design

Examining the structure of the five-canto version, we see a formal harmony of unity, symmetry, and proportion characteristic of classical beauty. The seizure of the lock centers and unifies all action; the balance between morning and afternoon events, the upperworld of sylphs and the underworld of gnomes, and inner passions of coquette and of prude reinforces a pervasive symmetry of antithesis enlarged from the two-canto version.[22] Cantos 2, 3, and 4—roughly equal in length, each containing a brief opening, a narration, and a brief summing up—proportion and balance the poem internally and establish a harmonious pattern of formal repetition, calling to mind the classical lines of Palladian architecture. In addition, the broader perspectives of the introduction and of the conclusion of the poem contribute to its appearance of balance and completeness. The unity, symmetry, and proportion of the five cantos parallel a dramatic action that, nevertheless, pulsates with activity. A homeostasis exists between the rigidity of form and the plasticity of content. Indeed, the fusion of formal and dramatic designs reflects the poetic character of Pope's couplet art, where word and image vie constantly against an inertia of unyielding metrics. More apparent than the five-canto version, the two-canto version, neatly divided by the cutting of the lock, exhibits a closer resemblance to the structural balance of the closed couplet, representing a kind of Rosetta stone that enables us to follow with greater clarity Pope's creative progression from couplet to poem.

As David B. Morris notices: "The central canto, with its vivid reversal, creates the pattern for Pope's elaboration of dramatic contrasts that extend even to such paired details as Belinda's 'Shouts' (iii.99) of victory at ombre and her 'Screams' (iii.156) of dismay following the rape."[23] Indeed, dramatic contrasts, paired antitheticals of character, action, and image, fuse the poem at all levels, generating an elaborate concentricity. The thematic strokes and counterstrokes that Morris perceives as part of a general dramatic pattern conform with Pope's structural harmony and underscore the insularity of the poem. Thus, the formal balance of the drama has more than aesthetic appeal, for we experience a sense of a completed action. The dramatic tension increases like a bowstring into canto 3, then it begins, inevitably, to snap back. A natural law of Newtonian physics controls Belinda's world, in which every action has an equal and opposite reaction. As a result, there is no real conflict between the dramatic core of the poem and its epic description.

The grandeur of epic description enriches the linguistic texture of the poem without competing with its referential substratum, words swirling about their objects like the sylphs and gnomes flitting in and out as illusory participants of human action. *The Rape of the Lock* exemplifies Dryden and Soames's description of epic style in their translation of Boileau's *Art of Poetry:*

> Thus in the endless Treasure of his mind,
> The Poet does a thousand Figures find,
> Around the work his Ornaments he pours,
> And strows with lavish hand his op'ning Flow'rs.[24]

Epic language becomes Pope's dress of thought, and we find that the same pictorial qualities are achieved through figurative language as in the Sarpedon episode discussed above. Compare the prosaic transparency of this direct statement: "With scissors the Baron cuts Belinda's lock" with the opacity of Pope's circumlocution designed to decrease the scale of action:

> The Peer now spreads the glitt'ring *Forfex* wide,
> T'inclose the Lock; now joins it, to divide.
> Ev'n then, before the fatal Engine clos'd,
> A wretched *Sylph* too fondly interpos'd;
> Fate urg'd the Sheers, and cut the *Sylph* in twain,
> (But Airy Substance soon unites again)
> The meeting Points the sacred Hair dissever
> From the fair Head, for ever and for ever!
>
> (3.147–54)

Rhetorical virtuosity transforms the mundane into the marvellous. The linguistic surface of poetic description becomes prominent through its figurative richness, adjusting our perspective from a previously human to a sylphan dimension and initiating a new range of clarity at the moment the sylph is cut in two. The rhetorical repetition of "for ever and for ever!" again increases opacity, signaling another shift in scale and preparing us for Belinda's subsequent reaction. As seen in this example, this pictorial technique is the same found in Pope's serious epic style. In addition, here we see how Pope uses epic technique to enhance dramatic action.

Within Belinda's fictive world, there are two modes of "real," one functioning according to the physical laws of the reader's world and the other according to the laws of poetic imagination. They do not compete, but rather coexist. The dramatic action moves the reader forward logically in a horizontal sequence of cause and effect; while the patently fanciful action provides an illusory plenitude matching the expressive flourish of epic description and creating qualitative diversions in a vertical movement of playfulness. The purposiveness of dramatic structure provides a logical groundwork, a centripetal counterpart to the centrifugal dalliance of epic festoonery. That Pope's epic description does not vie with his dramatic method shows how gracefully he has conjoined one literary structure with another; and unlike Garth's *The Dispensary*, Pope's dramatic structure coheres with a larger epic structure and avoids Garth's epic sprawl.

Pope may have found his model for an epic drama in actual dramas on stage or in the descriptions found in William Davenant's preface to his *Gondibert* or Dryden's *Of Dramatick Poesie*.[25] He was certainly aware of dramatic models, for he converts a familiar dramatic pattern for his poetic purpose in *The Rape of the Lock* and, in doing so, makes it delightfully new. As Johnson declares: "In this work are exhibited in a very high degree the two most engaging powers of an author: new things are made familiar, and familiar things are made new."²⁶ A comparison of Davenant's remarks in his preface with the dramatic structure of *The Rape of the Lock* will illustrate how indeed "familiar things are made new," as well as exhibit the conventional character of Pope's dramatic design.

Davenant was unable to fulfill his own "receit" for *Gondibert*, a proposed epic of five books, each containing six cantos. He managed to publish two books in 1651 and later added a third book. Pope tells Spence in 1736: "Sir William Davenant's *Gondibert* is not a good poem, if you take it in the whole, but there are a great many good things in it."²⁷ As did Dryden, Pope entertained an idea of writing an epic and had more than a casual interest in the mediocre successes of epic writers such as Davenant and Cowley; and he had read Davenant's preface with care, as evidenced by several lines in his *An Essay on Criticism*.²⁸ On the far less ambitious scale of mock-epic, Pope succeeds where Davenant fails. Davenant's preface to his *Gondibert*, which if not a direct source for Pope, suggests rather completely the dramatic design of *The Rape of the Lock*:

> The first *Act* is the general preparative, by rendring the chiefest characters of persons, and ending with something that looks like an obscure promise of design. The second begins with an introducement of new persons, so finishes all the characters, and ends with some little performance of that design which was promis'd at the parting of the first *Act*. The third makes a visible correspondence in the underwalks (or lesser intrigues) of persons; and ends with an ample turn of the main design, and expectation of a new. The fourth (ever having occasion to be the longest) gives a notorious turn to all the underwalks, and a counterturn to that main design which chang'd in the third. The fifth begins with an intire diversion of the main, and dependant Plotts; then makes the general correspondence more discernible, and ends with an easy untying of those particular knots, which made a contexture of the whole.²⁹

Let us compare Davenant's formula with the dramatic architecture of *The Rape of the Lock*.

Canto 1 supplies the proposition of the poem ("What dire Offence from am'rous Causes springs, / What mighty Contests rise from trivial Things"), the dream vision in which Ariel speaks, and the "chiefest character," Belinda at her dressing table metaphorically arming herself. Davenant's "obscure promise of design" lies in Ariel's prophetic warning:

> Late, as I rang'd the Crystal Wilds of Air,
> In the clear Mirror of thy ruling *Star*
> I saw, alas! some dread Event impend,
> Ere to the Main this Morning Sun descend.
>
> (1.107–10)

In canto 2, we see Belinda sailing up the Thames, which commences the chain of events. It also introduces "Th' Adventrous *Baron*," who sees her locks, aspires to have them ("By Force to ravish, or by Fraud betray"), and makes a sacrificial offering to Love; the answer to his supplication adds a dark undertone of dramatic inevitability ("The Pow'rs gave Ear, and granted half his Pray'r, / The rest, the Winds dispers'd in empty Air"). Canto 3 contains "an ample turn of the main design" with the rape of the lock and an "expectation of a new" through Belinda's violent change of humor from exultation to distress. This action is paralleled by the departure of the sylphs. Prior to these events, we are given "a visible correspondence" with the dramatic design through the "lesser intrigues" of the card table, foreshadowing the eroding punctilio in the splenetic speeches of canto 4 and the donnybrook in canto 5.

Only two lines short of being "the longest" as Davenant prescribes, canto 4 does provide "a notorious turn to all the underwalks." Umbriel replaces Ariel, marking Belinda's transformation from coquette to prude, and his journey to the Cave of Spleen serves as a rhetorical gloss of Belinda's repressed "Rage, Resentment, and Despair" (9). In addition, Umbriel's descent to the gnomic underworld neatly reverses the visionary ascent to the sylphic upperworld of canto 2.[30]

Finally, in canto 5, we find a dramatic sequence paralleling canto 1. Clarissa, who provided the baron with the fateful scissors, hypocritically chastizes Belinda with her insincere admonition ("Charms strike the sight, but Merit wins the Soul"), which is followed by Thalestris's call to arms and Belinda's violently prudish reaction. In canto 1, the poem had moved from speech to *action*, with Ariel's speech ("Whoever fair and chaste / Rejects Mankind, is by some *Sylph* embrac'd") and with Belinda's subsequent awakening and performance of her coquettish duties. In canto 5, the poem moves from speech to *reaction*. As Davenant's formula suggests, Clarissa's speech acts as "an intire diversion of the main, and dependant Plotts"; while the subsequent melee "makes the general correspondence of the persons more discernible"; finally, with the transformation of the lock, the poem "ends with an easy untying of those particular knots, which made a contexture of the whole."

In canto 1, Belinda, rested and composed, seems in control of her harmonious world. This is not the case in the chaotic world of canto 5, which is a formulaic reversal that does not, however, return us to where Belinda began. Her world appears destroyed, like a delicate bubble. Yet, like the regenerating cycles of the sun, a supernal reordering of life occurs through the transformation of the lock. The movement has a completeness to it. A natural sequence of action, reaction, and a return to inertia reverberates with a dramatic sequence of blindness and folly, conflict and suffering, and reprieve by *deus ex machina*. Thematically, we have a qualitative manifold of antithetical pairs: rising and falling, light and darkness, sylph and gnome, upperworld and underworld, coquette and prude, possession and loss, sun and star. Thus, Pope has fleshed out Davenant's design to create a unitary whole, fulfilling his own conception of beauty described in *An Essay on Criticism*:

> In Wit, as Nature, what affects our Hearts
> Is not th' Exactness of peculiar Parts;
> 'Tis not a *Lip*, or *Eye*, we Beauty call,
> But the joint Force and full *Result* of *all*.
> Thus when we view some well-proportion'd Dome,
> (The *World's* just Wonder, and ev'n *thine* O *Rome!*)
> No single Parts unequally surprize;
> All comes *united* to th' admiring Eyes;
> No monstrous Height, or Breadth, or Length appear;
> The *Whole* at once is *Bold*, and *Regular.*
>   (243–52)

Boileau's and Garth's Mock Epics

In *The Rape of the Lock*, Pope uses epic method with a formal integrity that surpasses Boileau's *Le Lutrin* (1674; 1683) and Samuel Garth's *The Dispensary* (1699), immediate predecessors in the "heroi-comical" tradition. Pope's greater success lies in sustaining his jest from beginning to end. For all of John Dennis's invective against the poem, he is right when he says: "That his *perpetual Gravity*, after the *Promise* of his Title, makes the whole Poem one continued *Jest.*"[31] Unlike Boileau and Garth, Pope never removes his poetic mask.

Pope's *persona* uses epic devices in a consistently serious effort to elevate his subject. On the other hand, we find in *Le Lutrin* an inconsistent tone when the poet drops his epic voice. This results in a dissociation of form and content, especially in the direct moralizing of canto 6 in Boileau's final version.³² For all his seriousness, it seems that Boileau's poet cannot take himself seriously when he should. For example, in canto 1, we find Boileau's poet being self-consciously absurd, which is evident in a contemporary translation:

> And thou Great *Heroe*, whose wise conduct stifled
> The growing Schisme which else thy Church had rifled,
> With favour influence my Advent'rous Verse,
> Nor dare to laugh, whilest I thy Acts rehearse.³³

Boileau has pressed his subjective rhetorical foil into excessive humility, and his poet's stance becomes that of a jester rather than of a court poet.

In *The Dispensary*, Garth employs epic convention with uneven skill and appropriateness. Tillotson remarks that he "lacks the control for fine mockery either of people or of a literary form"—and this criticism rings true.³⁴ Garth's poet at times displays a sarcasm that undermines the steadiness of his epic voice, questioning his real need for an epic style by collapsing into denunciatory satire; as in canto 1:

> Not far from that most celebrated Place,
> Where angry Justice shews her awful Face;
> Where little Villains must submit to Fate,
> That great Ones may enjoy the World in State.³⁵

The tone of these lines, one that intrudes periodically throughout the poem, too closely resembles the bickering posture of Garth's physicians. By vacillating in his point of view, Garth's poet blunts the comic force of his action. The humorous effect of describing the physicians' vices in epic style arises through indirection, and the direct statement of denunciatory satire can only subvert this effect. In relinquishing his epic distance, Garth's poet reduces his epic style to merely incongruous garniture. Pope "corrects" these lapses in Boileau's and Garth's poetry by creating a perfectly disciplined voice within a finely wrought poetic structure. In doing so, he produces a classic example of satire achieved through dramatic irony.

Epic Allusion

We have already discussed how the ironical nature of an insular *persona* relies on comparison. At its most fundamental level, such irony requires a comparative scrutiny of the poetic *logos;* and the hermetic aspect of Belinda's world allows us to place it against the backdrop of our own world. Through pictorialization, we are able to witness logical miscues and mistaken motives erupting from societal foibles or more serious moral errantry. The indecorous conjunction of epic style and comic action in *The Rape of the Lock* also increases our risibility; and a knowledge of literary norms enables us to see the jest of deliberate violation and to appreciate the "heroi-comical." Allusion, another important comparative device, elicits a more sophisticated response from a reader because it demands an erudition matching that of Pope's fellow Scriblerians.[36]

Allusion plays a vital role in Pope's poetry, as Reuben Brower's *Alexander Pope: The Poetry of Allusion* has shown.[37] Undoubtedly, the wealth of epic allusion in *The Rape of the Lock* enriches the texture of the poem for Pope's more literate reader. More importantly, however, epic allusion provides another level of comparison that further illuminates the complex irony in the poem.

In completing this discussion of *The Rape of the Lock,* I shall explore the Homeric allusion of Belinda's ritual preparations in canto 1 (121–48), comparing them with Juno's similar preparations in Book 14 of Pope's *Iliad* translation (191–218).[38] Tillotson considers Belinda's dressing scene a parody of the arming of the epic hero.[39] More to the point, however, Pope makes a parody of Homer's own parody of the arming of the epic hero, namely, his description of Juno's preparations to seduce Jove, a goddess going to war with her husband.[40]

Recalling the context of this Homeric episode, the tide of battle has now turned against the Greeks. Juno, who favors the Greek cause, cannot persuade Jupiter (Jove) against favoring Thetis, Achilles's mother, in her wish for Agamemnon and the Greeks to suffer for taking Briseïs from Achilles. She must resort to the deceit of wooing Jupiter to sleep with her beauty and the power of Venus's cestus, but Juno must borrow the cestus from Venus, and since Venus supports the Trojans, Juno must deceive her with a pretense of resolving a marriage dispute between her parents, Ocean and Tethys. If Juno can succeed in putting Jupiter to sleep, the tide of battle can be turned to the side of the Greeks without fear of his interference.

Drawing on Eustathius, Pope comments about the need for Juno's preparations:

> Thus the Goddess comes from her Apartment against her Spouse in compleat Armour. The Pleasures of Women mostly prevail by pure cunning, and the artful Management of their Persons; For there is but one way for the weak to subdue the mighty, and that is by Pleasure. The Poet shews at the same time, that Men of Understanding are not master'd, without a great deal of Artifice and Address. There are but three ways, whereby to overcome another, by Violence, by Persuasion, or by Craft: *Jupiter* was invincible by main Force; to think of persuading was as fruitless, after he had pass'd his Nod to *Achilles*; therefore *Juno* was obliged of necessity to turn her Thoughts entirely upon Craft; and by the Force of Pleasure it is, that she insnares and manages the God.[41]

Therefore, when Juno ponders: "*Jove* to deceive, What Methods shall she try, / What Arts, to blind his all-beholding Eye?" (Book 14:186–87), she decides on the charms of her sex.

According to Homeric logic, Belinda's strength lies in craft. In fact, when she relies on her craft, she is most victorious, whether through "the *Cosmetic* Pow'rs" (1.124) of her sylphan reign or intricate strategy in the game of ombre. Her sexual opponent, the baron, incapable of matching her subtlety, requires the wile of another female, Clarissa, to gain his prize:

> Just then, *Clarissa* drew with tempting Grace
> A two-edg'd Weapon from her shining Case;
> So Ladies in Romance assist their Knight,
> Present the Spear, and arm him for the Fight.
>
> (3.127–30)

Through Clarissa's cunning, the baron then resorts to his own sex's virtue—"Violence"—and snips Belinda's lock while she exults victoriously at the card table, her most vulnerable moment. Her and Sir Plume's ludicrous appeals for restoration of the lock in canto 4 are ineffectual. Equally fruitless are her and Thalestris's recuperative efforts through violence in canto 5.

Both dressing scenes are metaphorical versions of arming for the purpose of sexual confrontation, and each is portrayed as a ceremony of beautification; for Belinda: "Now awful Beauty puts on all its Arms / The Fair each moment rises in her Charms"

(1.139–40); for Juno: "Against his Wisdom to oppose her Charms, / And lull the Lord of Thunder in her Arms" (189–90). In both poems, there is a brilliant punning on "arms" (arms of Beauty; arms of Jove; arms of the epic hero) and "charms," a word containing "arms," evoking an intricately complex parody on the level of expression that echoes the thematic thrust of the episodes. Pursuing the comparison further, however, we begin to see that significant divergences from Juno's ceremony taint Belinda's virtue.

When Juno goes to her apartment, she goes alone and locks herself behind an impenetrable door:

> Swift to her bright Apartment she repairs,
> Sacred to Dress, and Beauty's pleasing Cares:
> With Skill divine had *Vulcan* form'd the Bow'r,
> Safe from Access of each intruding Pow'r.
>
> (191–94)

Solitary, solemn, and sacred, the majesty of Juno's conduct is not lost on Pope, who remarks:

> This Passage may be of Consideration to the Ladies, and, for their sakes, I take a little Pains to observe upon it. *Homer* tells us that the very Goddesses, who are all over Charms, never dress in Sight of any one: The Queen of Heaven adorns herself in private, and the Doors lock after her. In *Homer* there are no *Dieux des Ruelles*, no Gods are admitted to the Toilette.
>
> I am afraid there are some earthly Goddesses of less Prudence, who have lost much of the Adoration of Mankind by the contrary Practice.[42]

Belinda is one of these "earthly Goddesses of less Prudence," with her host of assistants, as well as her lapdog, Shock, wandering somewhere about her:

> The busy *Sylphs* surround their darling Care;
> These set the Head, and those divide the Hair,
> Some fold the Sleeve, whilst others plait the Gown;
> And *Betty*'s prais'd for Labours not her own.
>
> (1.145–48)

In addition, the solitude of Juno in her chamber and the presence of her Betty, sylphs, and Shock in Belinda's suggest the contrasting penetrability of their virtue.

Before consecrating herself with oils, Juno bathes herself: "Here first she bathes; and round her Body pours / Soft Oils of Fragrance, and ambrosial Show'rs" (197–98). Pope notes: "The Practice of *Juno* in anointing her Body with perfumed Oils was a remarkable part of ancient *Cosmeticks*, tho' entirely disused in the modern Arts of Dress. It may possibly offend the Niceness of modern Ladies; but such of 'em as paint ought to consider that this Practice might, without much greater Difficulty, be reconciled to Cleanliness."[43] Belinda's failure to bathe and her application of cosmetic paint in lieu of Juno's perfumed oils implies her antithetical superficiality to Juno's honest beauty; and unlike Juno, Belinda goes directly from her bed to the cosmetic table, unwashed, to sit before a mirror and paint herself:

> A heav'nly Image in the Glass appears,
> To that she bends, to that her Eyes she rears;
> Th'inferior Priestess, at her Altar's side,
> Trembling, begins the sacred Rites of Pride.
>
> (1.125–28)

Notice here that Belinda's pride lacks the qualifying adjective of Juno's pride: "Thus while she breath'd of Heav'n, with decent Pride" (203). Through dissimilarities of detail, Pope allusively generates an increasingly stronger reprobation of Belinda's character.

Like Belinda, Juno proceeds to dress from head to foot. Whereas Belinda devotes herself entirely to painting her face, leaving her hair and gown for the sylphs, Juno ignores her face and gives equal attention to all other aspects of her dress:

> Her artful Hands the radiant Tresses ty'd;
> Part on her Head in shining Ringlets roll'd,
> Part o'er her Shoulders wav'd like melted Gold.
> Around her next a heav'nly Mantle flow'd,
> That rich with *Pallas*' labour'd Colours glow'd;
> Large Clasps of Gold the Foldings gather'd round,
> A golden Zone her swelling bosom bound.
> Far-beaming Pendants tremble in her Ear,
> Each Gemm illumin'd with a triple Star.
> Then o'er her Head she casts a Veil more white
> Than new fal'n Snow, and dazling as the Light.
> Last her fair Feet celestial Sandals grace.
>
> (204–15)

About this passage, Pope comments:

> May I have leave to observe the great Simplicity of *Juno's* Dress, in Comparison with the innumerable Equipage of a modern Toilette? The Goddess, even when she is setting herself out on the greatest Occasion, has only her own Locks to tie, a white Veil to cast over them, a Mantle to dress her whole Body, her Pendants, and her Sandals. . . . The good *Eustathius* is ravish'd to find, that here are no Washes for the Face, no Dies for the Hair, and none of those artificial Embellishments since in Practice; he also rejoices not a little, that *Juno* has no Looking-Glass, Tire-Woman, or waiting Maid.[44]

As such notes make clear, Belinda suffers severe criticism through Pope's rhetorical strategy of allusive irony.

Through epic allusion, a similar vitiation of Clarissa's speech in canto 5 occurs. Though her speech parodies the nobility of Sarpedon's speech to Glaucus (*Iliad*, Book 12:371–96), the character of Sarpedon works as a foil to Clarissa's. Sarpedon is brave, prudent, not a meddler, and generous in his sentiments; as Pope tells us: "Neither rash nor boisterous . . . neither timorous nor tricking . . . neither talkative nor boasting. . . . He never reproaches the living, or insults the dead."[45] Clarissa certainly has none of Sarpedon's moral attributes, nor does she have the worldly knowledge (she seems only a lesser attractive Belinda), which makes her otherwise noble sounding speech hollow and hypercritical; as Cicero remarks: "It is from knowledge that oratory must derive its beauty and fullness, and unless there is such knowledge, well-grasped and comprehended by the speaker, there must be something empty and almost childish in the utterance."[46]

These are only two examples of Pope's rhetorical use of epic allusion, in these instances meant to undermine the *ethos* of his characters through delicately indirect irony. Indeed, this rare combination of delicacy and impressive poetic machinery make *The Rape of the Lock* such a unique poem. Thus, we have seen how Pope with a mighty force manages to lift a feather. Trifling, airy, amusing, and fantastic as the poem appears, Pope still renders to his enchanted reader, through masterful use of rhetorical strategies, a powerful condemnation of a viciously skewed logic and moral perception.

5
Expression, Emotion, and Forsaken Women

In *The Rape of the Lock*, we saw Belinda's world of "Self-Love" and distorted morality reflected in the perspective of its poet *persona*. In *Elegy to the Memory of an Unfortunate Lady* and *Eloisa to Abelard*, the speakers are also victims of a ruling passion that subverts the otherwise stabilizing powers of reason. Each speaker suffers from a loss of someone dear; the *Elegy* poet mourns the death of his lady; and Eloisa laments with a sense of futility her loss of Abelard. Both speakers, overwhelmed by a powerful *pathos*, engender an emotional appeal of sublime intensity. To accomplish this, Pope turns to rhetorical strategies found in Longinus's *On the Sublime*, a work he refers to frequently in his translation of the Homeric poems.[1]

Though Pope reshapes classical methods for his unique purposes, he strives to capture their spirit. In his preface of 1717, introducing the volume containing the *Elegy* and *Eloisa to Abelard*, he declares: "All that is left us is to recommend our productions by the imitation of the Ancients: and it will be found true, that in every age, the highest character for sense and learning has been obtain'd by those who have been most indebted to them."[2] Pope's words resonate with those of Longinus: "There is another road, besides those we have mentioned, which leads to sublimity. What and what manner of road is this? Zealous imitation of the great historians and poets of the past."[3]

In the spirit of Longinus, Pope acknowledges different roads to the sublime. In a letter to Ralph Bridges, 5 April (ca. 1708), we find Pope praising the Homeric sublime, "that Rapture and Fire, which carries you away with him, with that wonderful Force, that no man who has a true Poetical spirit is Master of himself, while he reads him"; he also tells Bridges that there are other kinds of sublimity, such as that of Virgil: "Homer makes you interested and concern'd before you are aware, all at once;

whereas Virgill does it by soft degrees."[4] In this chapter, we shall explore how Pope ventures on one of the lesser traveled roads to the sublime. In the *Elegy* and *Eloisa to Abelard*, he attempts a form of emotional absorption that Longinus hails in the poetry of Sappho—a "Sapphic" sublimity with formal qualities that eighteenth-century interpreters of the sublime generally ignored or rejected outright.[5]

The *Elegy* and *Eloisa to Abelard* contain tragic elements—a fateful event, dramatic conflict, and suffering—through which Pope achieves a powerful *pathos* in his vividly portrayed speakers. As Kenneth Burke has observed in the Greek proverb "*ta pathemata mathemata* [the suffered is the learned]," an agonistic relationship between suffering and learning underlies tragedy;[6] and such a tragic view of life informs the rhetorical spirit of Pope's two poems. In *Spectator*, no. 418, one of a series of periodical essays collectively entitled "The Pleasures of the Imagination," Joseph Addison describes an "action of the mind" that relies on the rhetorical appeal of *pathos*, providing us a view of eighteenth-century psychology shared by Pope's contemporaries:

> In the like manner, when we read of Torments, Wounds, Deaths, and the like dismal Accidents, our Pleasure does not flow so properly from the Grief which such melancholly Descriptions give us, as from the secret Comparison which we make between our selves and the Person who suffers. Such Representations teach us to set a just Value upon our Condition, and make us prize our good Fortune which exempts us from the like Calamities. This is, however, such a kind of Pleasure as we are not capable of receiving, when we see a Person actually lying under the Tortures that we meet with in a Description; because, in this Case, the Object presses too close upon our Senses, and bears so hard upon us, that it does not give us time or leisure to reflect on our selves. Our Thoughts are so intent upon the Miseries of the Sufferer, that we cannot turn them upon our own Happiness. Whereas, on the contrary, we consider the Misfortunes we read in History or Poetry, either as past, or as fictitious, so that the Reflection upon our selves rises in us insensibly, and over-bears the Sorrow we conceive for the Suffering of the Afflicted.[7]

Addison sees the distancing of history or poetry, "either as past, or as fictitious," as palliative, allowing the reader to suffer and learn, but without the devastating effects of first-hand experience. These general remarks, reminiscent of Aristotle, describe an emotional displacement and a *catharsis* of the reader similar to that sought by Pope in the *Elegy* and *Eloisa to Abelard*.

Through rhetorical strategies of expression and emotional appeal, Pope pulls the reader into the speakers' worlds of anguish and turmoil. He creates an imaginative *agon* in the Elegy and *Eloisa to Abelard* that gives each poem a tragic tone, moving the reader with the *pathos* of his speakers and producing a form of catharsis. Through an *agon* experienced vicariously, the reader is provided a wisdom lying beyond the mere accretion of knowledge, a wisdom such as that possessed by the poet's father in *Epistle to Dr. Arbuthnot:* "Un-learn'd, he knew no Schoolman's subtle Art, / No Language, but the Language of the Heart. / By Nature honest, by Experience wise" (398–400). In these early poems, the reader is drawn into the personal agony of each speaker; and how Pope obtains a union between reader and speaker belongs to a domain of poetical practice essentially rhetorical.

Longinian Ecstasy

We have seen how readers of *Windsor-Forest* are transported through a series of traditionally associated topics, across a symbolical mapping of patriotically affecting *loci*. While the poet elevates his reader emotionally through his laudatory rapture, he still situates his imagery *ut pictura poesis* in recognizable spatial and temporal frames that are public in nature. *Windsor-Forest*, like panegyric, relies on a historical moment in which its eighteenth-century reader, Whig or Tory, is predisposed to a theme of national glory and more willingly participates in the laudator's exaltation. But the public themes of *Windsor-Forest* require a use of *pathos* categorically different from that in the Elegy and in *Eloisa to Abelard*, poems which deal with themes of private anguish.

The personal lamentations of Eloisa and the Elegy poet must be made accessible to the unfamiliar reader. To accomplish this, Pope relies on rhetorically formulaic progressions for expressing his speakers' passionate states of mind. Whereas the laudator of *Windsor-Forest* seeks to lift his audience intellectually and emotionally into a shared national *ethos*, the speakers in the Elegy and *Eloisa to Abelard* pull the reader into their private *ethos*, into a sympathetic understanding of their self-imposed tribulations. The vicarious suffering of the reader through imaginative participation, functioning as in classical tragedy, then becomes the basis for a renewed perception; and, as in our Greek proverb, "the suffered is the learned."

The emotional displacement of a reader sought in these poems is a rhetorical form of *ecstasis,* an irresistible ecstasy, that Longinus circumscribes in his treatise *On the Sublime.* In the final section of this chapter, I shall explore briefly how this version of *ecstasis* was rejected or ignored by eighteenth-century proponents of the sublime, an exclusion promulgated by Romantic writers and continued into this century.

The English word *ecstasy* comes from the Greek *ecstasis,* meaning literally "to put out of place" (OED). In his note to a Greek edition of Longinus, D. A. Russell explains: "A condition of *ecstasis* is one of being out of one's senses, or being no longer the same person."[8] For Longinus, *ecstasis* is a dynamic expression for the corollary effect of *hypsos,* the "true sublime." An eighteenth-century translator of Boileau provides us this version:

> The Sublime is in effect that which forms the Excellence and Sovereign Perfection of Discourse; that 'tis by the Sublime that great Poets and the most famous Writers have gain'd the Prize, and fill'd Posterity with the Fame of their Glory; for it does not, properly speaking, perswade, it charms, it transports and produces in us a certain Admiration mingled with Astonishment and Surprize, which is quite another Thing than pleasing or perswading only. We may say of Persuasion, that it generally has no more Power over us than we please our selves. 'Tis not thus with the Sublime; it gives Discourse a certain noble Vigour, an invincible Force which ravishes the Souls of all that hear us.[9]

Being charmed, transformed, and placed in a state of "Admiration mingled with Astonishment and Surprize" is a "paraphrase" (using Dryden's term) of *ecstasis,* a rather free translation of the concept.[10] One modern translator provides a "metaphrase" of *ecstasis* as "to transport them [the audience] out of themselves";[11] but even this attempt, in its generality, does not suggest the functionally different forms of transport with which we are concerned. D. A. Russell's explanation, "being out of one's senses, or being no longer the same person," better defines the state of rapture Longinus describes.

The English word *ecstasy* provides a valuable connotative fund for explicating the particular kinds of emotional displacement Pope himself seeks in his poems and enables us to find a connection with Longinus's conception of *ecstasis*. Johnson's *Dictionary* definition for *ecstasy* contains five eighteenth-century connotations:

1. Any passion by which the thoughts are absorbed, and in which the mind is for a time lost
2. Excessive joy; rapture
3. Enthusiasm; excessive elevation of the mind
4. Excessive grief or anxiety
5. Madness; distraction

The first and third definitions represent two kinds of ecstasy relevant to the act of reading, in that they concern a relationship between the reasoning mind and emotions. We shall set aside from this discussion the other definitions.[12] The first and the third definitions are useful paradigms for distinguishing emotional engagement in *Windsor-Forest*, the *Elegy*, and *Eloisa to Abelard*.

The laudator of *Windsor-Forest* seeks to move, not to persuade. He accomplishes this by further stimulating an already incipient patriotic enthusiasm that elevates but does not disorient his British readers, since they are already linked by a common subject. This relationship must be preserved while a reader's emotional state is elevated. This "laudatory ecstasy" fits Johnson's third definition. The *Elegy* and *Eloisa to Abelard*, however, do not have such a historically adventitious node from which to move their readers. In these poems speaker and reader do not share initially a common orientation. The emotional appeal of the poems develops rhetorically through a calculated disorientation of a reader's incipient state of mind and a subsequent emotive involvement with the speaker's state of mind. This psychological effect fits Johnson's first definition of ecstasy and resembles an *ecstasis* Longinus considers paramount in achieving a "Sapphic" form of sublimity. Before inspecting this topic further, however, we should see how Pope achieves this form of ecstasy within the generic possibilities of the *Elegy* and *Eloisa to Abelard*.

English Elegy and the Unfortunate Lady

By the eighteenth century, English elegy no longer possesses the generic variety of its classical progenitor. To Greek and Roman writers, elegy was characterized by its metrical form, the elegiac couplet, a distich of hexameter and pentameter. As a metrical form, classical elegy included a family of generic types identified by subject matter; for example: *propemptikon* ("speech to the departing traveller"); *phonetikon* ("speech of the welcomer"); *syntaktikon* ("speech of the departing traveller"); *paraclausithyron* ("the song and actions of a lover who is usually excluded"); and so on.[13] In terms of subject matter, even the verse epistle *Eloisa to Abelard* fits within the broad spectrum of classical elegy.

In the seventeenth century, we find Milton's Latin elegies, written in elegiac meter, reflecting his classical use of generic types.[14] Other seventeenth century poets, such as Jonson, Donne, and Marvell, use the pentameter couplet as an English equivalent of Latin elegiac meter and employ the form somewhat in the liberal manner of Roman elegy. Nevertheless, the range of subject matter of elegy narrows as certain types of English elegy become prominent. Alastair Fowler writes: "But Elizabethan and Jacobean critics, while they retained the ancient term, often distinguished 'mourning elegies' and 'anniversaries' (with lamentation of funeral elegies omitted) from love elegies."[15] Boileau in his *Art poétique* (1674) marks an authoritative narrowing of the genre in terms of subject matter; and in 1683 with Sir William Soames and John Dryden's translation of Boileau's *Art of Poetry*, we are told that elegy either "loves a mournful stile" or "paints the Lovers Torments, and Delights," and, above all, "The Heart in *Elegies* forms the Discourse."[16] In the eighteenth century, love elegies find their way into genres of lyric and ode and become divorced from generic elegy.[17] By 1755, love elegies are excluded from Johnson's definitions of elegy: "A mourning song"; "A funeral song"; "A short poem without points or turns." Thus, in Pope's lifetime, English elegy undergoes a metamorphosis, and his *Elegy* follows in this pattern of change.

Yet, the transitional character of elegy would not be as puzzling to an eighteenth-century reader as, perhaps, this synopsis might suggest. By 1717, before revision to its present title, Pope's *Verses to the Memory of an Unfortunate Lady* would certainly be recognized as a mourning elegy, and Pope could assume a reader's familiarity with elegy as an expression of passionate lamentation. Pope, though quite aware of classical models, seems to reflect a growing acceptance of elegy as a native form. In 1736 when he adds "Elegy" to his title, it appears that only an assured connotative specificity would warrant a change from "Verses."[18]

Neither did poems that had become divorced from elegiac tradition pose a problem to less classically oriented readers. For example, Johnson's *London*, published a year after Pope's title change, was clearly viewed as imitation or satire, even though it, as well as its model, Juvenal's *Third Satire*, may be considered an inverse *syntaktikon*, a generic type of elegy serving as a vehicle for satire.[19] Though sensitive to contemporary opinion, Pope's strong understanding of broader classical forms still would have enabled him to see a fundamental connection between his *Elegy*, *London*, and *Eloisa to Abelard* and how they share classical strategies of *pathos*. In his *Elegy*, as in *Windsor-Forest*, Pope takes advantage of a contemporary understanding of poetic kind, both as a disciplined starting point for poet and reader and as a creative resource for classical strategies.

Recognition of the poem as elegy tentatively establishes the reader's rhetorical expectations. Samuel Johnson, though not fond of the *Elegy* on moral grounds, grants that the poem satisfies expectation: "They [the verses] must be allowed [that is, admitted] to be written in some parts with vigorous animation, and in others with gentle tenderness; nor has Pope produced any poem in which the sense predominates more over the diction."[20] Accordingly, Pope conforms to elegiac practice by subordinating rational argument *(logos)* to *pathos* as his primary appeal to the reader. The character *(ethos)* of his poet also serves as a secondary source of appeal. Given the brief compass of the *Elegy*, the poet's extreme passion precludes any functional elaboration of *ethos*. Despite the censure of later critics, Pope is justified in not providing us with a moral deliberation, because such an addition would distend and weaken the forcefulness of the poet's passion. With the *Elegy*, as with his other original poems, Pope wishes to tackle a poetic form previously unattempted. The elegy allows Pope a concentrated focus on *pathos* and challenges his imaginative use of familiar rhetorical strategies for effecting a mimesis of passions.

Pope "was the first Homeric translator in English to make abundant use of Longinus's treatise *On the Sublime*."[21] His understanding of Longinus enabled him to recognize the necessity of *Iliad* Books 23 and 24, the funeral of Patroclus and the redemption of Hector's body, as a necessary resolution of Homeric *pathos*. In his introductory note to Book 23, Pope explains: "What he [Homer] undertook to paint was the *Anger of* Achilles: and as that Anger does not die with *Hector*, but persecutes his very remains, so the Poet still keeps up to his Subject; nay it seems to require that he should carry down the Relation of that Resentment, which is the Foundation of His Poem, till it is fully satisfy'd."[22] As in Homer's paradigmatic completion of *pathos*, the speaker in the *Elegy* moves from an "inexorable resentment" to a "perfect tranquility";[23] and we see again the resemblance of *pathos* to tragedy in the poet's empassioned movement through his vivification of the lady's terrible fate, his personal suffering, and his renewed perception.

Reuben Brower warns us away from biographical interpretation of the *Elegy:* "It might be said that critics have paid too little attention to the first word of the title, and too much to the last two."[24] That Pope never attempts to fix his poem within a historical context should key us to his implied poetic purpose. The heart of the poem lies in the poet's empassioned state of mind, his reaction to the suicide, not the suicide itself. Johnson believes that the uncle's character, insufficiently described by Pope, cannot logically justify his proclaimed wickedness. But given Pope's elegiac purpose, the uncle's character is not really germane to the poem. Furthermore, even if the uncle is not as obviously responsible as Johnson would have him, the suicide of the poet's dear friend could very naturally entail his unreasonable condemnation of the uncle.[25] Indeed, the poem relies on an incompleteness of fact, for the logical basis of the poem, in following elegiac practice, extends beyond the poem itself; that is, the reason for the poet's suffering, for his passionate state of mind, lies outside of the poetic frame, and a reader familiar with the elegiac mode would expect that the poem begin *in medias res*, after the decisive act accounting for the poet's present emotional state. It is enough for the reader to know that the lady has suffered from unfortunate circumstances, on foreign soil, away from home and friends, and that she has been driven to self-destruction, for whatever reasons. Biographical particulars need not be present, nor have they cause to exist.

Let us return to Johnson's observation about the rational inconsistency of the speaker, whom Johnson considers as Pope himself:

But the tale is not skilfully told: it is not easy to discover the character of either the lady or her guardian. History relates that she was about to disparage herself by marriage with an inferior; Pope praises her for the dignity of ambition, and yet condemns the unkle to detestation for his pride: the ambitious love of a niece may be opposed by the interests, malice, or envy of an unkle, but never by his pride. On such an occasion a poet may be allowed to be obscure, but inconsistency never can be right.[26]

In chapter 8 of *Rasselas,* Imlac declares, "Inconsistencies cannot both be right, but, imputed to man, they may both be true"; Imlac's (or, ironically, Johnson's?) words make Johnson's complaint about the inconsistency of Pope's speaker sound hollow. Pope uses a *persona* and, in doing so, is perfectly consistent in his speaker's inconsistency. Moreover, his poet *persona* illustrates by example how allowing passion free reign can subvert reason, a recurring theme in Pope's poetry (and, I might add, Robert Browning's monologues, which modern readers more readily acknowledge). Johnson is really more concerned about Pope's audience and, for this reason, is motivated to censure on moral, not truly aesthetic, grounds.[27]

Yet, Johnson's criticism underscores the relationship of *pathos* in the *Elegy* to tragedy and, even more fundamentally, to ritual. Since the poet's character manifests itself through his passions, we know little about him. We do know, however, of his capacity for excessive passion, which may be the best indicator of his character. He, as did the lady, allows passion to get the best of him, and his illogical scorn represents an elegiac form of *hamartia,* or tragic flaw. So, it appears the inconsistency that Johnson observes is not an oversight on Pope's part; the poet's intellectual blindness increases the philosophical significance of the poem. If it were obvious that the uncle's "interest, malice, or envy" had led the lady to suicide, then the poetic justice of the poet's curse would have reduced the poem to melodrama. But life is neither neatly balanced nor poetically just, and the incongruity of tragic events compels one to search for meaning.

The dramatic irony of the poet's blindness, which mirrors the lady's, allows us to see that his own expiation through personal suffering functions as a ritual expiation for the lady's sin of suicide, a mimetic reenactment through which they will both be atoned. Thus, at the end of the poem we are told: "Poets themselves must fall, like those they sung" (75); and the poet's recognition in the final line that the lady's fate is tied to his own—"The Muse forgot, and thou belov'd no more!"—implies his philosophical understanding of their tragic insignificance within a cosmic order, a perception that the reader also shares if the poem has succeeded in its elegiac purpose.[28] After all, the *Elegy* must establish a sympathetic engagement of its reader that justifies the poet's flights of passion and prevents them from falling flat, from sounding bombastic and appearing unwarranted. Now let us see how Pope achieves such engagement of the reader.

Pope wishes to move the reader from an initial position of detachment at the very outset of the poem, when the sudden arrival of the lady's ghost, a sensational and frightening event, reifies her fateful act in the mind of the poet.[29] The speaker's first words—"What beck'ning ghost"—emphatically reveal his state of mind and also trigger in the reader's imagination a natural sequence of questions: from What does the poet see? to Why does he see it? Using a familiar, but effective, device, Pope has thrust us into the mind of the poet:

> What beck'ning ghost, along the moonlight shade
> Invites my step, and points to yonder glade?
>
> (1–2)

Just like the poet frozen in his tracks by wonder, the reader is expected to be held in suspension by his astonishment and curiosity. Pope captures his reader by what Longinus calls *phantasia* (in Ozell's translation of Boileau's): *"Wherein by an extraordinary Enthusiasm and Emotion of Soul, it seems as if we saw the things we speak of, and put them before the Eyes of those that hear us."*[30]

Longinian ecstasy requires the reader to become absorbed in the thoughts of the speaker. Pope manages this through the speaker's immediate answer to his own question: " 'Tis she!" (3); a rhetorical figure Longinus considers especially effective: "The inspiration and quick play of the question and answer, and his way of meeting his own words, as if they were someone else's, make the passage, through his use of the figure, not only loftier but more convincing."[31] The answer also fulfills three functions by appealing to the reader's incipient rationality: first, it addresses the reader's curiosity; second, it suggests why the ghost no longer remains a frightful apparition to the poet; and, third, in knowing her, it explains why he is drawn to her.

A succession of rhetorical questions follows, directed to the ghost and corresponding with the speaker's physical movement toward the lady. Similarly, we are invited by steps to abandon our sober detachment and witness at close hand the speaker's emotionally charged bewilderment:

> 'Tis she!—but why that bleeding bosom gor'd,
> Why dimly gleams the visionary sword?
> Oh ever beauteous, ever friendly! tell,
> Is it, in heav'n, a crime to love too well?
> To bear too tender, or too firm a heart,
> To act a Lover's or a *Roman's* part?
> Is there no bright reversion in the sky,
> For those who greatly think, or bravely die?
>
> (3–10)

These questions proceed from the factual to the philosophical, anticipating the poet's apostrophe in the next paragraph to "ye Pow'rs!"[32] The repetition of words *why, ever, to/too* and of end-stopped lines, in addition to the resonating rhyme, formally suggest his dramatic movement toward the ghost. They also invite an increasing empathy within us, as we track the progressive mental states leading to his passionate questioning.

With Ovidian ingenuity, Pope uses the same words to represent different realities.[33] The speaker's language becomes an aural mimesis echoing his traumatic recollection of her gruesome stabbing, made especially clear in the following repetitions:

> By foreign hands thy dying eyes were clos'd,
> By foreign hands thy decent limbs compos'd,
> By foreign hands thy humble grave adorn'd,
> By strangers honour'd, and by strangers mourn'd!
>
> (51–54)[34]

This powerful union of sound and sense reinforces within our own minds the horrific nature of the lady's suicide, while we visualize her unpropitious burial. Seductively invited to enter the poet's world of shadow and mystery, of "moonlight shade," we now find ourselves no longer detached spectators but engaged witnesses.

The antitheses of darkness and light and of "too tender, or too firm a heart" of the first paragraph (1–10) set in motion the speaker's emotional *stichomythia*, pitting the ghost's spirituality against his own reality, heaven against earth, death against life, past against present. These qualitative progressions create an intricate fabric of passions that characterize "Sapphic" sublimity.[35] With only a change of gender Longinus's remarks about Sappho's ode would apply: "See, with how many contrary Emotions she's agitated; she Freezes, she Burns, she's Mad, she's Wise; she's either entirely out of her Wits, or is Dying."[36]

Inversion of a traditional figure, "the imaginary second person," also plays a central role in the poem. Pope's poetry seems to thrive on inversions of all kinds; recall how in *Windsor-Forest* Pope inverts topics: the forest becomes the traditional city of panegyric; and in his other poems he inverts genres: panegyric for satire, epic for mock-epic, and so on. In the *Elegy*, he accomplishes a brilliant inversion of "the imaginary second person," a figure in which, as Longinus describes, "sometimes a writer, while speaking of his characters, suddenly turns and changes into the actual character."[37] The purpose of the figure lies in vivifying a speaker's presence by switching from narrative speech to direct speech.

Pope reverses the order of this figure by switching the speaker's voice from the actual character to the writer speaking of the character. At the dramatic outset of the poem, the poet self-consciously refers to himself with a first-person possessive pronoun, "my step" (3); then caught up by his emotions, he seems to obliterate his sense of self through direct speech; and, finally achieving a state of calm, in his coda he refers to himself in a narrative third-person voice:

> Ev'n he, whose soul now melts in mournful lays,
> Shall shortly want the gen'rous tear he pays;
> Then from his closing eyes thy form shall part,
> And the last pang shall tear thee from his heart.
>
> (77–80)

This inversion from direct to narrative speech results in a diminuendo signaling the fulfillment of ritual expiation. The poet circles back to the mood of detachment with which his reader began. As with the ending of *Windsor-Forest*, an emotional relaxation allows the reader to reflect back on the poet's transport, place it in perspective, and realize the significance of the occasion. There are numerous other figures and tropes that, however minor, function in this integral fashion. They are not merely stylistic ornamentation.[38]

By recognizing the rhetorical appeal through *pathos*, the function of Longinian ecstasy, and the generic expectations of elegy in this poem, we attend to Pope's brilliant execution of rhetorical technique in a well-wrought poetic display of passion.[39] Such rhetorically controlled passion had a place in the Renaissance and the eighteenth century, as George Puttenham's remarks on the function of lamentation tell us:

Lamenting is altogether contrary to reioising, euery man saith so, and yet is it a peece of ioy to be able to lament with ease, and freely to poure forth a mans inward sorrowes and the greefs wherewith his minde is surcharged. This was a very necessary deuise of the Poet and a sine, besides his poetrie to play also the Phisitian, and not onely by applying a medicine to the ordinary sicknes of mankind, but by making the very greef it selfe (in part) cure of the disease.[40]

Sublime Eloisa

If the *Elegy* may lay claim to a form of sublimity, *Eloisa to Abelard* with its wider appeal has an even stronger claim: "The Equal Judgment and Approbation of so many Minds, otherwise so different from one another, is a certain and undoubted Proof that the Marvellous and Sublime are there."[41] Like the *Elegy*, *Eloisa to Abelard* portrays a concourse of passions seeking to evoke a Longinian ecstasy; but by virtue of its length, *Eloisa to Abelard* requires a complexity of technique that surpasses that of the *Elegy*.

Eloisa to Abelard has no projected authorial voice or poet *persona*. Pope frames his poem with "The Argument" preceding it and subsumes his poetic self within a fictional Eloisa. Loosely basing his poem on historical fact, Pope presents Eloisa's mind at a particular moment of crisis, after reading Abelard's letter to a friend.[42] The challenge of a poet to imagine what a historical person would do at a significant moment or under a particular set of conditions has antecedents in the rhetorical exercises of *progymnasmata*, but more directly in the Ovidian epistle.[43]

Pope wishes to lose himself in Eloisa's psychological states. In following the tradition of Ovid's *Heroides*, he begins where Ovid left off and introduces a subjective complexity that outreaches the *Heroides*. Eloisa is so powerfully portrayed that we easily lose a sense of the poet's presence, which Pope seeks to achieve. Geoffrey Tillotson writes in his Twickenham introduction to *Eloisa to Abelard*: "The reader will judge the letter as he judges a fugue on a given subject. Eloisa becomes for him the 'artist,' the intellectual master co-ordinating times, places, and moods, the 'artist' of emotion rather than the experiencer of it"; but Tillotson oversimplifies the reader's perspective in calling Eloisa the "artist" of the poem and, thereby, equating Eloisa with Pope.[44] The reader no more confuses Eloisa with "the intellectual master" of the poem than he mistakes Hamlet for Shakespeare, for *Eloisa to*

Abelard functions as poetic drama. As with Hamlet, Eloisa's lines are choreographed, but neither Hamlet nor Eloisa is the maker of his own dramatic illusion. They are, after all, fictions; and given a reader's willing suspension of disbelief, Eloisa experiences her emotions with the same credibility that Hamlet does on the stage. She is the dramatic artifact, and Pope is the well-concealed artist of emotion. In the manner of a stage direction, Pope declares in "The Argument" to his poem: "This [Abelard's letter to a friend] awakening all her tenderness, occasion'd those celebrated letters *(out of which the following is partly extracted)* which give so lively a picture of the struggles of grace and nature, virtue and passion" [italics added].⁴⁵ Thus, Pope creates for us a *phantasia* of Eloisa's mind and, through selection and refraction, transforms a historical Heloise into an existential Eloisa.

Pope takes advantage of placing a well-known subject within a familiar genre, the heroic epistle. Attentive to the rhetorical properties of the poem, Tillotson writes: "This historical derivation means that the reader, without effort, knows as much of the past as the writer and the recipient. . . . The reader, therefore, expects not to be told the story and persuaded of the passions, but to see a use made of the known materials, to see as good a letter as possible made out of them."⁴⁶ Again, the reader expects "as good a letter as possible" from Pope the artist, not Eloisa; and if Tillotson refers to Eloisa as putative writer of the poem in his succeeding sentence, he seems to agree that Eloisa also is "the experiencer of it": "The writer sees the past through the present, which is not only its result but its unforeseen and unfortunate result." Indeed, Eloisa's emotional torment arises from her experience of the uncharted present; and her response to Abelard's letter suggests how Pope would like us to read her own epistle, as Eloisa tells us:

> Heav'n first taught letters for some wretch's aid,
> Some banish'd lover, or some captive maid;
> They live, they speak, they breathe what love inspires,
> Warm from the soul, and faithful to its fires,
> The virgin's wish without her fears impart,
> Excuse the blush, and pour out all the heart,
> Speed the soft intercourse from soul to soul,
> And waft a sigh from *Indus* to the *Pole*.
>
> (51–58)

Thus, the epistolary form of *Eloisa to Abelard* also stands as a poetic declaration of the power of language.

The *Elegy* and *Eloisa to Abelard*, published together in Pope's first collected *Works* of 1717, aesthetically complement one another; and Eloisa's final words might well have been those of the Unfortunate Lady:

> And sure if fate some future Bard shall join
> In sad similitude of griefs to mine,
> Condemn'd whole years in absence to deplore,
> And image charms he must behold no more,
> Such if there be, who loves so long, so well;
> Let him our sad, our tender story tell;
> The well-sung woes will sooth my pensive ghost;
> He best can paint 'em, who shall feel 'em most.
>
> (359-66)

An intertextual linking of these poems suggests that Eloisa does not achieve relief at the end of the poem.[47] The expiatory function remains for the "future Bard" to complete, and Eloisa's final words are not a *consolatio* but a suspension of her inner turmoil. Pope "paints" here what he tells us in "The Argument": "a picture of the struggles of grace and nature, virtue and passion." Moreover, he has already told us: "The Strength of the Passions will never be accepted as an Excuse for complying with them; they were designed for Subjection, and if a Man suffers them to get the upper Hand, he then betrays the Liberty of his own Soul."[48] *Eloisa to Abelard* reveals Pope's commiseration with a natural human weakness, not a justification for it. As in the *Elegy*, his conclusion has a rhetorical purpose; by employing an inversion of Longinus's figure of "the imaginary second person" in Eloisa's change of mood and tone, Pope signals a poetic diminuendo, but not, in this poem, to suggest a form of expiation. This emotional relaxation provides the reader a perspective from which to gauge the sublimity of Eloisa's passions.

Poetic "'geometry' of situation" also accounts for Eloisa's inability to resolve her conflicts.[49] In the *Elegy*, the poet's imaginative distance from the inspirational center of his grief—the lady's torment, suicide, and burial—enables him through compressed action, on the brink of symbolism, to complete a tragic cycle. The *Elegy* poet projects himself into his subject; and the short compass of the *Elegy* enables Pope to minimize the complexifying and, in this case, distracting use of *ethos* for a purer expression of *pathos*. On the other hand, Eloisa, inverting the psychodynamics of the *Elegy*, brings her subject into herself. She seems as if under a magnifying glass, and though we view her emotional trek over a longer metrical course, the emotional distance she traverses is, finally, less than that of the *Elegy* poet. Pope sustains the power of Eloisa's *pathos* by a greater focus on her character, from which he generates character foils that enlarge the drama of her inner struggle. Though her mental flights sweep across time, Eloisa still experiences a narrower slice of pathetic action than the poet of the *Elegy*. Our closer perspective of Eloisa provides Pope an imaginative opportunity to explore subtle links between her character and her passions and achieve a fruitful interplay of *ethos* and *pathos*.

Eloisa's first words in the poem are both literal and metaphorical. Literally, she places us within the darkly melancholic and contemplative gloom of the Paraclete, where she seems imprisoned. But "these deep solitudes and awful cells, / Where heav'nly-pensive, contemplation dwells" (1–2) can also be a metaphor for her mind. An impressionistic sequence of synecdochic references to heart, lips, hand, and tears in the first two verse paragraphs seem to correspond perfectly to Eloisa's self-perceptions; and we feel as if we were inside her skin. Through her eyes, we seem to view for a moment her own interior: her thoughts "rove . . . beyond this last retreat" (her mind), cause a "tumult" in her veins, and rekindle her heart, hearth-like, with "long-forgotten heat." In the third verse paragraph (17–28), her expression wells outward in apostrophes to the imprisoning "Relentless walls!" "rugged rocks!" and "grots and caverns shagg'd with horrid thorn!" Passionately alive, "I have not yet forgot my self to stone" (24), she seems now under seige: "Still rebel nature holds out half my heart" (26). The piously balanced equilibrium of mind and heart has been overturned by her memory of Abelard, and we are given immediately its effect on her through an effusion of images.

As does the *Elegy*, *Eloisa to Abelard* opens with rhetorical questioning. Eloisa directs her questions to herself, a figure of "Reasoning by Question and Answer" (*ratiocinatio*) in which "we ask ourselves the reason for every statement we make, and seek the meaning of each successive affirmation":

> What means this tumult in a Vestal's veins?
> Why rove my thoughts beyond this last retreat?
> Why feels my heart its long-forgotten heat?
>
> (4–6)

"This figure is exceedingly well adapted to a conversational style, and both by its stylistic grace and the anticipation of the reasons, holds the hearer's attention."[50] With progressively increasing emotion, the rational appeal of this series of questions holds a reader's attention, while the repetitive progression subtly shifts us into Eloisa's *pathos*. As in the *Elegy*, Pope allows us an extremely disciplined entrance into Eloisa's passionate state of mind. Even her answer comes in a dramatically halting manner intended to excite pity: "Yet, yet I love!"[51]

The discourse is broken off in the second verse paragraph (9–16) by apostrophes to "Dear fatal name," "my heart," "my hand," and "my tears." Quintilian tells us that "the term *apostrophe* is also applied to utterances that divert the attention of the hearer from the question before them."[52] These diversions reflect Eloisa's distracted state, but also pull the reader into a similar pattern of thought, which subserves Pope's need to bring his reader ever closer to Eloisa. Repetitions of "my" ("my heart"; "my hand"; "my tears") and of "her" ("her heart"; "her hand") are figures of *conduplicatio*, as similarly seen in the *Elegy*, that make "a deep impression upon the hearer" and inflict "a major wound upon the opposition."[53]

Aside from the mimetic effect of these repetitions, a thematic resonation occurs. The religious themes clearly have been established, both by the reader's familiarity with the well-known tragedy of Heloise and Abelard and by internal echoes: "heav'nly-pensive, contemplation" (2), "Vestal's veins" (4), "holy silence" (10), "Where, mix'd with God's, his lov'd Idea lies" (12). The resonation elicited by these religious themes and repetitions of *conduplicatio* ushers in images, perhaps, of the piercing of Christ's body, of self-flagellation, or of the brutal castration of Abelard. These themes of punishment seem to permeate the poem, giving Eloisa an aspect of martyrdom, though, as we shall see, a misdirected one.

The sublime compression of "Dear fatal name!" (9) evokes a congeries of associations. Pope ingeniously turns an overworked eighteenth-century convention of *periphrasis* into a *metalepsis* that brings to mind the wit of metaphysical poetry. Henry Peacham defines *metalepsis* in *The Garden of Eloquence* (1577; 1593):

> The orator in one word expressed, signifieth another word or thing removed from it by certain degrees . . . a kind of *metonymia* signify-

ing a cause far off by an effect nigh at hand . . . seldom used. . . . It teacheth the understanding to dive down to the bottom of sense.[54]

The "Dear fatal name!" that now produces such torment in Eloisa was written by the hand of Abelard, that "cause far off." A number of other associations arise. Name (9), hand (13), and heart (16) symbolically link language, body, and spirit, thematically embracing the poem. The hand discerned in the signature of Abelard joins metaphorically to Eloisa's "my hand" (13) now writing his name, and there is a dark memory of another fateful hand in the background, that which was ordered by her Uncle Fulbert to castrate Abelard.

In the same verse paragraph, Eloisa seems to fear naming Abelard directly. He is her god, and as her god, he, who has determined her past, now conditions her present state of mind and will control her future. The adjectives "Dear" and "fatal" carry both a historical and a prophetic meaning. Their love brought them a form of death in life; and in his castration and their physical separation, their love has been forcibly reduced to the spirit. That she still responds with physical passion creates a logical paradox that can only be resolved for her in physical death: "Death, only death, can break the lasting chain" (173).

One of the more interesting rhetorical aspects of the poem lies in Pope's interplay of *ethos* and *pathos*. Eloisa's character manifests itself in a number of ways. Historically and as the presumed writer of the epistle before us, she is keenly intelligent and capable of the hair-splitting scholastic reasoning Abelard made famous: "How shall I lose the sin, yet keep the sense, / And love th' offender, yet detest th' offence?" (191–92); she is proud and self-sacrificing: "Should at my feet the world's great master fall, / Himself, his throne, his world, I'd scorn 'em all" (85–86); she is dutiful: "Yet here for ever, ever must I stay; / Sad proof how well a lover can obey!" (171–72); and she is capable of pious humility:

> While prostrate here in humble grief I lie,
> Kind, virtuous drops just gath'ring in my eye,
> While praying, trembling, in the dust I roll,
> And dawning grace is opening on my soul.
>
> (277–80)

Admirably, Eloisa acts out of moral strength, not weakness, while heroically, she wars with herself, and her nobility becomes a test case for the Christian paradox of renouncing mortal love for the absolute love of God. Yet, her sublime capacity for embracing absolutes dooms her from the beginning. Were she to give herself completely to God in the way she gives herself to Abelard, she would be a saint. We are drawn to her plight because of her strength of character, but like Milton's Satan, she is sublimely wrong, and it is easy to confuse the author's aesthetic purpose for a moral statement of approval. In retrospect, Pope realized the blinding power of lofty passion in his poem, and the implied metaphor of a "stooping" falcon in his lines from *An Epistle to Dr. Arbuthnot* would seem to illustrate not only his eschewal of fancy's flight, but of the liberated excesses of passion as well: "That not in Fancy's Maze he wander'd long, / But stoop'd to Truth, and moraliz'd his song" (340–41).

An example of Pope's ability to move from the tender emotions of Eloisa's attractive *ethos* to the overwhelming power of her *pathos* are to be found in lines 59 to 106. She begins by describing their first meeting: "how guiltless first I met thy flame" (59); then the growth of her innocent love for Abelard: "Those smiling eyes, attemp'ring ev'ry ray, / Shone sweetly lambent with celestial day: / Guiltless I gaz'd" (63–65); and her delight in the pleasures of their love: "Back thro' the paths of pleasing sense I ran / Nor wish'd an Angel whom I lov'd a Man" (69–70). She further shows how completely she gave herself in love for Abelard: "Curse on all laws but those which love has made!" (74); and forsook marriage and all ties but those of the heart: "Oh happy state! when souls each other draw, / When love is liberty, and nature, law" (91–92). But the powerful hold of her memory overtakes her as she reenacts Abelard's horrible castration, and Pope makes the past deed vividly present through Longinus's figure of *phantasia*:

> Alas how chang'd! what sudden horrors rise!
> A naked Lover bound and bleeding lies!
> Where, where was *Eloise*? her voice, her hand,
> Her ponyard, had oppos'd the dire command.
> Barbarian stay! that bloody stroke restrain.
>
> (99–103)

Finally, out of her senses and completely overtaken by passion, Eloisa drives herself beyond expression: "I can no more; by shame, by rage supprest, / Let tears, and burning blushes speak the rest" (105–106).[55]

Pope also uses character foils to generate *pathos*. Eloisa contrasts her turmoil caused by her overpowering memory to that of the dispassionate Vestal who is never plagued by recollection:

> How happy is the blameless Vestal's lot!
> The world forgetting, by the world forgot.
> Eternal sun-shine of the spotless mind!
> Each pray'r accepted, and each wish resign'd;
> Labour and rest, that equal periods keep;
> 'Obedient slumbers that can wake and weep';
> Desires compos'd, affections ever ev'n.
>
> (207–13)

There are internal foils as well: "Assist me heav'n! but whence arose that pray'r? / Sprung it from piety, or from despair?" (179–80).

The success of Pope's use of *ethos* lies in his sensitive anticipation of the reader's emotional fatigue from sustained flights of passion. In this poem, he wishes to display the minutest sinews of Eloisa's turmoil, which begins and ends unresolved. Through the interplay of *ethos* and *pathos*, therefore, Pope creates a poetic rhythm of tension and distension that has some affinity to the panegyrical method we explored in *Windsor-Forest*. But, unlike *Windsor-Forest*, *Eloisa to Abelard* achieves a neglected form of "Sapphic" sublimity.

Pope's Longinus

Boileau's translation of Longinus's *Peri Hypsous* (1674) accounts for the rapid popularization of the sublime throughout Europe. By Pope's time, the sublime already has many interpreters, and the numbers multiply rapidly in the eighteenth century.[56] In the process of dissemination, the concept of the sublime undergoes radical transformations that depart from Longinus's original articulation, and it appears Pope's sense of the sublime was closer to Longinus's than to that of his contemporaries. The *Elegy* and *Eloisa to Abelard* meet the requirements of Longinus's original conception of the sublime, which, in its richness, included a sublimity exemplified in Sappho's *Ode to Anactoria*.

The technical control that Longinus praises in his examples of the "true" sublime and the rhetorical strategies he recommends to achieve that control suggest that, aside from an author's innate ability for conception and passion, the sublime is a rhetorical product. For Longinus, sublime expression must induce a concomitant effect of *ecstasis* to be the "true" sublime; and though an author must possess innate faculties for sublime invention, those faculties are not enough. Sublime expression also requires an artistic use of figures and tropes, of diction, and of invention and arrangement:

> We may affirm that there are Five Original or Principal Causes of the Sublime; but these Five Causes presuppose a common Foundation to all, *A Faculty of Speaking well*, without which all the rest is worth nothing.
> The *First* and Chiefest of those Causes *is that Elevation of Mind, by which we think happily on every thing.* . . .
> The *Second* consists in the *Pathetick*. By Pathetick I mean that Enthusiasm and Natural Vehemence which touch and move. These two Causes are almost entirely the Gift of Nature, and must be Born with us; whereas the other three depend in some Measure upon Art. The *Third* is nothing *but a happy Turn of Figures*. Now Figures are of two Sorts; Figures of Thought, and Figures of Diction.
> For the *Fourth* we put *Nobleness of Expression*, which has two Parts; Choice of Words, and an elegant and Figurative Diction.
> The *Fifth* is that which properly speaking, produces the Sublime, and contains all the others in it self; being *the Composition and Disposition of Words with all the Magnificence and Dignity they are capable of.*[57]

The first two "Causes" of the sublime, "*Elevation of Mind*" and "the *Pathetick*," properly belong to an author's innate ability, "the Gift of Nature"; but having the *capacity* for great conception and elevated emotion is not actually possessing them: "Though of the Five Causes I have mention'd, *A Natural Elevation of Wit*, the First and Chiefest of 'em all, be rather a Gift of Heaven, than a Quality that may be acquir'd; yet we ought as much as we can, to accustom our Thoughts to the Sublime, and keep 'em always full and puff'd up, as we may say, with a certain Noble and Generous Boldness."[58] A poet, therefore, must intoxicate himself with sublimity.

In addition, he must train himself in rhetoric, since he seeks through expression to convey his sublime emotion to his reader: "Every thing that's truly Sublime, has this Property in it; when we hear it, it elevates the Soul, and gives it a higher Opinion of it self; filling it with Joy and a certain noble Pride, as if it had it self brought forth the things which it only heard."[59] Not only must he himself experience a sublime ecstasy, he must also rhetorically fashion an objective correlative. Even the sublime silence of Ajax in the *Odyssey* (11:543–67), which Longinus praises so highly for its naked thought, functions *via negativa* within a rhetorical frame. Ajax's words are missing, but Homer's rhetoric is not. Homer relies on a stock response from his auditors, who expect Ajax's vilification of Ulysses. Through the surprise of omission, a sublimity of silence is evoked.

Eighteenth-century commentators increasingly underplay the necessity of rhetorical art for producing the sublime and emphasize Longinus's own claims for the overriding importance of an author's innate powers of sublimity. They begin to refashion Longinus. Boileau's influential prefatory remarks to his translation deserve some attention:

> It must be observed then that by the Sublime he does not mean what the Orators call the *Sublime Stile*, but something *extraordinary* and *marvellous* that strikes us in a Discourse and makes it elevate, ravish and transport us. The *Sublime Stile* requires always great Words, but the *Sublime* may be found in a Thought only, or in a Figure or Turn of Expression. A Thing may be in the *Sublime Stile*, and yet not be *Sublime*, that is, have nothing *extraordinary* nor *surprising* in it.[60]

Boileau applies the tag "the Sublime Stile" to the lifeless expression of an author who lacks a natural talent for the sublime. He gives us an example of such tumidity in: "The Sovereign Arbiter of Nature with one Word only form'd the Light," comparing it to Longinus's famous example of sublimity in Genesis when "God said, 'Let there be Light,' and there was Light."[61] Boileau criticises a sterilizing separation of form from content. He does not, as Samuel H. Monk declares, insist that the sublime is "above rhetoric."[62] According to Longinus, as already seen in his five "Causes" of the sublime, a poet must experience sublime thoughts *in addition* to having the rhetorical skill for expressing them. Sublime inspiration and powers of expression are each indispensable: "For our virtues and vices spring from much the same sources. And so while beauty of style, sublime expression, yes, and agreeable phrasing all contribute to successful composition, yet these very graces are the source and groundwork no less of failure than of success."[63] In his prefatory remarks, Boileau has an eye on those contemporaries who divorce style from the rhetorical processes of invention and arrangement and consider it a lush garden of tropes and figures.[64]

Pope recognizes that there exists a truly sublime style, but not everyone is capable of achieving it: "The *sublime* style is more easily counterfeited than the *natural;* something passes for it, or sounds like it, is common in all false writers"; he goes on to describe the not so easily counterfeited *natural* style, which in his later satirical poems he will develop to a high state of perfection: "But nature, purity, perspicuity, and simplicity, never walk in the clouds; they are obvious to all capacities; and where they are not evident, they do not exist."[65] His *Peri Bathous,* in its ironic inversion of Longinus, represents his disgust and unwillingness to compete with this deluge of "false writers."

We must keep in mind, however, that Longinus is only concerned with sublime poetry and how it may be accomplished: "Besides when one treats of any Art there are Two Things which ought to be study'd. The First is to render the Subject very intelligible: The Second, which in truth I take to be the Chief, consists in shewing how and by what means the Thing taught is to be acquired." Other kinds of poetry, relying on "the Art of the *Invention,* the Beauty of the Œconomy and Disposition," are not his main concern.[66]

For critics to appropriate the "true sublime" as a sole criterion for judging "true" poetry is to mistake Longinus's purpose. John Dennis, lampooned as "Sir Tremendous Longinus" by Gay, Arbuthnot, and Pope in *Three Hours after Marriage* (1717), was guilty of this excess: "Under the guidance of the great Greek, Dennis is led to reduce art to the expression of passion, and to maintain that the highest art—the sublime—is the expression of the greatest passion."[67] Longinus provides a practical treatise for achieving a particular element in literary art, even if he esteems that element over others: "Invariably what inspires wonder casts a spell upon us and is always superior to what is merely convincing and pleasing." He never abnegates the value of other artistic expression:

> Again inventive skill and the due disposal and marshalling of facts do not show themselves in one or two touches: they gradually emerge from the whole tissue of composition, while, on the other hand, a well-timed flash of sublimity scatters everything before it like a bolt of lightning and reveals the full power of the speaker at a single stroke.[68]

Windsor-Forest, for example, relies on "the whole tissue of composition" for its grandeur, not on "a single stroke." One might argue for passages of Longinian sublimity in the poem, such as the visionary speech of a personified Thames rising from "his Oozy Bed"; but, again, the unity of author and reader obtains essentially from a historical occasion and requires a laudatory form of ecstasy. *Windsor-Forest*, therefore, draws its merit from a set of criteria quite different altogether from what Longinus describes. Rhetorically, it appears that the experience of laudatory ecstasy in reading *Windsor-Forest* generally has been lost on the modern reader; but the same disassociation through time affects readings of Pindar's poems and other occasional poetry as well. Recall again Pope's Scriblerian appraisal of dedication and panegyric in *Peri Bathous* as "but the *Praise of a Day* . . . by the next useless, improper, indecent, and false." Yet, Pope knew his Longinus well and would have realized that *Windsor-Forest* does not fall under Longinus's criticism. On account of its occasional nature and in not attempting a Longinian form of ecstasy, *Windsor-Forest* is not "falsely" sublime. The emotive power of *Windsor-Forest*, as we have seen, issues explicitly from a different source, and it is for us to recognize the original rhetorical intention of the poem.

Longinus focuses his criticism on poetry attempting a sublimity that requires for success an *ecstasis* of an extreme emotive transport, of a temporary erasure of self, perhaps similar to Keats's negative capability. He gives such attempts the following test:

> Imagine that to be Sublime, which pleases universally and in every Part of it. For when a great Number of Persons, of different Professions and Ages, having no manner of Relation to each other by Humour or Inclination, shall be equally touch'd with any Part of a Discourse; the Equal Judgment and Approbation of so many Minds, otherwise so different from one another, is a certain and undoubted Proof that the Marvellous and Sublime are there.[69]

He is concerned with the practical success or failure of works attempting an ecstasy "in which the mind is for a time lost." A panegyric in which amplification is essential for elevation, such as *Windsor-Forest*, which requires an "excessive elevation of the mind" (Johnson's definition) does not really concern him. In "The Argument of Longinus' *On the Sublime*," Elder Olson describes Longinus's purpose:

> The author enters into the discussion [of stylistic qualities] not as one possessed or not possessed of the sources of sublimity but as one

who aimed at sublimity and in some way missed in each case; and his introduction depends upon the necessity for illustrating his failure—a failure in art, in the strictest sense, since the intention of sublimity is actually present—to achieve that unification of author and audience which is *ecstasis*.[70]

On the other hand, the *Elegy* and *Eloisa to Abelard* do attempt a Longinian ecstasy "by which the thoughts are absorbed, and in which the mind for a time is lost." From this rhetorical perspective, these poems achieve a sublimity that lies within Longinus's broader conception, though it may not be the refined and more restricted sublimity of eighteenth-century reinterpretation.

For Longinus, emotion is one of the five sources of the sublime, but not the sublime itself. The sublime must be independent of emotion, for there are occasions of great sublimity without emotion. Longinus tells us: "Now if he [Cecilius, author of a treatise of the sublime, now lost] thought that sublimity and emotion were the same thing, and that one always essentially involved the other, he is wrong."[71] Emotion may or may not be present in the sublime itself: "In Prose, *Panegyricks*, and all Discourses made only for Ostentation, have every where the *Great* and *Sublime*; tho' there commonly is no Passion in 'em; insomuch that those Orators who are most *Pathetick*, are generally least proper for *Panegyricks*, and those on the contrary, who succeed best in *Panegyricks*, know little enough of the Passions, and how to touch them."[72] On this point concerning the emotional content of the sublime, many eighteenth-century interpreters of the sublime diverge from Longinus.[73] Through an epistemological shell game, the rhetorical sublime becomes a psychological sublime.

According to Longinus, sublimity necessarily entails *ecstasis*, which functions as a manifestation of its power. The reader recognizes sublimity by its powerful emotional effect on him; but if emotive absorption of the reader is a necessary effect and not a cause of sublimity, how can one separate the sublime from the words evoking *ecstasis*? Longinus saw how easy it was to mistake the passionate effect of sublime ecstasy for the sublime itself. Here, I believe, Longinus recognized the instrumental power of language, that is, the importance of rhetoric to the sublime writer. The sublime in literature must be an objective correlative of the "true sublime" experienced by the author. The relationship of a sublime passage to the reader's ecstasy, as cause is to effect, mirrors the innate relationship of sublime conception to sublime ecstasy within the author himself. Like the author, the reader too must achieve a corresponding passionate elevation that allows him to realize the greatness of a conception; and language functions as the reader's bridge to the sublime. In language, the sublime exists as an ideational potential in a poetic universe until it is experienced by a reader. Saying this another way, for Longinus, despite his claims for "natural genius," the literary sublime is ultimately as much a matter of rhetorical expression, of arrangement and style, as sublime invention.

In the eighteenth century, interpretations emerge that ignore Longinus's stricture against equating the sublime with emotion, leading finally to *ecstasis* becoming an artistic cause, rather than an effect, of sublimity. The sublime reduces, therefore, to the sublime effect, to a psychological sublime. With the increasing dominance of associationism in the eighteenth century, the sublime becomes a pictured ecstasy as an end in itself.

John Dennis exemplifies how eighteenth-century interpreters of the sublime begin to diverge from Longinus's treatise. Monk sees in John Dennis a developing focus on the more extreme passions: "Admiration, terror, horror, joy, sadness, and desire."[74] Dennis, especially in his emphasis on the sublimity of terror, anticipates a major preoccupation of the late eighteenth-century literary imagination:

> With its insistence on strong emotion it [Dennis's view of the sublime] goes beyond Longinus, and is certainly quite different from Boileau's theory, for Dennis is willing to subordinate all qualities to emotion. In view of the prominence of terror, both in later theories of the sublime and in much eighteenth-century literature, the most interesting aspect of Dennis's treatment of the sublime is his introduction of that emotion.[75]

Dennis's insistence on a specified set of strong emotions initiates a narrowing systematization of the sublime method.

With further developments, the literary sublime becomes limited as a subject, and the fertile range of traditional rhetorical method gives way to stylistic mannerism. The sublime subject becomes that which conduces best to a pictured ecstasy. An example may be readily found in Edmund Burke's *On the Sublime and Beautiful* (1757):

> But let it be considered that hardly anything can strike the mind with its greatness, which does not make some sort of approach towards infinity; which nothing can do whilst we are able to perceive its bounds; but to see an object distinctly, and to perceive its bounds, is

one and the same thing. A clear idea is therefore another name for a little idea.[76]

Burke narrows, ironically, the sublime to those subjects which invite obscurity. Burke's poet, therefore, becomes a conceptually passive agent of the sublime, representing something of a reversal of Longinian psychology. The poet searches for, not conceives, topics to match or to substantiate his sublime ecstasy. What follows is a *post-hoc-ergo-propter-hoc* use of figured language; and Burke's literary sublime reduces to a picture of passion, a stylistic display of language teetering on the brink of expressibility.

Boileau, Dennis, and Burke represent a growing preoccupation with sublime topics and forms of expression and contribute to a general departure from traditional rhetorical method toward a rhetoric of style, which romantic theorists will later attack as ornamentally vacuous. As a poetical master of rhetorical method, Pope remains closer to the Longinian spirit. For him P. W. K. Stone's comments on classical expression would apply:

> Figures are obviously useful only as they *demonstrate* feeling: they are signs of a state of mind in the speaker which his audience will readily interpret, and instinctively react to. Such figures of thought as exclamation, interruption, apostrophe and the rest, such figures of language as asyndeton or tautology, clearly cannot convey feeling by exploring and defining it: they are merely indications of its presence in the speaker.[77]

Thus, the *Elegy* and *Eloisa to Abelard* attempt a form of sublimity—Sapphic sublimity—with themes that Pope's contemporaries no longer consider acceptable. Dennis, for one, overlooks Longinus's appraisal of Sappho, whose sublimity "is drawn from Circumstances."[78] Perhaps the most authoritative voice against Sapphic sublimity can be found in Hugh Blair's *Lectures on Rhetoric and Belles Lettres* (1783). He complains that "sublime" too often has been applied "in a sense too loose and vague" very improperly "applied to signify any remarkable and distinguishing excellency of composition; whether it raise in us ideas of grandeur, or those of gentleness, elegance, or any other sort of beauty." Blair believes that Longinus has nodded in praising Sappho:

> I am sorry to be obliged to observe, that the Sublime is too often used in this last and improper sense, by the celebrated critic Long-

inus, in his treatise on this subject. He sets out indeed, with describing it in its just and proper meaning; as something that elevates the mind above itself, and fills it with high conceptions, and a noble pride. But from this view of it he frequently departs; and substitutes in the place of it, whatever, in any strain of composition, pleases highly. Thus, many of the passages which he produces as instances of the Sublime, are merely elegant, without having the most distant relation to proper Sublimity; witness Sappho's famous Ode, on which he descants at considerable length.[79]

We see here that late eighteenth-century opinions on the sublime radically depart from Longinus.

As a practicing poet and translator of Ovid's epistle *Sapho to Phaon*, Pope would have disagreed with Blair, as he often did with John Dennis. According to Longinus, in her *Ode to Anactoria*, Sappho achieves the sublime by making "a right Choice of the most considerable, and by connecting them well together" and forming "'em into one Body: For this Choice on one Hand, and the Connection of select Circumstances together on the other, are as a Powerful Charm upon the Mind." This manner of rhetorical composition designed to evoke sublime ecstasy in a reader characterizes Pope's poetical efforts in the *Elegy* and *Eloisa to Abelard*, as we have seen, demonstrating again how Pope employs his imaginative genius within a rhetorical tradition of poetry.

6
Rhetorical Irony in *The Dunciad Variorum*

The *Dunciad* poet, despite advocating dullness, remains a master of language, and Pope allows him the best of both poetic worlds—of dullness and brilliance—by having his poet scourge unknowingly, yet magnificently, a burgeoning world of dullards and deviators through his reflexive acts of self-flagellation; as in this passage where Pope gives his *Dunciad* poet an irony of expression that undercuts itself as it mimetically captures the enthusiasm of his "mobile" dunces:

> There motley Images her fancy strike,
> Figures ill-pair'd, and Similes unlike.
> She sees a Mob of Metaphors advance,
> Pleas'd with the Madness of the mazy dance:
> How Tragedy and Comedy embrace;
> How Farce and Epic get a jumbled race;
> How Time himself stands still at her command,
> Realms shift their place, and Ocean turns to land.
> (A 1.63–70)

Through his demented *persona*, Pope portrays a world wildly spinning like a child's whirligig and achieves an ironic voice of supreme confidence and imaginative independence, writing with a rhetorical control so complete that his poem, like Shakespeare's plays, appeals to audiences at different levels of appreciation.[1] Beneath the delightful chaos, however, there lies a somber warning.

An apocalyptic inversion occurs in the final couplet of the four-book *Dunciad* of 1743: "Thy hand, great Anarch! lets the curtain fall; / And Universal Darkness buries All" (B 4.655–56). With the ultimate demise of literate culture portrayed in Book 4, Pope completes the vision of cultural eclipse, the "Pisgah-sight" Tibbald cuts short in the three-book *Dunciad Variorum* of 1729.

In a world overwhelmed by enervating chaos and obliterating night, "the mazy dance" of dullness will exhaust itself, as we see at the beginning of Book 4:

> Now flam'd the Dog-star's unpropitious ray,
> Smote ev'ry Brain, and wither'd ev'ry Bay;
> Sick was the Sun, the Owl forsook his bow'r,
> The moon-struck Prophet felt the madding hour:
> Then rose the Seed of Chaos, and of Night,
> To blot out Order, and extinguish Light,
> Of dull and venal a New World to mold,
> And bring Saturnian days of Lead and Gold.
> (B 4.9–16)

The light of "right reason and good taste" will be quenched; and "As Eastern priests in giddy circles run," the world of dunces will drop into itself in an act of uncreation and leave behind a new world of intellectual silence and spiritual nothingness.[2]

The final couplet of the 1743 *Dunciad* is a modification of the penultimate couplet in Book 3 of the 1729 variorum poem. In *The Dunciad Variorum*, this couplet precedes Tibbald's awakening from his prophetic vision and reads: "Thy hand great Dulness! lets the curtain fall, / And universal Darkness covers all." In his final version, Pope replaces the goddess "Dulness" with "Anarch" and the verb "covers" with "buries," a metaphorical transformation that closes the expanded poem and encloses its poetic universe with an eschatological finality in which nothing more can be said.

Both couplets contain an image of a falling curtain, which serves as a theatrical ending to the visionary drama, more pointedly spoofing Cibber the dramatist, who replaces Tibbald the critic, in the expanded version of the poem; but given the "sleepiness" of both heroes, the image is also suggestive of a bed curtain. In his 1755 *Dictionary*, Johnson defines *curtain* as: "A cloath contracted or expanded at pleasure, to admit or exclude the light; to conceal or discover any thing; to shade a bed; to darken a room." In the 1743 couplet, the image of a falling curtain has an internal logic that conforms with Johnson's descriptive sequence of *expansion* (when "the curtain fall[s]"), *exclusion* (of light), *concealment* (of the dunces), and *darkness* (when it "buries All"). The final verb of the poem, "buries," however, goes beyond any domestic sense of enclosure—or of sleep, a prevailing metaphor for dullness[3]—and describes a form of death in life. "Buries" suggests the finality of intellectual death, the nadir of civilization, "the *non plus ultra*" to which the *Dunciad* poet has sunk. Pope allows his *Dunciad* poet to reach in these last lines the profound bottom of his rapturous praise for Grub Street poets, party writers, critics, and booksellers.[4] His vision of the great Anarch's hand letting the curtain fall, following the line: "Light dies before thy uncreating word" (B 4.654), refers back to the poet's own uncreative act of self-extinction. With his own hand (or pen), he lets the curtain fall before his reader in a form of self-annihilation.

Caught in an "epidemical conspiracy for the destruction of paper" (Johnson's words), both the poet and his editors have buried themselves in paper with the mechanical relentlessness that the press has allowed them.[5] As Martinus Scriblerus tells the reader: "He [the poet] lived in those days, when (after providence had permitted the Invention of Printing as a scourge for the Sins of the learned) Paper also became so cheap, and printers so numerous, that a deluge of authors cover'd the land."[6] This final act is not played out in *The Dunciad Variorum*, but the logical implications of the 1729 poem anticipate the dramatic unraveling in Pope's fourth book.[7] The poem with all its critical appendages becomes a mimesis of the very insanity Pope wishes to censure.

Pope's Irony

The structural irony that Pope employs in *The Dunciad Variorum* has its source in Quintilian. According to D. C. Muecke: "By the middle of the eighteenth century the concept of irony in England, and, as far as I know, in other European countries, had scarcely evolved in its broad outlines beyond the point already reached in Quintilian."[8] Like Pope, Swift was well-grounded in Quintilian and classical rhetoric, already having demonstrated what irony could achieve, for example, in such works as *A Tale of a Tub*, *Gulliver's Travels*, and "A Modest Proposal."[9] With Swift's recognition of the instrumental value of such irony, we might easily believe the variorum note claiming that he "snatch'd from the fire" Pope's poem and "persuaded his friend to proceed in it."[10] Pope's rhetorical irony in *The Dunciad Variorum*, therefore, shall be better understood by first reviewing Quintilian's conception of figurative irony.[11]

Quintilian's distinction between tropes and figures appears to be tentative and unsatisfactory.[12] Nevertheless, his discussion of figurative irony rather clearly describes how it functions:

> In the *figurative* form of irony the speaker disguises his entire meaning, the disguise being apparent rather than confessed. . . . In the *trope* the conflict is purely verbal, while in the *figure* the meaning, and sometimes the whole aspect of our case, conflicts with the language and the tone of voice adopted, as was the case with Socrates, who was called an *ironist* because he assumed the rôle of an ignorant man lost at wonder in the wisdom of others. Thus, as continued *metaphor* develops into *allegory*, so a sustained series of tropes develops into this *figure*.[13]

Quintilian's remarks point to a correlation between the Socratic ironist and Pope's poet *persona*, who also may be described as an ignorant man "lost at wonder" but in the dullness of others; as in Pope's words "Fools *Admire*, but Men of Sense *Approve*," Pope and Socrates each assume a role of foolish admiration to reveal the unreasonable nature of their satirical subjects.[14]

Particularly suggestive about this passage is Quintilian's view of allegory as a series of sustained metaphors, creating a double level of meaning. The relationship between these levels in allegory differs from that in figurative irony. Quintilian describes how metaphor has two functions: "A noun or a verb is transferred from the place to which it properly belongs to another where there is either no *literal* term or the *transferred* is better than the *literal*. We do this either because it is necessary or to make our meaning clearer or . . . to produce a decorative effect."[15] For Quintilian, metaphor operates as a tool either to increase the clarity of discourse or to embellish it. Since allegory consists of a chain of interconnected metaphors, it follows that the allegorical meaning does not conflict with the literal meaning of a discourse, though it may depart from it in a more crystalline way.[16] On the other hand, irony departs from the literal meaning to subvert it, rather than to enhance it, by the substitution of an entirely different meaning. It might be useful to place in this context John F. Ross's comments on irony: "Irony exists not alone in the 'literal' meaning, nor alone in the 'hidden' or 'intended' meaning; it is the effect of the two meanings emerging in simultaneous relationship. That is, A (the 'literal' meaning) + B (the 'intended' meaning) make up C (the ironic effect). In this regard irony has the same basic structure as metaphor."[17]

Keeping in mind Quintilian's definition of allegory, we can

now better understand Pope's recurring joke on criticasters with an allegorizing compulsion. In his prefatory remarks, "Of the Poem," to the variorum edition, Martinus Scriblerus attempts to explicate the poem thus:

> First, taking things from their original, he [the *Dunciad* poet] considereth the Causes creative of such authors, namely *Dulness* and *Poverty*; the one born with them, the other contracted, by neglect of their proper talent thro' self conceit of greater abilities. This Truth he wrapp'd in an *Allegory* (as the constitution of Epic poesy requires) and feigns, that one of these Goddesses had taken up her abode with the other, and that they jointly inspir'd all such writers and such works.[18]

Scriblerus obviously misses the irony of the poem by treating it allegorically. If one has written an allegory as Quintilian prescribes, the allegory would clarify or embellish, but in no way enwrap, the "Truth" of the work. *The Dunciad*, therefore, is either a poorly written allegory or not one at all; and, of course, Scriblerus's mistaking irony for allegory is Pope's joke. That Pope's ironic praise of Dulness and Poverty through his poet *persona* is readily seen by the reader and not by Scriblerus suggests another level of dramatic irony in a *persona* entangled within the notes at the bottom of the poem (visual irony?). Scriblerus too is an insular *persona*, or a Swiftian obtuse speaker, as Martin Price would call him, whose discourse should always be suspect.

Inattentiveness to Pope's ironic use of the *persona* surely will result in misreading; we have seen in *The Rape of the Lock* how, for example, Clarissa's speech, despite its seeming virtue, is fruit of a poisoned tree. Blindness to ironic intent will result in reading too seriously and, perhaps, as with Scriblerus, mistaking irony for allegory; another of Pope's pseudocritics, Esdras Barnivelt, exhibits Scriblerus's allegorizing impulse in *A Key to the Lock* (1715): "How many Artifices have been made use of by Writers to obscure the Truth, and cover Designs, which may be detrimental to the Publick; in particular, it has been their Custom of late to vent their Political Spleen in Allegory and Fable."[19] Ironic writing surely requires careful reading for success; and even the best of readers can be caught off guard, as seen in Johnson's criticism of Pope's sylphs and gnomes: "The employment of allegorical persons always excites conviction of its own absurdity: they may produce effects, but cannot conduct actions; when the phantom is put in motion, it dissolves; thus Discord may raise a mutiny, but Discord cannot conduct a march, nor besiege a town."[20] Johnson did not see Pope wink.

Recognition of rhetorical signals is essential for reading irony. Let us again turn to Quintilian's use of irony and compare it with that of Pope. As a result of his exclusive concern with oratory, Quintilian groups irony as a special subclass of allegory, probably because of its functional ambiguity. A better rhetorician than a systematizer of tropes and figures, however, he perceives how irony can be employed:

> That class of allegory in which the meaning is contrary to that suggested by the words, involve an element of irony, or, as our rhetoricians call it, *illusio*. This is made evident to the understanding either by the delivery, the character of the speaker or the nature of the subject. For if any one of these is out of keeping with the words, it at once becomes clear that the intention of the speaker is other than what he actually says.[21]

Quintilian's words apply to Pope, for whom the nature of the subject, the character of the speaker, and the speaker's tone (a literary kin to *deliberatio*, the orator's delivery) are only "correct" when in "keeping with the words." In Pope's serious poetry, all poetic *tours*—design, language, and versification—must function together, but in his ironic poetry this is not necessary; purposeful incorrectness is allowed, and through calculated subversions of propriety he can divert his knowledgeable reader in one direction and his unwitting reader in another.[22] Pope's clearest rhetorical signals are generic misuse, an inappropriate poetic passion, a poetic voice whose *ethos* is suspect, or poor or illogical reasoning, all of which can account for absurdity in a poem. To recognize Pope as jester, no doubt, requires sensitive reading, as Rebecca Price Parkin tells us:

> To consider first the psychological aspect, irony implies a sophisticated reader and a sophisticated poet, together with an awareness and acceptance, on the part of both, of their sophisticated status. In a poem it implies recognition of the poem as a deliberately made thing, an artifact, a pact in time into which two civilized men have entered. An ironic poem is, to a greater degree than some types of poems, a ceremonial, and in the broadest sense, a social occasion.[23]

In *The Dunciad Variorum*, Pope uses irony to include as well as exclude readers. Without other signals, the poem and variorum notes could be construed as merely splenetic lampoon. His purported real-life dunces, for example, are expected to react personally or simply to misread in the same myopic way they write; and by taking themselves too seriously, like Scriblerus, they become satirical victims. But unabashedly scatological subjects in epic "dress" that shock, anger, or promote belly laughs are not necessarily ironical. They establish, rather, the literal level of the poem, the overt absurdity; but once the covert levels of irony are recognized, the poem foliates, and "*Words* are like *Leaves;* and where they most abound, / Much *Fruit* of *Sense* beneath is rarely found" (*Essay on Criticism,* 309–10). The reader then can peer behind the poetic curtain and engage in wisdom that allows him to laugh not only at others but at his own hobbyhorsical self. Too often, Pope's Socratic sense of humor is overlooked. When the pure fiction of the poem and variorum notes are taken for caviling, backbiting scorn, the art is mistaken for the artist. Pope achieves through his rhetorical irony a poetic art that ranges in subject well beyond social satire and captures the spirit of archetypal lunacy, so that we might well wonder, Does "the mazy dance" of dullness belong only to Pope's London?[24]

The *Dunciad* Mask

"The ironist must also make clear that he is ironic. He must be recognizable but inacceptable; we must know who he pretends to be but we must know that he is only pretending. We must not only recognize the mask, we must also recognize that it is a mask."[25] That Pope's contemporaries confused the author with his *persona* was a source for more Scriblerian humor, as the notes variorum demonstrate. In *The Dunciad Variorum,* the rhetoric of Pope's irony operates by dissuasion, a form of repulsion and attraction. We are given a "clouded maze" of complexity that would truly stupify or lull us into sleep were it not for Pope's exquisite control. As with *The Rape of the Lock,* Pope relies on the reader's judgment for discerning miscues that serve to distance the reader from his *personae*—the *Dunciad* poet and his editors; but whereas Belinda's world is almost too attractive, the world of the Dunces is almost too repulsive, and Pope must tether his reader from a much greater distance. Quoting Martin Price again: "In irony we hear two voices, one saying what its limited character requires, the other what a different awareness must add or oppose. The quality of the ironic effect will be determined by the relationship of these two voices—the extent to which they differ, the degree to which one complements the other or simply discredits it, the range of attitudes which can be inferred as the ground for each."[26]

The *Dunciad* poem is perversely egocentric, as is *The Rape of the Lock*, and the ruling passion of each poem has its icon—books or Belinda's lock. Yet, the satire of *The Dunciad Variorum* clearly has greater severity. The difference between these two poems of ironical praise lies in their intended effects on the reader, which work in distinctly antithetical ways. The topics of *The Rape of the Lock* evoke pleasure and attraction, as opposed to displeasure and revulsion in *The Dunciad Variorum*.[27] In each poem, Pope corrupts the logic of the *persona*, which further damages character appeal and keeps the reader emotionally detached. Belinda's enraptured poet loves beauty to excess and magnifies the minuscule into delicate distortion. The *Dunciad* poet ennobles the ludicrous through an overwrought praise of dullness. Amazingly, Pope has anticipated the spirit of these two poems so many years before in *An Essay on Criticism:*

> Avoid *Extreams;* and shun the Fault of such,
> Who still are pleas'd *too little,* or *too much.*
> At ev'ry Trifle scorn to take Offence,
> That always shows *Great Pride,* or *Little Sense;*
> Those *Heads* as *Stomachs* are not sure the best
> Which nauseate all, and nothing can digest.
> Yet let not each gay *Turn* thy Rapture move,
> For Fools *Admire,* but Men of Sense *Approve;*
> As things seem *large* which we thro' *Mists* descry,
> *Dulness* is ever apt to *Magnify.*
>
> (384–93)

Each poem succeeds in its own way as a poetic coup and displays Pope's control over either excessively delicate or grotesque expression to thrust at foolish admiration and draw censure from the reader.

Aaron Hill, who is referred to as a *"Flying Fish"* in *Peri Bathous* and makes an appearance in the diving contest of dunces (A 2.283–86), predictably fails to understand Pope's poetics, especially his irony.[28] In a letter to Pope, 18 January 1730/31, Hill writes: "I have a gentle complaint to make to, and against you, concerning a paragraph in the notes of a late edition of the *Dunciad,* I fear, you would think your crime too little to deserve the punishment of so long a letter, as you are doomed to, on the subject."[29] The source of Hill's complaint lies in the addition of two asterisks in place of the 1728 version of "H——" believed by Edmund Curll to be "Harte" and by a Dublin edition to be "Hughes." The variorum note coupled with the "* *" and the former "H——" succeed in identifying Aaron Hill as the subject of the passage.[30] Pope's reply to Hill is suggestive on several different levels:

> I should imagine the *Dunciad* meant you a real compliment, and so it has been thought by many, who have ask'd, to whom that Passage made that oblique *Panegyrick*? As to the Notes, I am weary of telling a great Truth, which is, that I am not Author of 'em; tho' I love Truth so well, as fairly to tell you, Sir, I think even that Note a Commendation, and I should think myself not ill us'd *to have the same Words said of me:* Therefore, believe me, I never was other than friendly to you, in my own Mind.[31]

Pope's qualification "in my own Mind" implies his dissociation from his poet *persona*, who also has fun, though not so harshly, with Gay, Swift, and Pope himself throughout the poem; as, for example, in the dream vision of Book 3 where the Sibyl glances at the fates of Swift and Pope: "Hibernian Politics, O Swift, thy doom, / And Pope's, translating three whole years with Broome" (A 3.327–28).

Though the *Dunciad* poet's perception cannot be wholly trusted, we can see an inverted logic in the mock-epic games of Book 2. That is, whoever performs poorly or cannot compete in the ludicrous games is given token approval "in [Pope's] own Mind." He who cannot sink, shout, or tire adequately has inversely proportional merit; as in the case of "* *" whom Aaron Hill presumes to be himself:

> Then * * try'd, but hardly snatch'd from sight,
> Instant buoys up, and rises into light;
> He bears no token of the sabler streams,
> And mounts far off, among the swans of Thames.
>   (A 2.283–86)

And indeed the *Dunciad* poet, in leaving this poor diving competitor anonymous, does not admire him nearly so much as the more successful penetrators of the bottom that follow:

> True to the bottom, see Concanen creep,
> A cold, long-winded, native of the deep!

> If perseverance gain the Diver's prize,
> Not everlasting Blackmore this denies:
> No noise, no stir, no motion cans't thou make,
> Th' unconscious flood sleeps o'er thee like a lake.
>   Not Welsted so: drawn endlong by his scull,
> Furious he sinks; precipitately dull.
>
> (A 2.287–94)

But it is Smedley who takes the prize:

> Sudden, a burst of thunder shook the flood.
> Lo Smedley rose, in majesty of mud!
> Shaking the horrors of his ample brows,
> And each ferocious feature grim with ooze.
> Greater he looks, and more than mortal stares;
> Then thus the wonders of the Deep declares.
>
> (A: 2.301–6)

And we might compare Smedley's inglorious entrance with that of the river god in *Windsor-Forest:*

> In that blest Moment, from his Oozy Bed
> Old Father *Thames* advanc'd his rev'rend Head.
> His Tresses dropt with Dews, and o'er the Stream
> His shining Horns diffus'd a golden Gleam.
>
> (329–32)

Yet, ironic praise is not always so neatly inverted. After all, the *Dunciad* poet's misdirected reasoning fractures and complexifies his poetical intentions. The poem, figuratively speaking, is not a polished surface that reflects Pope's "light" with a Newtonian precision, but is sometimes rough-hewn, flat, and unreflective, suggesting the appropriateness of Pope's adjective in "that oblique *Panegyrick.*"

Martinus Scriblerus possesses a distinctly different *ethos* from the poet in the poem, as well as the denunciatory writer(s) of the unsigned notes. Quite complex, Scriblerus is often Pope's heartless parody of Tibbald with his hair-splitting verbal criticism and, at other times, a convenient vehicle for miscues and interpolations that create a morass of critical controversy. It is impossible to discover how much Pope is indebted to Swift for his Scriblerus character; but Martin Price's description of Swift's method would certainly apply to Pope's in his creation of Scriblerus:

> The ironic method allows the constant implication of motive: solecisms of language and solecisms of morals steadily reinforce each other. The character of the speaker discredits his words, and his words in turn characterize him. One value of the method is that its continuity is not broken by the striking local effects of false wit; the reversals which these might achieve individually are made an essential part of the whole design. The use of levels of meaning in irony—the vertical method of wit—keeps us aware of incongruity yet allows the individual solecisms to be woven into a fabric of consistent attitudes and character.[32]

And while Scriblerus serves as an example of one kind of dunce, the Scriblerian apparatus as a whole becomes an extratextual *exemplum* of the poem itself, a meeting place for the poetical and the real world, functioning like Aristotle's inartificial rhetorical proofs, "witness[es], tortures, contracts, and the like," to reify a world of dunces and to further Pope's ironical purpose of condemnation in a way indeed "oblique."[33] The *Dunciad Variorum* magnifies through a tireless use of methods of dullness, even more forcefully than the 1728 version, which lacked the literalization of editorial extremes, the front and back matter and the footnotes appended as extremities to the body of the poem. Through large scale accumulation *(accumulatio)*, or congeries, the major editions of *The Dunciad* continue to swell with Scriblerian apparatus. We are given layer upon layer of commentary and extratextual material that create a cacophonous chorus of voices drowning out both poem and poet in a welter of critical discussion.

Despite Pope's denial in his reply to Hill, it appears that Pope composed most of the variorum notes, though he had some help from his circle;[34] thus George Sherburn clarifies Pope's muted apology to Hill: "In spite of the reiterations of this 'great truth' it has been regarded as a great lie."[35] Quite so, the entire edition is "a great lie," and Pope's letter to Hill suggests that Pope continues to have fun with his correspondent. Indeed, Pope cannot relinquish his mask. Scriblerus's inaccurate comment on the *Dunciad* poet shows how Pope's layers of irony extend beyond the poem itself: "Our good Poet, (by the whole cast of his work being obliged not to take off the Irony) where he cou'd not show his Indignation, hath shewn his Contempt as much as possible: having here drawn as vile a picture, as could be represented in the colours of Epic poesy." Scriblerus is obviously blind to Pope's real satire; the *Dunciad* poet does not show indignation because he has none and, therefore, would not consider his poem a "vile picture"; furthermore, Scriblerus's words are ironically self-referential, "the whole cast of [Pope's] work" would include the learned Scriblerus and his associate editors.[36]

Scriblerus is clearly wrongheaded in calling Pope's poet *persona* a "good" poet, inviting us to see that Scriblerus himself is not a "good" editor, whose commentary proliferates with half-truths. To further delineate him as a distinct *persona*, Pope allows a naive Scriblerus to make jokes at Pope's own expense. The prefaces, notes, and appendixes continually remind the reader of personal and critical invective laid against Pope that would have been better left forgotten. Responding to critics and editors who have maligned Pope's intentions, Aubrey L. Williams describes how distortion subserves Pope's efforts at distancing himself (and, of course, the reader from the work *in toto*): "Pope's 'baseless' manipulation of history, his 'vicious' misrepresentations of the dunces' real characters, is not only a part of the joke's effectiveness in giving discomfort to the dunces (and hence undoubtedly related to personal motives), but it is also a necessary part of the 'distancing' of the ephemeral in art, of getting the bee into the amber."[37]

Ironic Foliation

In *The Dunciad Variorum*, Pope's irony possesses a "tropic" richness that generates more levels of irony than Quintilian had in mind for the orator. Taking advantage of the greater complexity of sound and imagery that poetry allows, Pope turns on its head Quintilian's advice in order to exemplify his theme of dullness:

> The usual result of over-attention to the niceties of style is the deterioration of our eloquence. The main reason for this is that those words are best which are least far-fetched and give the impression of simplicity and reality. For those words which are obviously the result of careful search and even seem to parade their self-conscious art, fail to attain the grace at which they aim and lose all appearance of sincerity because they darken the sense and choke the good seed by their luxuriant overgrowth.[38]

Through sustained tropes, he layers the surface meaning of his poem to create a manifold of ironies, like the leaves of his book.

One example of ironic foliation lies in Pope's use of puns, or *paranomasia*.[39] In his "Remarks on the *Rape of the Lock*" (1728), John Dennis criticises Pope's punning:

> There are a great many Lines, which have no *Sentiment* at all in them, that is, no *reasonable Meaning.* Such are the *Puns* which are every where spread throughout it. *Puns* bear the same Proportion to *Thought,* that *Bubbles* hold to *Bodies,* and may justly be compared to those gaudy Bladders which Children make with Soap; which, tho' they please their weak Capacities with a momentary Glittering, yet are but just beheld, and vanish into Air.[40]

The *Dunciad* poet, as we readily see, is an unregenerate punster, who with "one poor Word a hundred clenches makes" (A 1.61), not unlike Dennis himself, who brutalizes Pope's name.[41] Punning on names to the point of absurdity, the *Dunciad* poet drives Dennis's remarks home; in *Peri Bathous,* Pope defines this trope:

> The PARANOMASIA, or PUN, where a Word, like the tongue of a jackdaw, speaks twice as much by being split: As this of Mr. Dennis,
>
> *Bullets that wound, like Parthians, as they fly.*[42]

Using Dennis's bubble-metaphor, name puns suddenly effervesce, and the dunces represented by them "may justly be compared to those gaudy Bladders which Children make with Soap." Thus, Pope has his fun puncturing his dunces and Dennis.

Pope's epic style in *The Rape of the Lock* creates an absurd exaltation of the trivial and charms us with a figurative pattern of elevation, which foreshadows Belinda's lock shooting to the heavens; the poem achieves mock-epic grandeur by a magnification of minutiae. On the other hand, *The Dunciad Variorum* acquires a mock-epic enormity inside the poem, through a morbid pattern of ironical sinking "With all the Might of gravitation blest," and outside the poem, through an annotative extrapolation by Pope's duncified *personae,* a territorial expansion allowed by printing and obsessive madness. Repetitions by man and his printing machine, therefore, play a vital role in this world of dullness.

In portraying the "customary" activity of his dunces, it appears that Pope has fun with Locke's well-known notion of the "habitual train" of thought:

> Custom settles habits of thinking in the understanding, as well as of determining in the will, and of motions in the body: all which seems to be but trains of motions in the animal spirits, which, once set a going, continue in the same steps they have used to; which, by often treading, are worn into a smooth path, and the motion in it becomes easy, and as it were natural.[43]

Locke provides a "curious instance" of the effect of custom, which, as we shall soon see, resembles the compulsive behavior of Pope's dunces:

> It is of a young gentleman, who, having learnt to dance, and that to great perfection, there happened to stand an old trunk in the room where he learnt. The idea of this remarkable piece of household stuff had so mixed itself with the turns and steps of all his dances, that though in that chamber he could dance excellently well, yet it was only whilst that trunk was there; nor could he perform well in any other place, unless that or some other such trunk had its due position in the room.[44]

Now let us compare the variorum note describing Edmund Curll, the notoriously prolific printer and Pope's *bete noire*:

> We come now to a character of much respect, that of Mr. *Edmond Curl*. As a plain repetition of great actions is the best praise of them, we shall only say of this eminent man, that he carried the Trade many lengths beyond what it ever before had arrived at, and that he was the envy and admiration of all his profession.
>
> ... The tribute our author here pays him, is a grateful return for several unmerited obligations: Many weighty animadversions on the Publick affairs, and many excellent and diverting pieces on Private persons, has he given to his name. If ever he ow'd two verses to any other, he ow'd Mr. *Curl* some thousands. He was every day extending his fame, and inlarging his writings: witness innumerable instances![45]

Ironic praise of Curll continues with mechanical relentlessness in this variorum note. Turning to the passage in the poem that, according to the annotator, is the *Dunciad* poet's "grateful return for several unmerited obligations," we can observe how Curll appears like Locke's "curious instance" when away from his press; Curll is racing for the "Saturnian gold" in Book 2:

> Swift as a bard the bailiff leaves behind,
> He left huge Lintot, and out-stript the wind.
> As when a dab-chick waddles thro' the copse,
> On feet and wings, and flies, and wades, and hops;
> So lab'ring on, with shoulders, hands, and head,
> Wide as a windmill all his figure spread.
>
> (A 2.57–62)

We can almost see Curll, a windmill of arms and legs, flying around his press, like Locke's "curious" gentleman dancing around his trunk, churning out "many lengths" of print with "a plain repetition" and "every day extending his fame."

Pope's manifold jest with the philosopher Locke and the printer Curll stands among other examples of ironic foliation created by the metaphorical interplay of poem and variorum notes; some of these are seen in metaphors of darkness and light, sleep, shouting and silence, and circularity. This section concludes by examining Pope's ironic use of metaphorical fire.

In *The Dunciad*, allusions to *The Aeneid* are clear but not always facile. For example, Aeneas leaves the ashes of Troy to create a new civilization, and giving this epic allusion a twist of cosmic irony, Pope's dunces embark on a procession from London to *uncreate* an old civilization. The dunces, as Aubrey L. Williams has shown, mimic the lord mayor's procession but with a calculated imprecision: "The correspondence between the progress of the dunces and the progress of the Lord Mayor's procession through the streets is not exact, but there are many remarkable similarities in the routes followed by the two processions."[46] The inexact correspondence noticed by Williams engenders another link in a circular chain of allusions—the Great Fire of 1666.

The word "fire" or "fires" recurs throughout the four-book *Dunciad*.[47] The march of the dunces toward Westminster suggests a human conflagration of insipidity as an intellectual counterpart to the physically destructive Great Fire of London. Their route is roughly along that of the Great Fire's destructive path.[48] *The Dunciad* begins "Where wave the tatter'd ensigns of Rag-Fair" (A 1.27), described as "a place near the *Tower* of *London*, where old cloaths and frippery are sold,"[49] and this imaginative location of "The cave of Poverty and Poetry" could not have been far from "no. 25 Pudding Lane, site of the house where the fire was believed to have started in the kitchen of Thomas Farynor the king's baker."[50] In this context, one of Pope's debts to Dryden's *MacFlecknoe* (1682) suddenly emerges. The baker's oven, a symbolic if not actual source for the Great Fire, is fueled by those forgettable books Dryden describes: "From dusty shops neglected Authors come, / Martyrs of Pies, and Reliques of the Bum." In Book 1 of *The Dunciad Variorum*, the night before the dunces begin their procession, melancholic Tibbald sits engulfed by the books that have escaped "the martyrdom of jakes and fire" (A 1.124) and have been "Redeem'd from tapers and defrauded pyes" (A 1.136). Thus, in "great affliction" Tibbald begins his sacrificial bibliocaust:

> "Adieu my children! better thus expire
> Un-stall'd, unsold; thus glorious mount in fire
> Fair without spot; than greas'd by grocer's hands,
> Or shipp'd with Ward to ape and monkey lands,
> Or wafting ginger, round the streets to go,
> And visit alehouse where ye first did grow."
> With that, he lifted thrice the sparkling brand,
> And thrice he dropt it from his quiv'ring hand:
> Then lights the structure, with averted eyes;
> The rowling smokes involve the sacrifice.
> (A 1.197–206)

Tibbald's book burning rouses "old Dulness" from her bed, and his great sacrifice prompts her to anoint him as king. From the smoking ashes of forgettable books, therefore, the fateful procession of the dunces draws its inspiration and obliquely provides a ritual remembrance of the Great Fire.

With Scriblerian tenacity, we might further perceive another irony in this historical allusion—Pope was born on Lombard Street, only a few blocks from where both the Great Fire and the journey of the dunces began. The irony does not end here, however, as suggested by Maynard Mack's description of Pope's birthplace: "In Pope's day this whole area swarmed with shops, well-stocked markets, taverns, coffee houses . . . and residences of substantial merchants, many of whom had been or one day would be Lord Mayor."[51]

Peroration: Fair Rhet'ric

The Dunciad Variorum marks a major shift in Pope's poetical career and in his use of rhetoric, and as I stated in the first chapter, rhetorical strategies in his later satire have received the most attention. My hope has been to chart an imaginative dimension in his poetry that has been neglected and, in so doing, contribute to a more comprehensive understanding of Pope's rhetorical art. Thus, with these final remarks about The Dunciad, my discussion will come to a close.

The Scriblerians witness with alarm how many of their contemporaries embrace the "rigor" of theoretical methods or of pseudoscientific projects. In Book 4 of The Dunciad, Pope prophesizes the end of classical humanism, envisioning the demise of traditional rhetoric in the pursuits of literature; he also predicts the serious encroachment of positivistic ideology on the areas of humanistic studies, visible already in John Locke's criticism of rhetoric in *An Essay concerning Human Understanding*:

> Since wit and fancy find easier entertainment in the world than dry truth and real knowledge, figurative speeches and allusion in language will hardly be admitted as an imperfection or abuse of it. . . . But yet if we would speak of things as they are, we must allow that all the art of rhetoric, besides order and clearness; all the artificial and figurative application of words eloquence hath invented, are for nothing else but to insinuate wrong ideas, move the passions, and thereby mislead the judgment; and so indeed are perfect cheats.[52]

Pope sees his world of humanistic tradition and learning crumbling about him. Dennis had complained that in *The Dunciad* Pope "sings Books, and not an Action," and he was quite right. For in the new world emerging about him, Pope sees no place for heroic action in letters or learning.

Fair Rhet'ric appears in Book 4 of *The Dunciad* (1743) when the goddess of Dulness mounts her throne in a fictive future realm naively presented as a vision by Pope's poet *persona*. From the reader's standpoint, however, the final vision possesses a deliberative character as an argument against a cultural Armageddon in which dunces will prevail. The four-book *Dunciad*, apotheosizing Cibberian dullness—or Cimmerian darkness—functions rhetorically like the Tibbaldian version, with the poet *persona* utilizing appeals of *pathos*, *ethos*, and *logos* as in the *Variorum* and the subject and manner of the poet's praise revealing his moral character and qualities as a poet. Pope, however, achieves his rhetorical irony with more subtlety in Book 4. The *Dunciad* poet's sophistry enables Pope to guide us through a completely ironic reversal of sense:

> Beneath her foot-stool, *Science* groans in Chains,
> And *Wit* dreads Exile, Penalties and Pains.
> There foam'd rebellious *Logic*, gagg'd and bound,
> There, stript, fair *Rhet'ric* languish'd on the ground;
> His blunted Arms by *Sophistry* are born,
> And shameless *Billingsgate* her Robes adorn.
> *Morality*, by her false Guardians drawn,
> *Chicane* in Furs, and *Casuistry* in Lawn,
> Gasps, as they straiten at each end the cord,
> And dies, when Dulness gives her Page the word.
> (B 4.21–30)

A chain of personifications—Science, Wit, Logic, and fair Rhet'ric, recognized champions of truth and protectors of Morality—pictures vanquished victims in a mad scene of oppression, punishment, and death. The antithetical pairings evoke laughter, but the viciousness of the captors invests our mirth with abhorrence. This double reaction distances us from the exulting poet, himself a sophister and a false rhetorician.

The *Dunciad* poet knows his rhetoric, but it is fouled because he has separated eloquence from sound thought, as Cicero tells us: "The undoubtedly absurd and unprofitable and reprehensible severance between the tongue and the brain . . . [leads] to our having one set of professors to teach us to think and another to teach us to speak."[53] And Quintilian has anticipated the spirit of the final act of *The Dunciad* and the influential proclamation of John Locke: "Of those who divorce eloquence from that yet fairer and more desirable title to renown, a virtuous life, some call rhetoric merely power, some a science, but not a virtue, some a practice, some an art, though they will not allow the art to have anything in common with science or virtue, while some again call it a perversion of art."[54]

The *Dunciad* poet is a sophist in his moral fraudulence. Underlying his depiction of the demise of fair Rhet'ric is an *enthymeme*, a rhetorical syllogism, resting on a commonly accepted premise of Aristotle's Law of the Excluded Middle: either fair rhetoric or foul sophistry will prevail, but not both. That fair Rhet'ric languishes implies that Sophistry flourishes, which is played out in the next lines: "His blunted arms by *Sophistry* are born, / And shameless *Billingsgate* her Robes adorn" (B 4.25–26). The either/or premise is irrefutable, and the flow of argument abides, but clearly we cannot accept the result. Herein lies Pope's ironical censure: subscribing to the poet's premise, yet averse to his pernicious application of it, the reader feels compelled to reverse the surface meaning of the poem and subvert the poet's own foul rhetoric.

Pope expects us to judge our speakers by what they say as well as how they say it. The "perfect cheats" to which Locke referred are not really the misleading artifices of language but their artificers. The *Dunciad* poet and Belinda's poet, for example, each have their false conception of eloquence or poetic "light." Belinda's photophilic poet loves the light of verbal ostentation and employs an eloquence similar to that scorned in *An Essay on Criticism*:

> *False Eloquence*, like the *Prismatic Glass*,
> Its gawdy Colours spreads on *ev'ry place;*
> The Face of Nature, we no more Survey,
> All glares *alike*, without *Distinction* gay.
>
> (311–14)

On the other hand, the photophobic *Dunciad* poet seeks to illuminate his eloquence with a darkness visible, supplicating in Book 4 to dwell for a moment longer in the twilight:

> Yet, yet a moment, one dim Ray of Light
> Indulge, dread Chaos, and eternal Night!
> Of darkness visible so much be lent,
> A half to shew, half veil the deep Intent.
>
> (B 4.1–4)

Pope leaves it to his readers to recognize and pass judgment on these delightfully defective rhetoricians.

Pope's rhetorical ability to experiment with the extreme possibilities of poetic language without losing his control places him among the great writers. That his poetry has eclipsed in popularity has as much to do with the rhetorical sensitivity, or insensitivity, of his readers as with revisionist influences concerning the nature of poetry. Pope shows ironically in *The Dunciad* how willfully Sophistry can subvert taste for good poetry or sound thought; and, in so doing, Pope succeeds in soliciting the graces of fair Rhet'ric, not through enslavement, but through just employment and good sense.

Recognizing Pope's rhetorical craftsmanship allows us to see his poetry with eyes more akin to those of his own time. Pope's eighteenth-century world is present in his poems, and we are expected to perceive his mimesis by viewing his poetry as he would have us view his world. Turning finally to the opening lines of *An Essay on Man*, we can now consider his words analogically as a directive for us on how to explore his poetical universe and vindicate his own poetical ways:

> A mighty maze! but not without a plan;
> A Wild, where weeds and flow'rs promiscuous shoot,
> Or Garden, tempting with forbidden fruit.
> Together let us beat this ample field,
> Try what the open, what the covert yield;
> The latent tracts, the giddy heights explore

Of all who blindly creep, or sightless soar;
Eye Nature's walks, shoot Folly as it flies,
And catch the Manners living as they rise;
Laugh where we must, be candid where we can;
But vindicate the ways of God to Man.

(1.6–16)

Appendix A: The Dionysius Rhetoric

The following Latin translation of chapter 1 of the "Art of Rhetoric," mistakenly included among the works of Dionysius of Halicarnassus, is from *Dionysii Halicarnassensis Opera Omnia*, 6 vols. (Lipsiae [Leipzig]: G. T. Georgi, 1774–77), 5:225–33. It accompanies a Greek text and has numerous annotations, which I have not included. On the title page, John Hudson is listed among several annotators:

Cap. I.

De Oratione Panegyrica

I. Panegyris est inuentum et donum deorum, ad intermissionem rerum maiorum, quae ad vitam attinent, tradita, (sicuti quodam in loco inquit Plato) cum dii humanum genus ad laborem natum miserati essent. Coacti autem fuerunt a sapientissimis hominibus conuentus, et a ciuitatibus publice communi decreto, ad recreationem atque oblectationem spectantium, constituti. Tributus vero, ad hos mutuo celebrandos, est a diuitibus quidem pecuniarum sumtus, a principibus magnifici apparatus, rerumque necessariarum copia. Athletae quidem corporum robore ornant Panegyrin; et Musarum ac Apollinis sectatores musica, qua pollent. At virum, qui in literarum et eloquentiae studiis versatus fuerit, ac vniuersum vitae tempus eis insumserit, in ornanda Panegyri ita sese gerere oportet, ac tanto inniti artificio, vti eius oratio a vulgari dicendi ratione abhorreat. Age igitur, o Echecrates, ad hoc tanquam duces viae plerisque intentatae facti, explicemus tibi, quae olim a nostratis sapientiae parentibus accepimus; illi vero, et illorum etiam superiores, a Mercurio et a Musis habuisse dixerunt; non secus, ac Ascraeus pastor ab eisdem in Helicone poësim est consecutus.

II. Age itaque, cum huiusmodi arte orationes sequere. Deus etenim vniuersae, quaecunque sit, panegyriως aliquo modo praeses est, eique cognominis: vt, Olympiorum, Olympius Iupiter; Pythiorum, Apollo. Principium igitur huiusmodi orationis, quaecunque fuerit, laus dei nobis sit, tanquam persona quaedam splendida in sermonis initio collocata. Exordium sit ab iis, quae deo insunt atque attribuuntur. Si quidem Iupiter fuerit, dicendum, deorum regem, rerumque omnium opificem esse: si vero Apollo, musices inuentorem exstitisse, et eundem esse cum Sole; Solem autem omnium omnibus bonorum auctorem: sin autem Hercules, Iouis esse filium; dein ea, quae mortalium vitae praebuit, enumerabis. Et locus ferme complebitur ex iis, quae quilibet aut inuenerit, aut hominibus tradiderit. Verum haec summa cum breuitate, ne praecedens oratio sequenti maior sit.

III. Deinceps vrbis laudes, vbi conuentus celebratur, vel a situ, vel ab ortu, recensere oportebit. In quo fane, quis deus, aut heros, eius conditor exstiterit, aut si aliquid habebis, quod de eo in medium possis afferre: si quid *viz.* ab eo vrbi praeclarum, vel bello, vel pace, gestum fuerit. Congruet etiam de magnitudine, si ampla, vel parua fit, aliquid dicere: quod pulchritudine excellit: quod, licet parua, potentia tamen cum amplissimis est adaequata: deinde quaecunque ad templorum, aut in his donariorum, publicorum priuatorumque aedificiorum ornamentum attinent: sicuti Herodotus quodam in loco, quinque et sex tabulatorum aedificia Babyloni esse dicit: dein si fluuius sit magnus, purus, et nitidus, vel regionem incolentibus vtilis: si itidem aliqua fuerit fabula de ciuitate; nam et hoc pacto multum suauitatis habebit oratio.

IV. Ad haec de ipso certamine dicendum erit, quodnam eius initium, et quae ipsius constitutio, vel quam ob caussam institutum sit. Si qua sit fabula, vel aliud priscum, horum nihil omittendum. Ad id vero cum veneris, non erit locus simpliciter transeundus: sed cum aliis certaminibus oportebit hoc comparare. Nam et hoc modo augebis orationem, vt ab anni partibus comparans. Si quidem veris tempore agatur, agi in temperatissimo, si in hyeme, in validissimo atque fortissimo (vt quispiam dixerit) tempore: si in aestate, ad exercitationem contemplationemque spectatorum constitui; et voluntatis indicium esse deficientibus athletis spectatores decertare debere. Poteris etiam autumnum a fructuum collectione non parum laudare; et ab eo, quod iam homines a laboribus quiescant.

V. Spectandum etiam, quo modo disposita sint certamina. Si enim musicum et gymnicum sit, plane perfectum esse, ac statim corporum robore et vocum concentu ac reliquis musicae partibus temperatum. Sin autem gymnicum sit, musicam tanquam animum effoeminantem abdicasse, corporum vero robur sumsisse atque retinuisse: et certaminis modum ad fortitudinem bellicam plurimum conferre.

VI. Coronam praeterea, quaecunque sit, ne silentio negligenter praetereas. Non enim, cum in hac re versaberis, tibi laudes deerunt. Nam si quercum laudare contigerit, eam Ioui sacram dices, et primum atque antiquissimum fuisse hominibus cibum; et nequaquam elinguem: vt quae in Dodona sit aliquando locuta. Si autem oliua fuerit celebranda, Palladi dicatam, laborum medelam, et ex hac planta antiquos erexisse tropaea; hancque arborem esse victoriae symbolum; Pallademque, cum superasset Neptunum, hac prima coronatam fuisse: atque certantium propriam esse; (athletarum enim certamina per oleum conficiuntur) necnon orationi sociam exsistere, eique multum conferre, qua publici conuentus exornantur. Laurum quoque celebrabis, dum Apollini sacram, plantamque vatibus dedicatam dices. Atque si

Daphnes fabulam attingere volueris, non vtique alienum videbitur. Similiter, si quid aliud affuerit; vt Cereris fructus: vel si fide non careas, circa vnumquodque istorum te poteris diffundere. Nec extra magnificentiam erit et gloriam, si certaminis coronam cum aliorum coronis comparaueris.

VII. Regis vero laus, a te veluti totius orationis fastigium, inducatur; et quod vere omnium certaminum praeses, qui pacem tuetur, propter quam certamina persici queunt. Nonnulli etiam eos, qui ludos disponunt, laudibus prosecuti sunt: si quidem hi gloria insignes sint, quod aliis ante in rebus vtiles fuerint, ac in his splendidissimi. Si vero nulla habeas antiquiora, ostendendum, principium gloriae, quae ad patriam pertinet, esse maximum, et Graecorum generi maxime innatum. Reliqua elocutio sit, vt vniuscuiusque natura et voluntas postulat.

VIII. Verum, si mea valeret opinio, nunquam auctor fuerim, vti elocutio sit vnius tantum modi, sed varia simul et mista: et alia sint cum simplicitate, alia oppositis et adaequationibus Isocratis respondentia, alia autem diuisis atque distinctis expressa. Scio enim, nostratis chori ducem et praesultorem hanc viam vel in pluribus (vt ita dicam) sectatum fuisse: nisi quidpiam in aliquo praecipuo genere scribere proposuisset. Cuiusque autem formae dicendi materia videtur facultatem praebere. Verum iis, quae excogitaueris, oportet et congruam elocutionem inducere: vti narrationes, et aliquid fabulae habentia, cum simplici oratione. Quaecunque autem de regibus, vel de diis, dicere volueris, sint cum dignitate, quae vero ad similitudines et comparationes pertinent, vrbano sermone: nisi quispiam ad hoc, dignum aliquod orationis genus in omnibus praebuerit. Quod tamen ante dictum plus habet ostentationis, et maiorem affert populo delectationem.

Appendix B: Juno's Dressing Scene in Pope's *Iliad* Translation

The following lines, 179–218, include Juno's dressing scene, from Book 14 of Pope's *Iliad* translation:

    Meantime *Saturnia* from *Olympus*' Brow,
High-thron'd in Gold, beheld the Fields below;   180
With Joy the glorious Conflict she survey'd,
Where her great Brother gave the *Grecians* Aid.
But plac'd aloft, on *Ida*'s shady Height
She sees her *Jove*, and trembles at the Sight.
Jove to deceive, what Methods shall she try,   185
What Arts, to blind his all-beholding Eye?
At length she trusts her Pow'r; resolv'd to prove
"The old, yet still successful, Cheat of Love";
Against his Wisdom to oppose her Charms,
And lull the Lord of Thunders in her Arms.   190
    Swift to her bright Apartment she repairs,
Sacred to Dress, and Beauty's pleasing Cares:
With Skill divine had *Vulcan* form'd the Bow'r,
Safe from Access of each intruding Pow'r.
Touch'd with her secret Key, the Doors unfold;   195
Self-clos'd behind her shut the Valves of Gold.
Here first she bathes; and round her Body pours
Soft Oils of Fragrance, and ambrosial Show'rs:
The Winds perfum'd, the balmy Gale convey
Thro' Heav'n, thro' Earth, and all th' aerial Way;   200
Spirit divine! whose Exhalation greets
The Sense of Gods with more than mortal Sweets.
Thus while she breath'd of Heav'n, with decent Pride
Her artful Hands the radiant Tresses ty'd;
Part on her Head in shining Ringlets roll'd,   205
Part o'er her Shoulders wav'd like melted Gold.
Around her next a heav'nly Mantle flow'd,
That rich with *Pallas*' labour'd Colours glow'd;
Large Clasps of Gold the Foldings gather'd round,
A golden Zone her swelling Bosom bound.   210
Far-beaming Pendants tremble in her Ear,

Each Gemm illumin'd with a triple Star.
Then o'er her Head she casts a Veil more white
Than new fal'n Snow, and dazling as the Light.
Last her fair Feet celestial Sandals grace. 215
Thus issuing radiant, with majestic Pace,
Forth from the Dome th' Imperial Goddess moves,
And calls the Mother of the *Smiles* and *Loves*.

Appendix C: Pope's Translation of Longinus

Pope's postscript to the *Odyssey* (1726) contains a loose translation of a passage from Longinus (*On the Sublime*, 9.12–15), and Pope credibly claims this translation as his own (*TE* 8:284–85 n. 1032). Elsewhere, Pope attributes to Elijah Fenton a translation of another passage of Longinus, in a note to Book 16 of his *Iliad* (1718). In his *Dunciad* edition of 1729 and quarto *Works* of 1735, "Pope specified as among his writings 'twelve books of the Odyssey, with the Postscript (not the Notes)' " (Sherburn, *Early Career*, 262; Mack, *Pope*, 415).

Given his experience as a Greek and Latin translator, it is unjustified, I believe, to assume that Pope's critical views of Longinus rely entirely on Boileau's version, as one editor indicates: "Scholars are generally agreed that Pope knew Longinus through Boileau—but whether directly from the French or at another remove through English translations has been debated" (Pope, *Prose Works*, 2:69 n. 11). Pope's customary method in translating for the Homeric poems was, he tells us, "to read carefully all [critics or commentators] I can procure, to make up that way for my own want of critical understanding in the original beauties of Homer" (*EC* 6:12; Warren, *Pope*, 79). Longinus was readily accessible to him in Greek and Latin, as well as in French and English. In fact, John Hudson, Latin translator of Dionysius of Halicarnassus and the Dionysius rhetoric (1704), produced a Latin translation of Longinus with a Greek text in 1710 and another edition in 1718 (*Dictionary of National Biography*). Pope probably read in all of these languages for his own understanding of Longinus.

I have collated a portion of Pope's translation of Longinus in his postscript with corresponding translations by Boileau (1674), John Ozell (1712), Leonard Welsted (1712), and W. Hamilton Fyfe (1927). A comparative analysis of these translations reveals that Pope probably used Boileau's, Ozell's, and Welsted's translations in making his own. Nevertheless, Pope gives his translation his own stamp and demonstrates his critical independence.

Ozell's 1712 edition bears on the title page Pope's verses on Longinus from *An Essay on Criticism* (675–80), which had appeared the year before. Welsted's translation was construed, allegedly, directly from Greek. Yet, it appears evident that Welsted followed closely Boileau's translation; and a similar parallel between Ozell's and Welsted's texts, both published in 1712, suggest one or the other's unacknowledged piracy. I could not ascertain which text preceded the other.

Boileau (Longinus, *Oeuvres*, 23–24):

Delà vient à mon avis, que comme Homere a composé son Iliade durant que son esprit estoit en sa plus grande vigeur, tout le corps de son Ouvrage est dramatique & plein d'action: au lieu que la meilleure partie de l'Odyssée se passe en narrations, qui est le genie de la vieillesse; tellement qu'on le peut comparer dans ce dernier Ouvrage au Soleil quand il se couche, qui a toûjours sa mesme grandeur, mais qui n'a plus tant d'ardeur ni de force. En effet il ne parle plus du mesme ton: on n'y void plus ce Sublime de l'Iliade qui marche par tout d'un pas egal, sans que jamais il s'arreste, ni se repose. On n'y remarque point cette foule de mouvemens & de passions entassées les unes sur les autres. Il n'a plus cette mesme force, & s'il faut ainsi parler, cette mesme volubilité de Discours si propre pour l'action, & mélée de tant d'images naïves des choses. Nous pouvons dire que c'est le reflus de son esprit qui comme un grand Ocean se retire & deserte ses rivages. A tout propos il s'égare dans des imaginations & des fables incroibles. Je n'ai pas oublié pourtant les descriptions de Tempestes qu'il fait, les avantures qui ariverent à Ulysse chez Polypheme, & quelques autres endroits qui sont sans doute fort beaux. Mais cette vieillesse dans Homere, aprés tout, c'est la vieillesse d'Homere: joint qu'en tous ces endroits-là il y a beaucoup plus de fable & de narration que d'action.

Ozell (Longinus, *Treatise*, 29–30):

From hence it is, in my Opinion, that as *Homer* wrote his *Ilias* during the greatest Vigour of his Mind; the whole Body of the Poem is Dramatick and full of Action; whereas the best Part of the *Odysses* is taken up with Narration, according to the Genius of Old Age; insomuch that we may compare him in this last Work to a Setting Sun, which has always the same Bigness with the Morning or Meridian, but has not the same Force nor the same Warmth. In short, he does not talk in the same Tone. We do not there meet with the *Sublime* of the *Ilias*, which goes on every where with an Equal Step, and without ever stopping or reposing it self: We do not perceive that Crowd of Emotions and Passions heap'd one upon another: There's none of that Strength, and if I may say, that Volubility of Discourse, so proper for actions mingled with so many Natural Images of things. We may term it the Ebb of his Wit, which, as in the Ocean, retires and deserts the Shore. He ev'ry now and then, flies out into incredible Fancies and Fables; and yet I do not forget the Descriptions he makes of Tempests, the Adventures which happen'd to

Ulysses at Polyphemus's, and some other Places, which are certainly very Fine. For this Old Age in *Homer,* is after all, the Old Age of *Homer.* The Fault is, that in all those Places there's much more Fable and Narration than Action.

Welsted (Longinus, Works, 32–33):

Hence is it, in my Opinion, that as *Homer* composed his *Iliad,* when his Mind was in its full strength and vigour, the whole Body of the Poem is Dramatical and full of Action; whereas the best part of the *Odysseis* is taken up in Narrations, which seems to be the Genius of Old Age; so that one may compare him, in this last Work, to the setting Sun, who still appears with the same Magnificence, but has no longer the same heat and force. In a word, he has quite lost his tone; he has no more that Sublime which marches on in one equal pace throughout the *Iliad* and never stops or sinks; there is not to be found that variety of Turns and Passions heap'd one upon another; there is not that force, nor, if I may use the Expression, that Volubility of Speech, so proper for Action, and intermixed with such a number of lively Images. It may be said, that the Piece is the reflux of his Genius, which, like the great Ocean, ebbs and deserts its Shores; at every turn he is running out into wild Notions and incredible Fables. In the mean time, I have not forgot his Descriptions of the Tempests, the Story of the Cyclops, and some other Passages which are undoubtedly very fine; but, after all, this is old age, yet still the old Age of *Homer;* besides I must insist upon it, that in the above-mentioned places there is much more of Fable and Narration than Action.

Pope (Prose Works, 2:51–52):

From hence in my judgment it proceeds, that as the Iliad was written while his *Spirit* was in its greatest vigor, the whole structure of that work is Dramatick and full of action; whereas the greater part of the Odyssey is employ'd in Narration, which is the taste of *Old Age*: So that in this latter piece we may compare him to the setting Sun, which has still the same greatness but not the same ardor, or force. He speaks not in the same strain; we see no more that *Sublime* of the Iliad which marches on with a constant pace, without ever being stopp'd, or retarded: there appears no more that hurry and that strong tyde of motions and passions, pouring one after another: there is no more the same fury, or the same volubility of diction, so suitable to action, and all along drawing in such innumerable images of nature. But *Homer,* like the Ocean, is always great, even when he ebbs and retires; even when he is lowest and loses himself most in Narrations and incredible Fictions: As instances of this, we cannot forget the descriptions of tempests, the adventures of *Ulysses* with the *Cyclops,* and many others. But tho' all this be *Age,* it is the *Age* of *Homer*—And it may be said for the credit of these fictions, that they are *beautiful Dreams,* or if you will, the *Dreams of* Jupiter *himself.*

Fyfe (Longinus, *On the Sublime,* 9.13–14):

It was, I imagine, for the same reason that, writing the *Iliad* in the heyday of his genius he made the whole piece lively with dramatic action, whereas in the *Odyssey* narrative predominates, the characteristic of old age. So in the *Odyssey* one may liken Homer to the setting sun; the grandeur remains without the intensity. For no longer does he preserve the sustained energy of the great *Iliad* lays, the consistent sublimity which never sinks into flatness, the flood of moving incidents in quick succession, the versatile rapidity and actuality, brimful of images drawn from real life. It is rather as though the Ocean had shrunk into its lair and lay becalmed within its own confines. Henceforth we see the ebbing tide of Homer's greatness, as he wanders in the incredible regions of romance. In saying this I have not forgotten the storms in the *Odyssey* and such incidents as that of the Cyclops—I am describing the old age of a Homer—yet the fact is that in every one of these passages reality is worsted by romance.

Appendix D: Sapphic Sublimity

The following portion of chapter 8, "Of the Sublimity which is drawn from Circumstances," in John Ozell's translation of Boileau's, contains Longinus's remarks on Sappho's *Ode to Anactoria* and Sapphic sublimity (Longinus, *Treatise*, 31–32):

> Let us now see whether there's no other way of rendering a Discourse Sublime. I say then, that as nothing happens naturally in the World, without being attended with certain Circumstances. 'Twou'd be an infallible Secret for us to reach the *Sublime*, if we knew how to make a right Choice of the most considerable, and by connecting them well together, form 'em into one Body: For this Choice on one Hand, and the Connection of select Circumstances together on the other, are as a Powerful Charm upon the Mind.
>
> Thus when *Sapho* wou'd express the Furies of Love, she gathers together from all Sides, the Accidents that follow and attend that Passion; but her Address appears chiefly, in that all those Incidents, she chooses those, which Denote most the Excess and Violence of Love, and connects them well together.
>
> > Happy! Who near thee, sighs alone for thee:
> > Who hears thy Charming Tongue, and hears like me:
> > Who sometime finds thee Tender as thou'rt Fair.
> > Can the God's Happiness with her's compare.
> > From Vein to Vein, I feel a Subtle Flame,
> > Whene'er I see thee, run thro' all my Frame.
> > And as the Transport seizes on my Mind,
> > I'm Dumb; and neither Tongue nor Voice can find.
> >
> > A Mist of Pleasure o'er my Eyes is spread:
> > I hear no more, and am to Reason dead.
> > Pale, Breathless, Speechless, I Expiring lie:
> > I Burn, I Freeze, I Tremble and I Die.
> > When Nothing's left us, we may venture All.
>
> Don't you admire how she collects all these things, and blends 'em together; Soul, Body, Hearing, Language, Sight, Colour, as if they were so many different Persons, and all ready to Expire? See, with how many contrary Emotions she's agitated; she Freezes, she Burns, she's Mad, she's Wise; she's either entirely out of her Wits, or is Dying: In a Word, we can't say she's seized with one particular Passion, but that her Soul is the

Rendezvous of all the Passions; which indeed is what happens to all that are in Love. You find there, that as I have observ'd, all the grand Circumstances distinguished *a propos*, and collected with Judgment, are the chief Beauty of her Poem.

Notes

Chapter 1. Pope's Rhetorical Art

1. "Pope was most deeply engaged in planning and executing his ethic scheme in the years 1729 to 1735," Miriam Leranbaum, *Alexander Pope's 'OPUS MAGNUM', 1729–1744* (Oxford: Oxford University Press, 1977), 6. Bolingbroke writes in a letter to Swift, 19 November 1729: "Bid him talk to you of the Work he is about. I hope in good earnest; it is a fine one: it will be in his hand an Original," *The Correspondence of Alexander Pope*, ed. George Sherburn, 5 vols. (Oxford: Clarendon Press, 1956), 3:71. See also Joseph Spence, *Observations, Anecdotes, and Characters of Books and Men, Collected from Conversation* (1820), ed. James Marshall Osborn, 2 vols. (Oxford: Clarendon Press, 1966), § 293.

A note on references: Lines to Pope's poetry will be cited parenthetically. Unless otherwise indicated, I refer to *The Twickenham Edition of the Poems of Alexander Pope*, ed. John Butt et. al., 11 vols. (London: Methuen; New Haven: Yale University Press, 1939–69), hereafter indicated as "TE." Also, *The Works of Alexander Pope*, ed. Whitwell Elwin and William John Courthope, 10 vols., 1871–89 (New York: Gordion Press, 1967) will be indicated as "EC"; and George Sherburn's edition of Pope's *Correspondence* as "*Corr.*"

2. Spence, § 321–21a.

3. A comprehensive analysis of Pope's rhetoric has yet to be written, but there are many excellent studies of his satire that treat aspects of his rhetoric, especially Pope's use of the *persona*; I have referred to some of these satirical strategies when relevant to my discussion. The following articles or essays make valuable contributions to our understanding of Pope's rhetoric: Ruth C. Wallerstein, "The Development of the Rhetoric and Metre of the Heroic Couplet, Especially in 1625–1645," *Publications of the Modern Language Association (PMLA)* 50 (1935): 167–209; George Williamson, "The Rhetorical Pattern of Neo-Classical Wit," *Modern Philology* 33 (1935): 55–81; Elder Olson, "Rhetoric and the Appreciation of Pope," *Modern Philology* 37 (1939): 13–35; Samuel Holt Monk, "A Grace Beyond the Reach of Art," *Journal of the History of Ideas* 5 (1944): 131–50; W. K. Wimsatt, Jr., "One Relation of Rhyme to Reason: Alexander Pope," *Modern Language Quarterly* 5 (1944): 323–38, and also "Rhetoric and Poems: Alexander Pope," in *English Institute Essays for 1948* (New York: Columbia University Press, 1949), 183ff.; Austin Warren, "The Mask of Pope," *Sewanee Review* 54 (1946): 19–33; William Empson, "Wit in the *Essay on Criticism*," *Hudson Review* 2.4 (1950): 559–77; Earl R. Wasserman, "The Inherent Values of Eighteenth-Century Personification," *PMLA* 65 (1950): 435–63; Maynard Mack, "The Muse of Satire," in *Collected in Himself: Essays Critical, Biographical, and Bibliographical on Pope and Some of His Contemporaries* (Newark: University of Delaware Press; London and Toronto: Associated University Presses, 1982); and *Yale Review* 51 (1951): 80–92; R. E. Hughes, "Pope's *Essay on Man*: The Rhetorical Structure of Epistle I," *Modern Language Notes*

70 (1955): 171–81; John M. Aden, "'First Follow Nature': Strategy and Stratification in *An Essay on Criticism,*" *Journal of English and Germanic Philology* 55 (1956): 604–17; Richard H. Douglass, "More on the Rhetoric and Imagery of Pope's Arbuthnot," *Studies in English Literature, 1500–1900* 13 (1973): 488–502; Simon Varey, "Rhetoric and *An Essay on Man,*" in *The Art of Alexander Pope,* ed. Howard Erskine-Hill and Anne Smith (London: Vision Press, 1979), 132–43; and Frederick V. Bogel, "Dulness Unbound: Rhetoric and Pope's *Dunciad,*" *PMLA* 97 (1982): 844–55.

4. For Pope's method of composition and revision, see George Sherburn, "Pope at Work," in *Essays on the Eighteenth Century, Presented to David Nichol Smith in Honour of his Seventieth Birthday* (Oxford: Clarendon Press, 1945), 49–64; John Butt, "Pope's Poetical Manuscripts," Warton Lecture on English Poetry, *Proceedings of the British Academy* 40 (1954): 23–39; Robert M. Schmitz, *Pope's Windsor Forest 1712, A Study of the Washington University Holograph,* Washington University Studies (New Series): Language and Literature 21 (Saint Louis: Eden, 1952); and David B. Morris, *Alexander Pope: The Genius of Sense* (Cambridge: Mass., and London: Harvard University Press, 1984), 75–102. Two important facsimile sources for Pope's manuscripts are *Pope's Epistle to Bathurst: A Critical Reading with an Edition of the Manuscripts,* ed. Earl R. Wasserman (Baltimore: Johns Hopkins Press, 1960); and *The Last and Greatest Art: Some Unpublished Poetical Manuscripts of Alexander Pope,* ed. Maynard Mack (London and Toronto: Associated University Presses; Newark: University of Delaware Press, 1984).

5. One particular exception is John M. Aden's treatment of *An Essay on Man* in "'First Follow Nature': Strategy and Stratification in *An Essay on Criticism.*" There are many approaches to these poems in terms of design or unity, but not from a rhetorical point of view; for example, Arthur Fenner Jr., "The Unity of Pope's *Essay on Criticism,*" *Philological Quarterly* 39 (1960): 435–56, which does consider verse paragraph structure; and Earl R. Wasserman's historical analysis of *Windsor-Forest* as a cosmological poem in *The Subtler Language: Critical Readings of Neoclassic and Romantic Poems* (Baltimore: Johns Hopkins Press, 1959), chap. 4. Rhetorically sensitive studies of the design of *The Dunciad* with emphasis on the four-book version may be found in two major studies: Aubrey L. Williams, *Pope's Dunciad: A Study of its Meaning* (London: Methuen, 1955), and John E. Sitter, *The Poetry of Pope's Dunciad* (Minneapolis: University of Minnesota Press; London and Bombay: Oxford University Press; Toronto: Copp Clark, 1971).

6. In attempting to understand Pope's poetics—or, if I may, rhetorical poetics—I have sought out literary conventions or "norms" that Pope would have recognized. I did initially consider other forms of rhetorical analysis, but I found them unsatisfactory, one being that proposed by Group μ: J. Dubois, F. Edeline, J.-M. Klinkenberg, P. Minguet, F. Pire, and H. Trinon, in *A General Rhetoric (Rhétorique générale,* 1970), trans. Paul B. Burrell and Edgar M. Slotkin (Baltimore and London: Johns Hopkins Press, 1981). Group μ refuses to recognize literary norms at all, "the famous definition of style as 'a deviation as compared with a norm,' a cream puff for all stylistics" (13). I consider Pope's poetry stridently referential, recognizing the philosophical difficulties in such a premise, but Group μ would have us toss out the baby with the bathwater: "Howsoever *poetic* language may be, poetic *language* is nonreferential, or it is referential only to the extent that it is not poetic" (12). Strange results would occur from a Group μ analysis; how could we begin to understand Pope's conception of God or of his poetic muse when "To determine the frequency of

the literary usage of the language, it would certainly be necessary to ask the Great Computer"? (14); there would be no hope for understanding Pope's sublimity: "Rhetoric is a set of operations made on language necessarily dependent on certain characteristics of language. We shall see that *all* rhetorical operations rest on a fundamental property of linear discourse—that discourse can be composed into smaller and smaller units" (25); and both Pope and his reader would disappear when a "universal Darkness buries All": "The final consequence of this distortion of language is that the poetic word is disqualified as an act of communication. In fact, it communicates nothing, or rather it communicates nothing but itself. We can also say that it communicates with itself, and this intracommunication is nothing other than the very principle of form. By inserting at each level of discourse, and between levels, the constraint of multiple correspondences, the poet closes discourse on itself. It is precisely this closure that we call the opus" (12).

7. For a historical study of Pope's audience covering the time frame of this study, see Ian Jack, "Pope and his Audience: From the *Pastorals* to *The Dunciad Variorum*," in *Studies in the Eighteenth Century IV: Papers Presented at the Fourth David Nichol Smith Memorial Seminar Canberra 1976*, ed. R. F. Brissenden and J. C. Eade (Canberra: Australian National University Press, 1979), 1–19.

8. [Cicero], *Ad C. Herennium, De Ratione Dicendi (Rhetorica Ad Herennium)*, trans. Harry Caplan, vol. 1, Loeb Classical Library, 1954 (Cambridge: Harvard University Press; London: William Heinemann, 1981), 6.10 n. b.

9. "Rhetoric—Old and New," *Journal of General Education* 5 (1951): 202–9.

10. "Towards Defining an Age of Sensibility," in *Eighteenth-Century English Literature: Modern Essays in Criticism*, ed. James L. Clifford, 1959 (New York: Oxford University Press, 1964), 312.

11. Trans. W. Hamilton Fyfe, vol. 23, Loeb Classical Library, 1927 (Cambridge: Harvard University Press; London: William Heinemann, 1982), 1.4.

12. *The Sublime, A Study of Critical Theories in XVIII-Century England*, 1935 (Ann Arbor: University of Michigan Press, 1962), 11.

13. Kenneth Orne Myrick has shown how the argument of the *Apology* follows the order of a classical oration in *Sir Philip Sidney as a Literary Craftsman* (Cambridge: Harvard University Press, 1935). For further concerning the rhetoric of Sidney and his contemporaries, primarily their poetic diction, see Veré L. Rubel, *Poetic Diction in the English Renaissance: From Skelton through Spenser* (New York: Modern Language Association; London: Oxford University Press, 1941), esp. 1–13 and 102–18.

14. *Criticism: The Major Texts*, ed. Walter Jackson Bate, 1952 (New York: Harcourt Brace Jovanovich, 1970), 85.

15. *The Selected Poetry and Prose of Percy Bysshe Shelley*, ed. Carlos Baker (New York: Random House, 1951), 496. Compare Pope's description of representative meter, "The Sound must seem an *Eccho* to the Sense" (*Essay on Criticism*, 365), to Shelley's much stronger claim:

> Sounds as well as thoughts have relation both between each other and towards that which they represent, and a perception of the order of those relations has always been found connected with a perception of the order of the relations of thoughts. (498)

16. For a discussion of the rhetorical nature of humanism in the eighteenth century, see Paul Fussell, *The Rhetorical World of Augustan Humanism: Ethics and Imagery from Swift to Burke*, 1965 (London, Oxford, and New York: Oxford

University Press, 1969). For a survey of "the progressive atrophy of rhetoric in modern times, in particular the reduction of tropes," see Brian Vickers, "The Atrophy of Modern Rhetoric, Vico to De Man," *Rhetorica* 6.1 (1988): 21–56.

An Essay on Man lies beyond the scope of this study, but not of Pope's rhetoric. Epistle 1 serves as an argument, "Of Man *in the abstract*" (a statement of facts, or extended *narratio*), leading to his major declaration that "The proper study of Mankind is Man" (2.2). Pope's point is that we must dissociate ourselves finally from metaphysical speculation. But he is too rhetorically emphatic in postulating at the end of Epistle 1 that "Whatever IS, is RIGHT" (1.294), for many of his readers have criticized him for making such an imperial claim. Yet, some of those readers fall into the same metaphysical quagmire, namely, by asserting that "Whatever IS" somehow cannot be right. Pope remarks to Spence: "The rule laid down in the beginning of the *Essay on Man* of reasoning only from what we know is certainly a right one, and will go a great way toward destroying all the school metaphysics," Spence, § 303.

17. From *Letter to* **** ******* [John Murray] (1821) in *Letters and Journals* 5 (1901): 552–53, quoted in *Discussions of Alexander Pope*, ed. Rufus A. Blanchard (Boston: D. C. Heath, 1960), 36. Byron is rebutting remarks made by W. L. Bowles in his *The Invariable Principles of Poetry* (1819); for a complete study of their controversy, see Jacob Johan Vann Rennes, *Bowles, Byron, and the Pope Controversy* (New York: Haskell House, 1966).

18. *The Anxiety of Influence: A Theory of Poetry* (New York: Oxford University Press, 1973). See also Walter Jackson Bate, *The Burden of the Past and the English Poet*, 1970 (New York and London: W. W. Norton, 1972).

19. *Lives of the English Poets*, ed. George Birkbeck Hill, 3 vols., 1905 (New York: Octagon Books, 1967), 3:251.

Chapter 2. Rhetoric and Poetics in *An Essay on Criticism*

1. *Principles of Literary Criticism*, 1925 (New York: Harcourt, Brace & World, n.d.), 115.

2. *The Prose Works of Alexander Pope*, vol. 2: *The Major Works, 1725–1744*, ed. Rosemary Cowler (Hamden, Conn.: Archon Books, 1986), 200.

3. TE, 1:212.

4. One discussion of the *Essay*'s design may be found in the Twickenham introduction to the poem, TE, 1:223–32.

5. Pope's understanding and use of Quintilian's *Institutio Oratoria* should not be underestimated. He was "an old favourite author" of Pope during his "great reading period," from about age thirteen to twenty-one (Spence, § 45 and 549). Aside from his praise of Quintilian within *An Essay on Criticism* (669–74), Pope quotes him in notes nine times: TE, 1:241 n. 25, 250 n. 98, 256 n. 146, 261 n. 180, 266 n. 233, 272 n. 297ff., 275 n. 324, 278 n. 345, and 309 n. 612; and his MS included another citation to him (TE, 1:274 n. 309).

Pope knew well the works of other classical rhetoricians. As was common in his time, he attributed the *Rhetorica Ad Herennium* to Cicero, quoting from the work in his notes to *An Essay on Criticism* twice (TE, 1:240 n. 15 and 278 n. 345); and he quotes from Cicero's *De Oratore* once (TE, 1:241 n. 20). Aristotle, Longinus, and Dionysius of Halicarnassus are other writers he certainly read. The works of these Greek and Roman rhetoricians are referred to throughout Pope's writings. The best evidence of Pope's knowledge of classical rhetoricians may be found in his commentary and notes for the Homeric translations; for a detailed study of Pope's notes, see Hans-Joachim Zimmermann, *Alexander Popes Noten zu Homer: Eine Manuskript- und Quellenstudie* (Heidelberg: Carl Winter, 1966).

6. *Lives*, 3:99.

7. While he praises the poem in *The Spectator*, no. 253 (1711), Joseph Addison declares: "The Observations follow one another like those in Horace's Art of Poetry, without that Methodical Regularity which would have been requisite in a Prose Author," *The Spectator*, ed. Donald F. Bond, 5 vols. (Oxford: Oxford University Press, 1965), 2:481–86.

8. "The term [*basis*, or *stasis*] seems to be derived from the fact that it is on it that the first collision between the parties to dispute takes place, or that it forms the *basis* or *standing* of the whole case. So much for the origin of the name. Now for its nature. Some have defined the *basis* as being the *first conflict of the causes*. The idea is correct, but the expression is faulty. For the essential *basis* is not the first conflict, which we may represent by the clauses 'You did such and such a thing' and 'I did not do it.' It is rather the kind of question which arises from the first conflict," *The Institutio Oratoria of Quintilian*, trans. H. E. Butler, 4 vols., Loeb Classical Library, 1920–22 (Cambridge: Harvard University Press; London: William Heinemann, 1979–86), 3.6.4–5.

9. Since the formal structure of *An Essay on Criticism* has been considered so often as a poetical platter for carrying his couplets, I hope my reader will see the justification for such a detailed outline. Pope was a consummate artist, as this outline seeks to show. For the same reason, a similar procedure is used to examine the rhetorical design of *Windsor-Forest* (see chap. 3).

10. *Journal of English and Germanic Philology* 55 (1956): 606.

11. The same considerations may be applied to understanding the rhetorical structure of *An Essay on Man*; see R. E. Hughes, "Pope's *Essay on Man*: The Rhetorical Structure of Epistle I," *Modern Language Notes* 70 (1955): "The first epistle is a rhetorical persuasion drawn up along the lines of the classical oration; for here is the *exordium*, preparing the minds of the audience to favor orator and oration, ll. 1–16; *narratio*, statement of the problem in brief, ll. 17–42; *probatio*, the bulk of the argument, setting up the terms, advancing the proofs, ll. 43–112; *refutatio*, objections to the argument and answers to those objections, ll. 113–280; *peroratio*, summation of the argument, ll. 281–294. Pope allows himself no variation on this scheme; it seems to be a conscious use of the rhetorical form" (347). For a different rhetorical approach, see also Simon Varey, "Rhetoric and *An Essay on Man*," who perceives Pope to be using the satirical *persona* of his denunciatory satires.

Pope's use of oratorical method would appear to be related to his initial composition of both poems in prose. See Spence, § 107, 302, and 307; and Sherburn, "Pope at Work," 52.

12. *Institutio Oratoria*, 7.1.2. The number of parts of an oration varies among rhetoricians. For a brief synopsis, refer to Richard A. Lanham, *A Handlist of Rhetorical Terms: A Guide for Students* (Berkeley, Los Angeles, and London: University of California Press, 1969), 112. Pope's knowledge of Aristotle, Cicero, the *Rhetorica Ad Herennium*, and Quintilian would have shown him how varied were opinions on what parts belong in an oration. Other poets like Pope were well aware that these models were designed primarily for prose or oratory, but could see their value in poetic argument since they are based on similar principles of effective argumentation; for example, see J. B. Broadbent,

"Milton's Rhetoric," *Modern Philology* 56 (1959): 225–42; Brian Vickers, *Classical Rhetoric in English Poetry* (London: Macmillan, 1970); and Lillian Feder, "John Dryden's Use of Classical Rhetoric," *PMLA* 69 (1954): 1258–78.

13. Ironically, when Pope resorts to rhetorical method to seek a more effective means of impressing his reader, he "does not follow the [rhetoricians] in everything," reversing Quintilian's admonishment to his orator regarding the dangers of following poets:

> We should, however, remember that the orator must not follow the poets in everything, more especially in their freedom of language and their license in the use of figures. Poetry has been compared to the oratory of display, and further, aims solely at giving pleasure, which it seeks to secure by inventing what is not merely untrue, but sometimes even incredible. (*Institutio Oratoria*, 10.1.28)

14. *The "Art" of Rhetoric*, trans. John Henry Freese, vol. 22, Loeb Classical Library, 1926 (Cambridge: Harvard University Press; London: William Heinemann, 1982), 1.3.1–3.

15. *Institutio Oratoria*, 3.8.15.

16. *Institutio Oratoria*, 3.8.12. Rhetorical postures of authoritative sanction and humility are called "subjective rhetorical foils" by Elroy L. Bundy in his analysis of Pindar in *Studia Pindarica I/II. The Eleventh Olympian Ode / The First Isthmian Ode*, University of California Publications in Classical Philology, 18.1–2 (1962): 1–34/35–92; in the next chapter, I will examine how Pope employs similar foils in *Windsor-Forest*.

17. *Institutio Oratoria*, 3.8.49; Quintilian then discusses the need for impersonation, or *prosopopoeia*, in order to achieve humility. He also connects this figure to its function in poetry: "It [impersonation] is a most useful exercise because it demands a double effort and is also of the greatest use to future poets and historians, while for orators of course it is absolutely necessary," 3.8.49–54.

18. See *Institutio Oratoria*, 6.1.9–55 and 6.1.2.

19. "Reflections on *An Essay upon Criticism*" in *The Critical Works of John Dennis*, ed. Edward Niles Hooker, 2 vols. (Baltimore: Johns Hopkins Press, 1943), 1:399.

20. *Institutio Oratoria*, 3.4.6.

21. See *Institutio Oratoria*, 3.9.4 and 3.8.6.

22. *TE*, 1:214–15. The playful use of words like "wit," "judgment," and "nature" also serves to characterize Pope's poet; see William Empson, "Wit in the *Essay on Criticism*."

23. George Kennedy, *Quintilian* (New York: Twayne, 1969), 56, 76, and 115.

24. *The Autobiography of William Butler Yeats, Consisting of Reveries over Childhood and Youth, The Trembling of the Veil, and Dramatis Personae*, 1916 (New York: Collier Books, 1967), 65, 317–18; see also Dustin H. Griffin, *Alexander Pope: The Poet in the Poems* (Princeton: Princeton University Press, 1978), 23.

25. "Phaedrus," in *The Collected Dialogues of Plato*, ed. Edith Hamilton and Huntington Cairns, trans. R. Hackforth, 1952 (Princeton: Princeton University Press, 1973), 517 (271c; 271e).

26. *The "Art" of Rhetoric*, 1.2.1; 3.1.8; 3.1.9.

27. Horace, *Ars Poetica*, in *Satires, Epistles, and Ars Poetica*, trans. H. Rushton Fairclough, Loeb Classical Library, 1926 (Cambridge: Harvard University Press; London: William Heinemann, 1978), 333–34. Of course, rhetorical tradition permeates the period, and Horace is not the only reason for the

confluence of rhetoric and poetics; see Alexander H. Sackton, *Rhetoric as a Dramatic Language in Ben Johnson* (New York: Columbia University Press; London and Bombay: Oxford University Press, 1948), esp. chap. 2; and Wilbur Samuel Howell's comprehensive study *Logic and Rhetoric, 1500–1700*, 1956 (New York: Russell & Russell, 1961).

28. The *"Art" of Rhetoric*, 1.2.2. Pope employs inartificial proofs as Scriblerian devices appended to *The Dunciad Variorum* (see chap. 6).

29. The *"Art" of Rhetoric*, 1.2.3.

30. George Kennedy perceives "several apparent inconsistencies" in the discussion of proofs and their organization in Aristotle's *Rhetoric*; see his *The Art of Persuasion in Greece* (Princeton: Princeton University Press, 1963), 82–87. About the later use of Aristotle's proofs, Kennedy remarks: "Aristotle's division of artificial proof into logical, ethical, and pathetical was largely abandoned by his successors. Cicero appreciated it, but did not succeed in reestablishing it. Quintilian thinks that knowledge of the case, conveyed by rational argument, is the fundamental thing (V, viii, 2–3). Presentation of the emotions, whether the gentle ones which had come to be equated with ethos, or the strong ones thought of as pathos, is at most an aid or ornament to the argument"; see his *Quintilian*, 68. This is an understanable development among Roman rhetoricians in their preoccupation with forensic argument. In the matter of using *ethos* and *pathos* in poetry, the poetic imagination naturally must depart from that of the rhetorician, since persuasion is not always the purpose of the poet and delight and "ornament" often are.

31. See George Kennedy, *Classical Rhetoric and Its Christian and Secular Tradition from Ancient to Modern Times* (Chapel Hill: University of North Carolina Press, 1980), 9–15. Kennedy sees imitation as a common phenomenon in the history of oratory:

> The would-be orator listens to speakers and acquires a sense of oratorical conventions and of what is effective. He does not work out a theory, but he imitates, and sometimes succeeds. He builds up a technique of organizing the subject and a collection of examples, of stock phrases, of themes. The Homeric orator is always understood as speaking extempore, and when he is at his best he has a gift of speech, an inspiration from the gods, which is something more than his own understanding. (*Classical Rhetoric*, 10)

Kennedy's remarks would apply to an oral poet as well. It appears likely that these poets had the first rank as effective speakers and, therefore, provided important models of effective uses of language.

32. See Walter J. Ong, *Orality and Literacy: The Technologizing of the Word* (London: Methuen, 1982), esp. chap. 5, for a related discussion of print closure and how "hearing-dominance yields to sight-dominance" in print technology. See Eric A. Havelock, *Preface to Plato*, 1963 (Cambridge and London: Harvard University Press, 1982), for a related discussion of the Platonic campaign against the poetic *paideia* of primary orality. In terms of rhetoric, I perceive Plato's efforts to be an assertion of the superiority of *logos*, and secondarily *ethos*, over *pathos*, as proofs rather than appeals: "There was a state of mind which we shall conveniently label the 'poetic' or 'Homeric' or 'oral' state of mind, which constituted the chief obstacle to scientific rationalism, to the use of analysis, to the classification of experience, to its rearrangement in sequence of cause and effect," Havelock, 47.

33. *The Singer of Tales*, 1960 (New York: Atheneum, 1978), 129–30.

34. *Singer of Tales*, 133.

35. This premise has been explored from different directions by Eric A. Havelock in *Preface to Plato* and Walter J. Ong in *Orality and Literacy* [with an excellent bibliography].

36. See Ernst Cassirer, *The Philosophy of Symbolic Forms*, vol. 2: *Mythical Thought*, trans. Ralph Manheim, 3 vols., 1925 (New Haven and London: Yale University Press, 1955), esp. 60–70, for an analysis of the transition from mythopoeic to empirical-scientific modes of thought.

37. "Among the Romans a poet was called *Vates*, which is as much as a diviner, foreseer, or prophet, as by his conjoined words *vaticinium* and *vaticinari* is manifest," Sidney, "An Apology," in Bate, *Major Critics*, 84.

38. The *"Art" of Rhetoric*, 1.9.40.

39. The *"Art" of Rhetoric*, 2.20.2; 2.21.2; 2.21.13; 2.21.15.

40. The *"Art" of Rhetoric*, 1.9.40.

41. *Institutio Oratoria*, 6.2.12; George Kennedy, *The Art of Rhetoric in the Roman World: 300 B.C.–A.D. 300* (Princeton: Princeton University Press, 1972), 41.

42. *Institutio Oratoria*, 6.2.9. Quintilian also states: "Ethos rather resembles comedy and pathos tragedy," 6.2.20. Pope echoes Quintilian's distinction in his postscript to the *Odyssey* when he translates Longinus:

> I spoke of the Odyssey only to show, that the greatest Poets when their genius wants strength and warmth for the *Pathetic*, for the most part employ themselves in painting the *Manners*. This *Homer* has done, in characterizing the Suitors, and describing their way of life; which is properly a branch of Comedy, whose peculiar business it is to represent the manners of men. (*Prose Works*, 2:52)

Like René Le Bossu in his *Traité du poëme épique* (1675): "Each Epic Poem has likewise some *peculiar Passion*, which distinguishes it in particular from other Epic Poems" [in Steven Shankman, *Pope's Iliad: Homer in the Age of Passion* (Princeton: Princeton University Press), 35], Pope recognizes that the Homeric poems have different appeals, the *pathos* of Achilles in the *Iliad* and the *ethos* of Ulysses in the *Odyssey*. Similarly, through a variation of emphasis on *ethos* and *pathos*, Pope distinguishes his own poems.

43. *The Prose Works of Alexander Pope*, vol. 1: *The Earlier Works, 1711–1720*, ed. Norman Ault (Oxford: Shakespeare Head Press, 1936), 45.

44. Arthur O. Lovejoy has schematized the many connotations of the term in "'Nature' as Aesthetic Norm," *Modern Language Notes* 42.7 (1927): 444–50.

45. *Institutio Oratoria*, 7. Preface. 3.

46. Spence, § 380; see also § 380n.

47. For an excellent study of Pope's "versification," see Jacob H. Adler, *The Reach of Art: A Study in the Prosody of Pope* (University of Florida Monographs, Humanities no. 16, 1964).

48. *Prose Works* 2:199. Frederic V. Bogel describes Pope's rhetoric of differentiation: "Rhetoric, in short, can as readily be considered an art of division working on a prior undifferentiated mass as it can an art of unification working on distinct items, and the same is true of larger double structures like the mockheroic (which draws forth both high and low from an antecedent confusion), irony (which divides a single voice into a problematic doubleness), and even rhyme"; in "Dulness Unbound: Rhetoric and Pope's *Dunciad*," *PMLA* 97 (1982): 845. For a deconstructive approach to this topic, see G. Douglas Atkins, *Quest of*

Difference: Reading Pope's Poems (Lexington: University Press of Kentucky, 1986).
49. Lives, 1:62; 3:231; 3:232.
50. See TE, 1:281 n. 365.
51. Wentworth Dillon, Earl of Roscommon, "An Essay on Translated Verse" (1684), in Critical Essays of the Seventeenth Century, vol. 2: 1650–1685, ed. J. E. Spingarn (Oxford: Clarendon Press, 1908), 307, line 246.
52. Corr., 1:107–8; Marco Girolamo Vida, The De Arte Poetica of Marco Girolamo Vida (1517), trans. Ralph G. Williams (New York: Columbia University Press, 1976), Book 3:329–32.
53. On Literary Composition, Being the Greek Text of the De Compositione Verborvm, ed. and trans. W. Rhys Roberts (London: Macmillan, 1910), 201.

Chapter 3. Design in *Windsor-Forest*

1. See John Chalker, *The English Georgic: A Study in the Development of a Form* (Baltimore: Johns Hopkins Press, 1969), esp. chap. 3.
2. *The Subtler Language: Critical Readings of Neoclassic and Romantic Poems*, chap. 4.
3. *The Poems of John Dryden*, ed. James Kinsley, 4 vols., 1958 (Oxford: Oxford University Press, 1970), 2:583 [I have reversed the italics].
4. Heather Dubrow, *Genre*, The Critical Idiom, series 42 (London and New York: Methuen, 1982), 10.
5. *Essays of John Dryden*, ed. W. P. Ker, 2 vols. (Oxford: Clarendon Press, 1900), 2:139.
6. Pat Rogers provides a valuable analysis of synchronic and diachronic "ingredients" in *Windsor-Forest*, stating "that the way these are blended has not been fully appreciated," in "Time and Space in *Windsor Forest*," in *The Art of Alexander Pope*, ed. Howard Erskine-Hill and Anne Smith (London: Vision Press, 1979), 41. He maintains, however, "*Windsor Forest* is rightly seen as a loco-descriptive poem" (40).
7. *A Dictionary of the English Language*, 1755 (New York: Arno Press, 1979).
8. *Critical Works*, 2:135–36.
9. *Lives*, 3:205.
10. As a loco-descriptive poem, see Joseph Warton, *An Essay on the Writings and Genius of Pope*, 2 vols. (London: T. Maiden for W. J. and J. Richardson et al., 1806), 1:29; Johnson, *Lives*, 1:78; and *TE*, 1:132; as a georgic, see Reuben A. Brower, *Alexander Pope: The Poetry of Allusion*, 1959 (Oxford: Oxford University Press, 1968), 49; and Chalker, *The English Georgic*, chap. 3; and as a cosmological poem, see Wasserman, *Subtler Language*, chap. 4.
11. E. D. Hirsch, Jr., describes this critical circularity: "Thus, while it is not accurate to say that an interpretation is helplessly dependent on the generic conception with which an interpreter happens to start, it is nonetheless true that his interpretation is dependent on the last, unrevised generic conception with which he starts. All understanding of verbal meaning is necessarily genre-bound," in *Validity in Interpretation* (New Haven: Yale University Press, 1967), 76.
12. See *TE*, 1:129–31; and Sherburn, "Pope at Work."
13. "Lord Lansdowne was at the zenith of his career when he persuaded

Pope to eulogise the Peace," writes Whitwell Elwin, *EC*, 1:325. Pope tells Joseph Spence: "Lord Lansdowne insisted on my publishing my *Windsor Forest*, and the motto shows it (*Non injussa cano*)," Spence, § 102.

14. *Critical Works*, 1:6.
15. *EC*, 1:326.
16. *Corr.*, 1:172.
17. "Tickell's Prospect of Peace went through six editions, and to judge by the sale was more popular than Windsor Forest, which was published four months later. The greater success of the far inferior poem was doubtless owing to the eulogium in the Spectator" [no. 523 by Joseph Addison], *EC*, 1:330.
18. *Prose Works*, 2:226.
19. *Dryden and the Tradition of Panegyric* (Berkeley: University of California Press, 1975), 43.
20. *TE*, 7:11.
21. *Art of Rhetoric in the Roman World*, 636; also, see Appendix A for Hudson's Latin translation.
22. *Corr.*, 1:12.
23. I have not incorporated Hudson's Latin translation of the Dionysius rhetoric into the text, deeming it unnecessary for my argument. The Latin translation of chapter 1 of the Dionysius rhetoric can be referred to in Appendix A.
24. Johnson would call this an "exemplification," see *Lives*, 1:130.
25. For historical background, see *TE*, 1:172–73 nn. 257–58; for Pope's friendship with Trumball, see Maynard Mack, *Alexander Pope: A Life* (New York: Norton; New Haven and London: Yale University Press, 1985), 104–9.
26. For Pope's personal associations with these monarchs, see Mack, *Pope*, 57–61.
27. "The allusion—youthfully ostentatious—implies that *Windsor Forest* is the poet's georgic phase, perhaps with the added suggestion that an *Aeneid* is coming next," Brower, *The Poetry of Allusion*, 48.
28. Kennedy, *Art of Rhetoric in the Roman World*, 636.
29. *Critical Works*, 1:42.
30. See Austin Warren, *Alexander Pope as Critic and Humanist*, 1929 (Gloucester: Peter Smith, 1963), 188; and Spence, § 533.
31. Compare Elijah Fenton's translation of Longinus, included in the commentary of Pope's *Iliad* translation: "Again, do you prefer the Odes of *Bacchilides* to *Pindar's*, or the Scenes of *Ion of Chios* to those of *Sophocles*? Their Writings are allow'd to be correct, polite, and delicate; whereas, on the other Hand, *Pindar* and *Sophocles* sometimes hurry on with the greatest Impetuosity, and like a devouring Flame seize and set Fire whatever comes in their way; but on a sudden the conflagration is extinguish'd, and they miserably flag when nobody expects it," in *TE*, 8:285.
32. See George N. Shuster, *The English Ode from MILTON to KEATS* (New York: Columbia University Press, 1940), 170.
33. *The English Ode to 1660: An Essay in Literary History* (Princeton: Princeton University Press; London: Oxford University Press, 1918), 28.
34. George Sherburn and Donald F. Bond, "New Voices in Poetry," in *A Literary History of England*, ed. Albert C. Baugh, 2d ed. (Englewood Cliffs, N.J.: Prentice-Hall, 1948), 943.
35. Shuster, 169.
36. *On the Poetry of Pope*, 1938 (Oxford: Clarendon Press, 1950), 22–23.

37. Robert M. Schmitz, *Pope's Windsor Forest 1712*, 50–68.
38. Schmitz, 54. In the 1712 holograph, the four alexandrines are found in ll.94, 114, 164, and 214; the three triplets in ll.118–19 (interlined), 233–35, and 266–68.
39. *Essays*, 1:267–68.
40. Lines 131–40.
41. *Essays*, 1:7; also cited in *TE*, 1:280 n. 361, where the editors also quote Dryden from *An Essay of Dramatic Poesy*: "They [the Elizabethans] can produce . . . nothing so even, sweet, and flowing, as Mr. Waller; nothing so majestic, so correct, as Sir John Denham"; see also *Essays*, 1:34–35.
42. *Essays*, 1:268.
43. See the editorial commentary to Dryden's "Translations from Horace," in *The Works of John Dryden*, vol. 3: *Poems 1685–1692*, ed. Earl Miner (Berkeley and Los Angeles: University of California Press, 1969), 291–94.
44. Lines 513–14. See *EC*, 360 n. 4, and *TE*, 181–82 n. 330.
45. See the editorial commentary to this poem in *Poems 1685–1692*, 317–19: "The vision of the immortality of art enlivens such traditional rhetorical 'places' of panegyric as worthy origins or ancestry (st. ii), superiority to one's fellows (st. iv), striking achievements (sts. vi and vii), comparison with great predecessors (ll. 29–33, 162–164), manner of death (ll. 149–161), and apotheosis (st. x)."
46. Edward Bysshe, *The Art of English Poetry (1708)*, ed. H. Richard Archer et al., with an introduction by A. Dwight Culler, Augustan Reprint Society 40 (Los Angeles: Clark Memorial Library, 1953), 8. Mark Van Doren recognized this tendency in Dryden's poetry: "Dryden's habit of dilating his heroic verse with Alexandrines not only grew upon him so that he indulged in flourishes when flourishes were not required, but it became contagious," *The Poetry of John Dryden* (New York: Harcourt, Brace and Howe, 1920), 241.
47. Introduction in Bysshe, i–ii. During Pope's lifetime, Bysshe's work was reprinted eight times, in 1705, 1708, 1710, 1714, 1718, 1724, 1725, and 1737; see A. Dwight Culler, "Edward Bysshe and The Poet's Handbook," *PMLA* 63 (1948): 858–85.
48. *Corr.*, 1:24.
49. *Corr.*, 1:17, 17 n. 1.
50. *The Complete Works of William Congreve*, ed. Montague Summers, 4 vols., 1924 (New York: Russell & Russell, 1964), 4:83.
51. Lines 80–83.
52. *Complete Works*, 4:84.
53. "Today Cowley has been acquitted of ignorance concerning the nature of Pindar's odes: he knew, as do we, that they were divided into strophe, antistrophe, and epode; knew, also, that their 'numbers' were not really irregular. Consciously, he sought to produce an equivalence in English verse to the dithyrambic effect he felt in the Greek," Austin Warren, *Richard Crashaw, A Study in Baroque Sensibility* (Kingsport: Louisiana State University Press, 1939), 161.
54. See Dionysius of Halicarnassus, *On Literary Composition*, 195. Robert Shafer describes Jonson's poem as "an ode in which we get a full English approximation of Pindaric form. . . . Jonson was the earliest Englishman to succeed in this; and he was also the only one to do so until the time of Congreve's effort some seventy-five years later," *English Ode to 1660*, 106.
55. "In 1657, Crashaw published his Pindaric Odes, which set the fashion for

a variety of poem much practiced during the sequent century. . . . From one point of view, it was a timid approach to a freer kind of verse, for the lines might vary in length, and without pattern or precedent, from two to six feet; from another, it might be regarded as anticipating the imminent reign of heroics, for it was prevalently rhymed, in couplets," Warren, *Crashaw*, 160.

56. *Corr.*, 1:110.

57. See Carol Maddison, *Apollo and the Nine: A History of the Ode* (London: Routledge and Kegan Paul, 1960), 350–51.

58. Spence, § 533.

59. Spence, § 192.

60. According to Shafer, the Pindaric ode "should have a distinguishable beginning, middle, and end. The beginning would concern itself with some indication of the poem's subject-matter, the middle would treat of one or more of the natural associations of this subject in such a way as to induce in the reader an appropriate emotion, and the end or the conclusion of the poem would refer the reader back once more to the immediate subject in hand, thus giving direction and clear meaning to the emotional state induced in him," *English Ode to 1660*, 27.

61. See sections 3.6.10 through 3.8.15. The epideictic mode in *Ad Herennium* abbreviates the usual six part arrangement that applies more appropriately to judicial argumentation (heard by a jury and concerning past deeds) and to deliberative modes (heard by an influential audience and concerning future events). The narration, confirmation, and refutation are missing in this epideictic mode. A brief overview of the process of rhetorical arrangement may be found in Richard A. Lanham, *A Handlist of Rhetorical Terms*, 112–13.

62. 3.7.13.

63. 3.7.13–14.

64. Compare Shafer on Pindar: "Praise, however, directed toward human beings, inevitably in Greece also entailed advice, caution, lest the blessings of victory be lost through increase of pride, with its fatal accompaniment, insolence. And so there is in Pindar's odes a very considerable element, which embodies both the essence of the practical wisdom of the Greek peoples and the nobility of Pindar's own nature," *English Ode to 1660*, 24. Compare also translator Harry Caplan's note in *Ad Herennium*: "Whereas in both deliberative and judicial causes the speaker seeks to persuade his hearers to a course of action, in epideictic his primary purpose is by means of his art to impress his ideas upon them, without action as a goal," 3.6.10 n. b.

65. Schmitz, MS, II.3–5.

66. About Pindar's use of subjective foils, Elroy L. Bundy explains: "If he seems embarrassed by irrelevance, or by the poverty of his expression, or by his failure to do justice, these inadequacies have been rigged as foil for the greatness of the laudator," *Studia Pindarica*, 1:4. This section of the chapter reflects my debt to Bundy's own descriptions of rhetorical devices in Pindar's odes.

67. The *Ad Herennium* author writes: "If we speak in praise, we shall say that we are doing so from a sense of duty, because ties of friendship exist; or from goodwill, because such is the virtue of the person under discussion that every one should wish to call it to mind; or because it is appropriate to show, from the praise accorded to him by others, what his character is," 3.6.11.

68. Bundy's name for this device, *Studia Pindarica*, 1:5 n. 18.

69. "Through the figure, Reasoning by Question and Answer [*ratiocinatio*], we ask ourselves the reason for every statement, and seek the meaning of each

successive affirmation," *Rhetorica Ad Herennium*, 4.16.23. See Lee A. Sonnino, *A Handbook to Sixteenth-Century Rhetoric* (London: Routledge & Kegan Paul, 1968), 154–55, for other historical definitions of this figure. Sonnino's *Handbook* is a valuable resource for seeking out historical examples of rhetorical terms.

70. Bundy, *Studia Pindarica*, 1:5; "The priamel, because it selects some one object for special attention, is a good prooimal device; it will highlight one's chosen theme," Bundy, 1:6.

71. *Complete Works*, 4:83.

72. Pope praises by associating a name to something great; in his satire he often inverts this method by ironically associating a name to something trivial or repulsive—a fool's form of praise. Pope also creates associations through names in his use of rhetorical figures as linking devices of sound or sense, such as antithesis, zeugma, rhyming, and punning; W. K. Wimsatt explores these strategies in "Rhetoric and Poems: Alexander Pope." Pope's satirical use of names as feigned attempts at disguise invites the question of that fine distinction between lampoon and satire and, unfortunately, revives again misdirected accusations that Pope denunciates unscrupulously; Earl R. Wasserman discusses this and the complexities of Pope's revision of names in "The Rhetorical Use of Names," a commentary in his edition of *Pope's Epistle to Bathurst*, 56–57.

73. *Essays*, 1:30.

74. "In the subjective group the foil often states or implies that the merits of the laudandus provide material in such abundance as to make it impossible for the laudator to recount, or the audience to hear, the whole story," Bundy, 1:12.

75. See TE, 1:152 n. 43ff.

76. "Finally, any gnome (generalizing as it does *many* human experiences illustrating by analogy or contrast the laudator's chosen theme) may serve as a foil," Bundy, 1:8.

77. Schmitz, MS, II.91–94. See TE, 1:159 n. 91, regarding Pope's ambiguous references to recent monarchs.

78. "In panegyric, then, we are dealing not only with two themes but with two audiences as well. The theme of restoration, elaborated in a ceremonial way, serves the function of popular propaganda. By celebrating the current monarch in relation to a historical pattern that is made to seem inevitable or providential, the orator solicits the obedience of the people. The theme of limitation, on the other hand, is directed toward the king," James D. Garrison, *Dryden and the Tradition of Panegyric*, 59.

79. In his note to 'Longinus' *On the Sublime* (Oxford: Clarendon Press, 1964), editor D. A. Russell refers to this rhetorical figure as "the imaginary second person," 144 n. 26. In describing this figure, Longinus observes: "Sometimes a writer, while speaking of his characters, suddenly turns and changes into the actual character," *On the Sublime*, 27.1. For a fuller discussion of Pope's use of transparency and opacity, see chap. 4.

80. See TE, 1:161 n. 110.

81. *Prose Works*, 2:227. For more on Pope's use of color, see Pat Rogers, " 'The Enamelled Ground': The Language of Heraldry and Natural Description in *Windsor-Forest*" (1973), in *Pope: Recent Essays by Several Hands*, ed. Maynard Mack and James A. Winn (Hamden: Shoe String Press, 1980), 159–76.

82. See TE, 1:163 n. 147.

Chapter 4. Persona, Drama, and Epic in *The Rape of the Lock*

1. *The Poetics*, trans. W. Hamilton Fyfe, vol. 23, Loeb Classical Library, 1927 (Cambridge: Harvard University Press; London: William Heinemann, 1982), 4.3.
2. *TE*, 2:142; for historical background, see *TE*, 2:83–105.
3. Pope critics are divided on the issue of his use of *personae*. I make my own case in this chapter for his use of this traditional device. For arguments against Pope's use of *personae*, see Irvin Ehrenpreis, *Literary Meaning and Augustan Values* (Charlottesville: University Press of Virginia, 1974), 49–60; and John M. Aden, *Something Like Horace: Studies in the Art and Allusion of Pope's Horatian Satires* (Kingsport, Tenn.: Vanderbilt University Press, 1969), 118.
4. James Boswell, *Boswell's Life of Johnson*, ed. George Birkbeck Hill, 1934, revised L. F. Powell, 6 vols. (Oxford: Clarendon Press, 1964), 3:251; see Frederick M. Keener, *An Essay on Pope* (New York and London: Columbia University Press, 1974), 13.
5. Pope's use of satirical *personae* has been given a great deal of attention; see Elder Olson, "Rhetoric and the Appreciation of Pope" (1939), a valuable essay on Pope's use of the *persona* and on other aspects of his rhetoric in *An Epistle to Dr. Arbuthnot*; and Maynard Mack, "The Muse of Satire" (1951), which revivified interest in this rhetorical aspect of Pope's poetry; see also Thomas E. Maresca, *Pope's Horatian Poems* (Columbus: Ohio State University Press, 1966); Howard D. Weinbrot, *The Formal Strain: Studies in Augustan Imitation and Satire* (Chicago and London: University of Chicago Press, 1969), esp. 129–64, who has treated this subject throughout his other studies of Pope's satire; Norman Callan, "Pope and the Classics," in *Writer's and Their Background: Alexander Pope*, ed. Peter Dixon (Athens: Ohio University Press, 1975), 242–48; Frederick M. Keener, *An Essay on Pope*, 12–15; and Dustin H. Griffin, *Alexander Pope: The Poet in the Poems* (Princeton University Press, 1978), esp. 22–25.
6. Samuel Johnson, The Oxford Authors, ed. Donald Greene (Oxford and New York: Oxford University Press, 1984), 419.
7. *Institutio Oratoria*, 9.2.33.
8. *A Rhetoric of Irony* (Chicago and London: University of Chicago Press, 1974), 53.
9. In *The Rape of the Lock*, Pope's own voice can be heard in his titulary description, "An Heroi-Comical Poem in Five Cantos."
10. Pope remarks in his "Observations on the Shield of *Achilles*," Book 8 of his *Iliad* translation, *TE*, 8:358:

> His [Homer's] Intention was no less, than to draw the Picture of the whole World in the Compass of this Shield. We see first the Universe in general; the Heavens are spread, the Stars are hung up, the Earth is stretched forth, the seas pour'd round: We next see the World in a nearer and more particular view; the Cities, delightful in Peace, or formidable in War; the Labours of the Countery, and the Fruit of those Labours, in the Harvests and the Vintages; the Pastoral Life in its Pleasures and its Dangers: In a word, all the Occupations, all the Ambitions, and all the Diversions of Mankind.

11. See *Literacy and the Survival of Humanism* (New Haven and London: University of California Press, 1983), esp. chaps. 4 and 5, and *The Motives of*

Eloquence: Literary Rhetoric in the Renaissance (New Haven and London: Yale University Press, 1976), esp. 25–28.

12. *Literacy and the Survival of Humanism*, 52.

13. *Literacy and the Survival of Humanism*, 58–59.

14. See *Pope's Iliad: Homer in the Age of Passion*, where Shankman also compares Aristotle's distinction between the open oratorical style of the public assembly and the close-quartered refinements of written style (in *The "Art" of Rhetoric*, 3.12) with Horace's pictorial analogy of "light" and "shade" (in *Ars Poetica*, 361); "Horace contrasted the bolder style of the painting which wishes to be seen in the light of day *(sub luce videri)* with the more meticulous, even precious style of the picture which courts the shade *(amat obscuram),*" Shankman, 169; see also Wesley Trimpi, "Horace's 'Ut Pictura Poesis': The Argument for Stylistic Decorum," *Traditio* 34 (1978): 29–73.

15. *Critical Works*, 2:364.

16. *Lives*, 3:436–37.

17. *Peri Bathous*, in *Prose Works*, 2:229. See Rebecca P. Parkin, "Mythopoeic Activity in the *Rape of the Lock*," *English Literary History* 21 (1954): 30–38.

18. Lines 1.9–10, in *Poems on Affairs of State: Augustan Satirical Verse 1660–1714*, vol. 6, ed. Frank H. Ellis, 7 vols., gen ed. George deF. Lord et al. (New Haven: Yale University Press, 1963–74), 58–128.

19. *TE*, 5:133 n. 258.

20. "The Preface of 1717," *TE*, 1:8.

21. In "The Limits of Allusion in *The Rape of the Lock*," Earl R. Wasserman also considers this passage a particularly severe moment in the poem: "But in the sheltered Petit Trianon world of conventionalized manners that the total poem constructs, the lines on the judges and the merchant are, as it were, the poet's one hard glance at the Hobbesian state of nature raging outside, so that he may expose the ugly alternative for Belinda and her friends if they shatter the fragile decorum that fences them in," in *Pope: Recent Essays by Several Hands*, ed. Maynard Mack and James A. Winn (Hamden, Conn.: Archon Books, 1980), 227.

Regarding the ploy of Clarissa's speech, consider Pope's remarks "For the MORAL and ALLEGORY" of an epic poem in *Peri Bathous*: "These you may extract out of the Fable afterwards, at your leisure: Be sure to *strain* them sufficiently," *Prose Works*, 2:229. Further discussion of Clarissa's character follows at the end of the section "Epic Allusion" in this chapter.

22. "For the MACHINES" of an epic poem, writes Pope in *Peri Bathous*, "Take of Deities, male and female, as many as you can use: Separate them into two equal parts, and keep Jupiter in the middle; Let Juno put him in a ferment, and Venus mollify him," *Prose Works*, 2:229.

23. *Alexander Pope, The Genius of Sense*, 89.

24. Lines 600–603.

25. See James L. Jackson, "Pope's *The Rape of the Lock* Considered as a Five-Act Epic," *PMLA* 65 (1950): 1283–87. In *Alexander Pope, The Genius of Sense*, 89–90 and 333 n. 18, David B. Morris examines *The Rape of the Lock* according to Dryden's account of dramatic structure in *Of Dramatick Poesie*; see *Essays of John Dryden*, 1:45.

26. *Lives*, 3:233.

27. Spence, § 440.

28. See *TE*, 1:255 n. 142, 258 n. 155–57, 272 n. 297ff; Spence, § 350; Warren, *Alexander Pope as Critic and Humanist*, 67–69.

29. In *Critical Essays of the Seventeenth Century*, vol. 2: 1650–1685, ed. J. E. Spingarn, 3 vols. (Oxford: Clarendon Press, 1908), 17–18. James L. Jackson in "Pope's *The Rape of the Lock* Considered as a Five-Act Epic" also uses this passage for an analysis of the poem. As Jackson points out, Pope's source, if any in particular, for the idea of an epic drama cannot be positively ascertained. Davenant's preface seems as likely a source as Dryden's remarks on drama, despite Pope's innumerable debts to his venerable predecessor; Davenant makes an explicit connection between epic and drama, and his fuller account of a five-act structure bears more points of conformity than does Dryden's.

30. Applying Dryden's dramatic nomenclature, Morris refers to this symmetry as the *epitasis* of canto 2 and the *catastasis* of canto 4, *Alexander Pope, The Genius of Sense*, 89.

31. "Remarks on Mr. Pope's *Rape of the Lock*" (1728), in *Critical Works*, 2:331.

32. In *An Essay on the Genius and Writings of Pope*, Joseph Warton expressed a similar criticism: "In reading the Lutrin, I have always been struck with the impropriety of so serious a conclusion as Boileau has given to so ludicrous a poem. PIETY and JUSTICE are beings rather too awful to have any concern in the celebrated Desk. They appear as much out of place and season, as would the archbishop of Paris in his pontifical robes in an harlequin entertainment," 1:240.

33. Lines 21–24 in a translation of the four-canto version by "N. O." (Nicholas Okes) published in 1682, *Contexts 2: The Rape of the Lock*, ed. William Kinsley (Hamden, Conn.: Archon Books, 1979), 133.

34. TE, 2:112.

35. Lines 7–10; for brief historical background, see Mack, *Alexander Pope*, 100–104.

36. "Pope looked back with veneration to the models of antiquity and cherished the ambition of writing a great epic; and like them he addressed himself to a highly educated and sophisticated audience, a fact to which Swift alluded when he reminded Pope that his epitaph on Gay, 'quite the contrary to your other writings, will have a hundred vulgar readers, for one who is otherwise,'" Ian Jack, "Pope and his Audience: from the *Pastorals* to the *Dunciad Variorum*," 1.

37. Studies of Pope's epic allusion are legion; two relevant examinations may be found in William Frost, "*The Rape of the Lock* and Pope's Homer," *Modern Language Quarterly* 8 (1947): 342–54; and in Earl R. Wasserman, "The Limits of Allusion in *The Rape of the Lock*" (1966).

38. Curiously, the two verse paragraphs are of identical length. Pope's translation of Juno's dressing scene may be found in Appendix B to facilitate comparison.

Thomas Parnell, who assisted Pope with his *Iliad* translation, once translated Belinda's dressing scene (1.121–48) into Latin verse (leonine hexameters) to play a trick on Pope as he read to a group of friends. Oliver Goldsmith describes this humorous episode in his "Life of Thomas Parnell" (1770), in *The Works of Oliver Goldsmith*, ed. J. W. M. Gibbs, 5 vols. (London: George Bell and Sons, 1885), 4:175-76:

> The translation of a part of the 'Rape of the Lock' into monkish verse, serves to show what a master Parnell was of the Latin: a copy of verses made in this manner, is one of the most difficult trifles that can possibly be imagined. I am assured that it was written upon the following occasion. Before 'The Rape of the Lock' was yet completed, Pope

was reading it to his friend Swift, who sat very attentively, while Parnell, who happened to be in the house, went in and out without seeming to take any notice. However, he was very diligently employed in listening, and was able, from the strength of his memory, to bring away the whole description of the Toilet pretty exactly. This he versified in the manner now published in his works; and the next day, when Pope was reading his poem to some friends, Parnell insisted that he had stolen that part of the description from an old monkish manuscript. An old paper with the Latin verses was soon brought forth, and it was not till after some time that Pope was delivered from the confusion which it at first produced.

See also TE, 2:154 n. 121.
39. See TE, 2: 155 n. 139ff.
40. Compare Dryden's parody of Milton's Satan in *Absalom and Achitophel*; see Michael Wilding, "Dryden and Satire: 'MacFlecknoe, Absalom and Achitophel, the Medall', and Juvenal," in *Writers and their Background: John Dryden*, ed. Earl Miner (Athens: Ohio University Press, 1975), 199–200, where Wilding points out that "Milton's portrayal of Satan has its own satiric dimension. Satan attempts to equal God but achieves only parody"; thus, another parody of a parody.
41. TE, 8:170–71 n. 216.
42. TE, 8:168 n. 191.
43. TE, 8:168 n. 198.
44. TE, 8:169 n. 203.
45. TE, 8:263 n. 512.
46. *De Oratore*, trans. E. W. Sutton and H. Rackham, vol. 3, Loeb Classical Library, 1942 (Cambridge: Harvard University Press; London: William Heinemann, 1976), 1.6.20.

Chapter 5. Expression, Emotion, and Forsaken Women

1. In his *Iliad* translation, for example: TE, 7:9 (preface), 160 n. 711, 233 n. 256, 244 n. 502, 287 n. 422, 312 n. 960, 356 n. 595; and TE, 8:64–65 n. 668, 105 n. 29, 212 n. 396, 224–25 n. 752, 284 n. 1032, 316 n. 731, 397 n. 75, 437 n. 405.
2. TE, 1:7.
3. On the Sublime, 13.2.
4. Corr., 1.44.
5. Longinus's remarks on Sappho's poetry are brief, but establishing their relevance to Pope's *Elegy* and *Eloisa to Abelard* requires some extended discussion of Longinus and later interpretations of the sublime. The reader might refer to Appendix D before proceeding in this chapter.
6. *A Grammar of Motives*, 1945 (Berkeley and Los Angeles: University of California Press, 1969), 39.
7. *The Spectator*, ed. Donald F. Bond, 3:568–69.
8. 'Longinus' On the Sublime, 62 n. 1.4.
9. Longinus, *A Treatise of the Sublime, or, The Marvellous in Discourse* in *The Works of Monsr. Boileau Despreaux*, trans. John Ozell, 2 vols. (London: E. Sanger and E. Curll, 1711–12), 2:12–13. This is John Ozell's translation of Boileau's French rendering of Longinus, which Pope knew. Pope himself relied on several texts, either translations or Greek, for his own understanding of Longinus. See Appendix C for further discussion.
10. Dryden's terms of "metaphrase," "paraphrase," and "imitation" are de-

fined in his "Preface to the *Translation of Ovid's Epistles*" (1680) in *Essays*, 1:237:

> All translation, I suppose, may be reduced to these three heads.
> First, that of metaphrase, or turning an author word by word, and line by line, from one language into another. . . . The second way is that of paraphrase, or translation with latitude, where the author is kept in view by the translator, so as never to be lost, but his words are not so strictly followed as his sense; and that too is admitted to be amplified, but not altered. . . . The third way is that of imitation, where the translator (if now he has not lost that name) assumes the liberty, not only to vary from the words and sense, but to forsake them both as he sees occasion; and taking only some general hints from the original, to run division on the groundwork as he pleases.

11. *On the Sublime*, trans. W. Hamilton Fyfe, 1.4.

12. Ecstasies of excessive joy or rapture (2), of excessive grief or anxiety (4), and of madness or distraction (5) could be construed as temporary rhetorical effects subsumed by the first definition: (1) "Any passion by which the thoughts are absorbed, and which the mind is for a time lost." The second and the fourth definitions are antithetical emotional states, the former (2) suggesting possession or a movement toward something, and the latter (4) suggesting loss or a movement away from something. The fifth definition, madness or distraction, unlike the other kinds of ecstasy, suggests an irrational disjunction of mind and reality, of thought and context.

13. Defined in Francis Cairns, *Generic Composition in Greek and Roman Poetry* (Edinburgh: Edinburgh University Press, 1972), 6 and 18. I perceive a theme of *separation* as a common denominator among the generic elegies that Cairns discusses. Thus, the elegiac distich appears an appropriate mimetic vehicle for accommodating examples of separation; a hexameter line followed by a shorter pentameter line visually, as well as aurally, invites such expression.

14. Milton's *Elegia Prima* and *Elegia Quarta* are forms of farewell *(propemptikon)*; *Elegia Quinta* of welcome *(phonetikon)*. *Elegia Secunda* and *Elegia Tertia* are the now familiar forms of mourning elegy, containing some elements found in Pope's *Elegy*: a visionary entrance (in *Elegia Tertia*, 3ff. and 51ff.) and an apostrophe to Death (*Elegia Secunda*, 17–20; *Elegia Tertia*, 16–30).

15. *Kinds of Literature: An Introduction to the Theory of Genres and Modes* (Cambridge: Harvard University Press, 1982), 136. Concerning the presence of epideictic rhetoric in the funeral elegy, Fowler writes:

> Under the influence not only of classical epicedium but of Christian sermon—and perhaps of Petrarch's elegies in the *In Morte* section of the *Canzoniere*—conventional topics of epideictic rhetoric developed in the English funeral elegy. And eventually these became quite distinct from anything in classical elegy.

But it may also be the case that funeral elegy has natural associations with tragedy. Tragic passion arises through a dramatic separation of an individual and the old order of his life, his society, or the world itself, and demands some form of reconciliation, a reordering of perception for a conditional acceptance of such a personal disruption. Epideictic rhetoric in English funeral elegy, broadly expressed, individuates and elevates someone's death, humanizes suffering, and invites a form of *catharsis* akin to the dynamics of tragedy.

16. From lines 269, 271, and 287, in *Poems of John Dryden*.

17. Fowler, 137.

18. I have not found any evidence of generic confusion among eighteenth-century readers about the *Elegy* being titled *Verses*.
19. Cairns treats Juvenal's third satire as an inverse *syntaktikon*, 47–49.
20. *Lives*, 3:226.
21. Shankman, xvi–xvii.
22. *TE*, 8:486n.
23. Shankman, 33.
24. *Poetry of Allusion*, 64. Compare Courthope in his *Life of Pope*, *EC*, 5:133–34: "The reality of the feeling has misled the critics into the belief that such an animated expression of feeling could only have been evoked by a series of facts corresponding with the story suggested in the poem. What the 'Elegy' really establishes, in spite of serious faults of taste by which it is disfigured, is Pope's right to be considered a creative poet of genuine pathetic power."
25. William Roscoe excuses the poet's condemnation thus: "It is, in fact a spontaneous burst of indignation against the authors of the calamity which it records. Throughout the whole poem, the author speaks as if he were under a delusion, and utters sentiments which would be wholly unpardonable at other times. It is only in this light that we can excuse the violence of many of the expressions, which border on the verge of impiety," *EC*, 2:200.
26. *Lives*, 3:226.
27. Despite ambiguous references to "Angels" (14; 67), the poem has a pagan cast. Pope's unchristian attitude toward the lady's suicide seems to affect Johnson's opinion: "Poetry has not often been worse employed than in dignifying the amorous fury of a raving girl," *Lives*, 3:101; "The *Verses on the unfortunate Lady* have drawn much attention by the illaudable singularity of treating suicide with respect," *Lives*, 3:226.
28. The poem had considerable success with Pope's readers, see *TE*, 2:336. For an opposing view of ritual in the poem, see Ian Jack, "The Elegy as Exorcism: Pope's 'Verses to the Memory of an Unfortunate Lady'" (1978), in *Pope: Recent Essays by Several Hands*, 266–84. Jack takes a different approach to Pope's design, comparing the "plan" of the *Elegy* with an outline plan for a funeral elegy in Julius Caesar Scaliger's *Poetics*. He also quotes from Joseph Trapp's lecture "De Elegia," possibly read by Pope: "[In the funeral elegy] every Thing that is epigrammatical, satirical, or sublime, is inconsistent," 279; therefore, according to Jack's argument, Pope does not seek sublimity in his poem.
29. In fairness to Pope, we should keep in mind the eighteenth-century fascination with ghosts and its relative shock value. The best known contemporary example may be the overwhelming popularity of Daniel Defoe's account of a purported ghost sighting in "A True Relation of the Apparition of Mrs. Veal" (1706). See *TE*, 2:340 n. 1–4 for literary analogues.
30. *A Treatise of the Sublime*, 40. W. Hamilton Fyfe translates this figure as "Imagination" in *On the Sublime;* and D. A. Russell refers to it as "visualization" in *'Longinus' On the Sublime*.
31. *On the Sublime*, 18.1.
32. Quintilian distinguishes these as "definite" and "indefinite" questions, *Institutio Oratoria*, 3.5.5–9. The clustering of these questions resembles a related figure, *quaestium*, defined in Henry Peacham, *The Garden of Eloquence* (1593): "A figure by which the orator doth demand many times together, and use many questions in one place, whereby he maketh his speech very sharp and vehement. . . . It serveth . . . to move affections and . . . should not be used to deceive the hearer by the multitude of questions," in Sonnino, 153.

33. See Howard Jacobson, *Ovid's Heroides* (Princeton: Princeton University Press, 1974), 8.

34. Two rhetorical figures are at work here, *anaphora* in the first word repetition of "By" and *conduplicatio* in the internal repetitions of "foreign," "hands," "thy," and "by." The metaphorical description of *conduplicatio* in *Rhetorica Ad Herennium*, 4.28.38, shows how skillfully Pope thematically integrates rhetorical figures into his poetry:

> The reiteration of the same word makes a deep impression upon the hearer and inflicts a major wound upon the opposition—as if a weapon should repeatedly pierce the same part of the body.

35. A "qualitative progression" occurs when "We are put into a state of mind which another state of mind can appropriately follow," Kenneth Burke, "Lexicon Rhetoricæ," in *Counter-Statement*, 1931 (Chicago: University of Chicago Press, 1957), 125.

36. *A Treatise of the Sublime*, 32.

37. *On the Sublime*, 27.1; D. A. Russell refers to this figure as "the imaginary second person" in *'Longinus' On the Sublime*, 144 n. 26.

38. See Brower, 63–84, for more discussion of rhetorical technique in the *Elegy* and in *Eloisa to Abelard*, poems that share many stylistic devices. In my treatment of both poems, I have tried to avoid duplicating discussion of tropes and figures that Brower and others have already pointed out.

39. Mack has a different opinion of the *Elegy*: "There are passages of great beauty in this poem.... Still, it is hard to resist the judgment that it is a pastiche of motifs and attitudes not very well accommodated to the whole in which they find themselves," *Alexander Pope*, 315.

40. *The Arte of English Poesie* (1589), 1906 (Kent, Ohio: Kent State University Press, 1970), 61–62.

41. Longinus, *A Treatise of the Sublime*, 21. See Appendix O in *TE*, 2:398–99 for a summary of the many "Replies, Imitations, and Parodies" inspired by *Eloisa to Abelard* during the eighteenth century.

42. Pope uses John Hughes's translation *The Letters of Heloise to Abelard* (1713) as the historical source for his poem, and both were later published in a single edition. The historical letters have a tradition of unfaithful translation. Hughes's "somewhat bowdlerized" translation of The Hague edition (1711) is based on "a wildly romanticized French version" of the letters by Roger de Rabutin, comte de Bussy, published posthumously in 1697, see *Eloïsa to Abelard with the letters of Heloise to Abelard in the version by JOHN HUGHES (1713)*, ed. James E. Wellington, with notes and introduction, University of Miami Critical Studies no. 5 (Coral Gables, Fla.: University of Miami Press, 1965), 20; Wellington's notes and introduction provide an excellent historical analysis of Hughes's translation and its relation to Pope's poem; see also the Twickenham editor's notes to the poem.

43. Howard Jacobson in *Ovid's Heroides* provides a detailed analysis of the elements of the Ovidian epistle. He demonstrates how the Ovidian epistle departs from rhetorical *prosopopoiia* and *ethopoiiae*. Though both the *Heroides* and *Eloisa to Abelard* by no means should be categorized as rhetorical exercises, Ovid and Pope appear to share the *attitude* a writer adopts in performing *progymnasmata*. In particular, Pope begins from the disciplined starting point of a prescribed problem; his genius lies not only in entangling

himself poetically in that problem but in working himself (or more accurately, Eloisa) out of it, snatching "a grace beyond the reach of art."

44. *TE*, 2:289.
45. *TE*, 2:298.
46. *TE*, 2:289.
47. Tillotson states otherwise: "The act of writing [Eloisa's] is a relief, and the relief is an intellectual, as well as an emotional, one," *TE*, 2:289.
48. *The Spectator*, no. 408, in *Prose Works*, 1:45.
49. Tillotson observes: "Hughes's letters are in prose and the change-over to verse, to couplets, meant also the change-over to tighter 'geometry' of situation. . . . This 'geometry' derives, of course, from Ovid, but Ovid's pointedness is enforced for Pope by the example of dramatic poetry, especially by the plays of Shakespeare, Corneille, and Dryden. . . . This 'geometry' implies rhetoric," *TE*, 2:281.
50. *Rhetorica Ad Herennium*, 4.16.23; see also Longinus, *On the Sublime*, 18.1.
51. The repetition of "yet" in lines 7–8 is a figure of *subjunctio (epizeuxis)*, characterized by Quintilian as able "to excite pity," *Institutio Oratoria*, 9.3.28.
52. *Institutio Oratoria*, 9.2.39.
53. *Rhetorica Ad Herennium*, 4.28.38.
54. Sonnino, 186.
55. Pope ludicrously defines this figure, *aposiopesis*, in *Peri Bathous*, in *Prose Works*, 2:207:

> An excellent figure for the Ignorant, as "What shall I say?" when one has nothing to say: or "I can no more," when one really can no more. Expressions which the gentle reader is so good as never to take in earnest.

We see that, in *Peri Bathous*, Pope pokes fun at those who cannot accomplish with rhetoric what he has managed with so much grace.

56. Warren, *Alexander Pope as Critic and Humanist*, 11; see Monk, *The Sublime*, esp. chaps. 2–3.
57. *A Treatise of the Sublime*, trans. John Ozell (1711–12), 22; compare Fyfe's modern translation of this passage in *On the Sublime*, 8.1:

> The first and most powerful is the command of full-blooded ideas . . . and the second is the inspiration of vehement emotion. These two constituents of the sublime are for the most part congenital. But the other three come partly of art, namely the proper construction of figures—these being probably of two kinds, figures of thought and figures of speech—and, over and above these, nobility of phrase, which again may be resolved into a choice of words and the use of metaphor and elaborated diction. The fifth cause of grandeur, which embraces all those already mentioned, is the general effect of dignity and elevation.

We might notice how John Ozell's translation of Boileau's Longinus reflects the strong influence of the three rhetorical processes (invention, disposition, or arrangement of parts, and style) as traditionally taught.

58. *A Treatise of the Sublime*, 24.
59. *A Treatise of the Sublime*, 21.
60. *A Treatise of the Sublime*, 7; I have reversed the italics.
61. *On the Sublime*, 9.9.
62. *The Sublime*, 45, where Monk summarizes:

Boileau . . . had read in Longinus that the sublime is a quality of art that does not depend for its existence on fine words and rhetorical devices. He had insisted that it is above rhetoric, and lives really in the grandeur of a great artist's thoughts, that it conveys emotions, that it is recognizable by its sudden overwhelming effect, and he had agreed with Longinus that it is the product of genius not rules.

63. *On the Sublime*, 5.
64. This is a complex and speculative area of study. The prevalent popularity of ornamental style in the Renaissance arises, it appears, from a confluence of Ramism and traditional interests in style. See Wilbur S. Howell, *Logic and Rhetoric*, esp. 116–37 and chap. 4, and *Eighteenth-Century British Logic and Rhetoric* (Princeton: Princeton University Press, 1971), throughout; Rosemund Tuve, *Elizabethan and Metaphysical Imagery, Renaissance Poetic and Twentieth Century Critics*, 1947 (Chicago and London: University of Chicago Press, 1965), esp. chaps. 4 and 12; Walter J. Ong, *Ramus: Method, and the Decay of Dialogue*, 1958 (Cambridge and London: Harvard University Press, 1983), esp. chaps. 12 and 13; and George Kennedy, *Classical Rhetoric*, 210–15.

The influence of Ramistic logic, in appropriating invention and arrangement to the domain of dialectic, delimits rhetoric to matters of style. This contributes to an eventual dissolution of the traditional overlapping of poetics and rhetoric. Tenacious adherents of classical rhetoric, such as Boileau and Pope, view a rhetoric of style as pernicious. I detect a note of irony in Boileau's references to "the Sublime Stile." In short, Boileau does not attack the style of classical rhetoric but the style of an *ars-gratia-artis* aesthetic, a rhetoric debased by the expropriations of Ramism and embraced by ornamentalists.

In Tuve's remarks concerning the metaphor of "style as a garment," I find particularly interesting her mention of "external Gorgiousness." The passage reads:

> Like the analogy with painting, it would seem to tempt poets to think of imagery as something added onto meaning, and of 'embroidered' prettiness as a desideratum, with one added temptation—to make garments that could stand alone, so stiff with 'external Gorgiousness' that they needed no body within. (61)

"Gorgiousness" has its root in the Old French *gorgias*, meaning "elegantly dressed, fashionable, gay," and is of uncertain origin (OED). In regards to this word, I find it remarkably coincidental that when the famous Greek sophist Gorgias (480–c.375 B.C.) arrived as an ambassador in Athens in 427 "his remarkable oratorical style became a fad," see Kennedy, *Classical Rhetoric*, 29. The "Gorgianic style" among ancient orators possessed an elaborate ornamental character similar in its excess to Boileau's "Sublime Stile" and the "Garden" style examined by Tuve. Long before Longinus, Gorgias had emphasized the importance of natural genius in an orator. It is, therefore, not surprising to see Longinus's strong-minded view of the relationship between innate and acquired powers of expression result, as was the case with Gorgias, in a misdirected preoccupation with ornamental style. The Gorgianic style also suffered adverse criticism from traditional rhetoricians. Thus, the Old French *gorgias* might have a richer historical origin than lexicographers have been able to prove.

65. *Prose Works*, 2:58.
66. *A Treatise of the Sublime*, 12–13.
67. Monk, *The Sublime*, 46.
68. *On the Sublime*, 1.4.

69. *A Treatise of the Sublime*, 21.
70. In *Critics and Criticism, Ancient and Modern*, ed. R. S. Crane (Chicago: University of Chicago Press, 1952), 242.
71. *On the Sublime*, 8.2; see *A Treatise of the Sublime*, 22–23.
72. *A Treatise of the Sublime*, 23.
73. In *The Spectator*, no. 339 (1712), 3:254–55; Joseph Addison also remains faithful to Longinus:

> Longinus has observed, that there may be a Loftiness in Sentiments, where there is no Passion, and brings Instances out of Ancient Authors to support this Opinion. The Pathetick, as that great Critick observes, may animate and inflame the Sublime, but it is not essential to it. Accordingly, as he further remarks, we very often find that those, who excell most in stirring up the Passions, very often want the Talent of Writing in the Great and Sublime manner; and so on the contrary.

Addison goes on in his essay to demonstrate how Milton has mastered both forms of the sublime.
74. *The Sublime*, 51.
75. Monk, *The Sublime*, 54.
76. *A Philosophical Enquiry into the Origin of Our Ideas of the Sublime and Beautiful* (1757), ed. James T. Boulton, 1958 (Notre Dame, Ind., and London: University of Notre Dame Press, 1968), 63.
77. *Art of Poetry 1750–1820: Theories of Poetic Composition and Style in the Late Neo-Classic and Early Romantic Periods* (New York: Barnes & Noble, 1967), 64.
78. Monk, *The Sublime*, 53; see Appendix D for Longinus's brief discussion of Sappho.
79. *Lectures on Rhetoric and Belles Lettres*, ed. Harold F. Harding, 2 vols., 1783 (Carbondale and Edwardsville: Southern Illinois University Press, 1965), 1:58–59.

Chapter 6. Rhetorical Irony in *The Dunciad Variorum*

1. Pope has fun not only with his dunces, but their audience as well, as his unsigned note suggests, *TE*, 5:60 n. 2:

> *Smithfield* is the place where Bartholomew Fair was kept, whose Shews, Machines, and Dramatical Entertainments, formerly agreeable only to the Taste of the Rabble, were, by the Hero of this Poem and others of equal Genius, brought to the Theatres of Covent-Garden, Lincolns-inn-Fields, and the Hay-Market, to be the reigning Pleasures of the Court and Town.

See Ian Jack, "Pope and His Audience: From the *Pastorals* to the *Dunciad Variorum*," esp. 20–30. According to Jack, success allows Pope to address a more select audience in the manner of Shakespeare: "In his early work [his Preface to *Shakespeare*], Pope informs his readers, Shakespeare 'writ . . . without patronage from the better sort, and therefore without aims of pleasing them'. Later, however, 'when his performances had merited the protection of his Prince, and when the encouragement of the Court had succeeded to that of the Town, the works of his riper years are manifestly raised above those of his former,'" 27.

2. "In the word 'dullness' Pope intended to include 'every sort of rebellion against right reason and good taste,'" editor's introduction, *TE*, 5:xxxvi; see also *EC*, 4:28. Pope's view of the episodic rising and falling of learning occurs in *An Essay on Criticism* (685–92). In *Pope's Dunciad: A Study of its Meaning*, Aubrey L. Williams notes a relationship between *The Dunciad Variorum* and "the hoax entitled *Epistolae Obscurorum Virorum*, which was executed in the early sixteenth century by a group of German humanists" who also scorned "monkish" learning, 61–62. The latter title is suggested for a proposed collection of letters in a separately published advertisement for *The New Dunciad*, *TE*, 5:411. Pope also mentions John Reuchlin, then believed one of the authors of the *Epistolae*, in a published letter to Caryll, 25 June 1711, *Corr.*, 1:122 n. 7; *EC*, 6:148 n. 2; see Williams, 61 n. 2.

3. *Sleep* occurs in *The Dunciad* nine times: 1.7, 1.56, 1.94, 1.318, 2.346, 2.373, 2.419, 3.100, and 4.69; *sleeping* one time: 4.440; *sleepless* one time: 1.94; and *sleeps* four times: 1.294, 2.304, 3.87, and 4.202.

4. For a study of Grub Street culture, see Pat Rogers, *Hacks and Dunces: Pope, Swift and Grub Street*, 1972 (London and New York: Methuen, 1980).

5. Marshall McLuhan states: "Pope had a very simple scheme for his first three books. Book I deals with authors, their egotism and desire for self-expression and eternal fame. Book II turns to the book sellers who provide the conduits to swell the tides of public confession. Book III concerns the collective unconscious, the growing backwash from the tidal wave of self-expression. It is Pope's simple theme that the fogs of Dulness and new tribalism are fed by the printing press," *The Gutenberg Galaxy: The Making of Typographic Man*, 1962 (Toronto: University of Toronto Press, 1968), 259. But, of course, Pope himself has been "fed by the printing press," and thus the complexities of irony go well beyond McLuhan's simplified summary. See also William Kinsley, "The Dunciad as Mock-Book" (1971), in *Pope: Recent Essays by Several Hands*, 707–28.

6. "Martinus Scriblerus of the Poem," *TE*, 5:49.

7. McLuhan considers Pope's fourth book prophetic: "The popular mesmerism achieved by uniformity and repeatability, taught men the miracles of the division of labour and the creation of world markets. It is these miracles that Pope anticipates in *The Dunciad*, for their transforming power had long affected the mind," *The Gutenberg Galaxy*, 261.

8. *Irony and the Ironic*, The Critical Idiom, series 13, 1970 (London and New York: Methuen, 1982), 17–18; see also Wayne C. Booth, *A Rhetoric of Irony*, 49.

9. See Charles Allen Beaumont, *Swift's Classical Rhetoric*, University of Georgia Monographs, no. 8 (Athens: University of Georgia, 1961), and Martin Price, *Swift's Rhetorical Art, A Study of Structure and Meaning*, 1953 (Carbondale and Edwardsville: Southern Illinois Press; London and Amsterdam: Feffer & Simons, 1973). For a discussion of Swift's use of instrumental, or stable, irony in "A Modest Proposal," see Wayne C. Booth, *A Rhetoric of Irony*, 137–38, 105–20.

10. *TE*, 5:201 n. a. For more about Swift's contributions to the poem, see *TE*, xiiiff., xx, and xxv.

11. "Rhetorical irony," as I apply the expression, requires purpose and deliberate control of language. Booth points out: "Some modern critics—for example, I. A. Richards, Cleanth Brooks, and Kenneth Burke—have suggested that every literary context is ironic because it provides a weighting or qualification on every word in it, thus requiring the reader to infer meanings which are in a

sense not in the words themselves: all literary meanings in this view become a form of covert irony, whether intended or not," *A Rhetoric of Irony*, 7. I do not consider unintentional irony as rhetorical.

12. Kennedy comments on Quintilian's poor account of tropes in *Quintilian*, 83–85; he explains: "One reason why he does not handle tropes well is perhaps the fact that he was accustomed to think of them as more poetic than oratorical and thus the business of grammarians, another is his lack of sympathy for any technical terms," 85. Pope notices this also, seeing his rhetoric aimed "less to please the Eye, than arm the Hand," *Essay on Criticism*, 673. Booth also expresses dissatisfaction with Quintilian's discussion of tropes that may be used ironically, see *A Rhetoric of Irony*, 67–68, 68n, and 138.

13. *Institutio Oratoria*, 9.2.46.

14. Rebecca Price Parkin writes: "Irony is a humanly significant disproportion between the thing itself and a limited perception of it. The intelligent observer (the Eiron) recognizes the disproportion. The unintelligent (the Dupe) takes the partial for the whole. The two intrinsic parts of irony, then, are the hidden 'real real' and an apparent but misleading real. The element of human observation and perception constitutes a third aspect of the Idea (in the Platonic sense) of irony," *The Poetic Workmanship of Pope* (Minneapolis: University of Minnesota, 1955), 31.

15. *Institutio Oratoria*, 8.6.5–6.

16. Quintilian concerns himself only with effective communication, and his concept of metaphor, therefore, subserves clarity of expression. He is prescribing a particular use of metaphor, which does not preclude the possibility that metaphor can be ironical and, through the rhetorical play of variation, can generate into symbol. Even for Quintilian, metaphor can function as an ironic trope.

17. *Swift and Defoe: A Study in Literary Relationship* (Berkeley: University of California Press, 1941), 81–82; quoted in Martin Price, *Swift's Rhetorical Art*, 57.

18. *TE*, 5:50.

19. *Prose Works*, 1:182.

20. *Lives*, 3:233.

21. *Institutio Oratoria*, 8.6.54.

22. In "Dulness Unbound: Rhetoric and Pope's *Dunciad*" (1982), Fredric V. Bogel observes: "The poem's rhetoric at once establishes and partly erodes the distinctions on which Pope's verse usually depends, and it does so not because Pope secretly envies the dunces but because the creation of meaning depends as much on the power to undo distinctions as on the power to establish them. This exemplary subversion suggests, in turn, that *The Dunciad*, before it is a poem about individual characters or forces or things, is a poem about relations, especially those relations whose relationship to each other, in *The Dunciad* as in rhetorical structuring, makes meaning possible at all: the relations of sameness and difference," 846.

23. *Poetic Workmanship of Pope*, 31–32.

24. About madness, Locke declares: "I shall be pardoned for calling it so harsh a name as madness, when it is considered that opposition to reason deserves that name, and is really madness; and there is scarce a man so free from it," *An Essay concerning Human Understanding*, ed. L. A. Selby-Bigge, Great Books of the Western World, vol. 35 (Chicago: Encyclopaedia Britannica, 1952), 2.33.4. For a discussion of the "belligerent sanity" of Pope in *The*

Dunciad, see Max Byrd, *Visits to Bedlam: Madness and Literature in the Eighteenth Century* (Columbia: University of South Carolina Press, 1974), esp. 12–57.

25. Martin Price, *Swift's Rhetorical Art*, 63.
26. *Swift's Rhetorical Art*, 57.
27. For a comparison of the two poems, see B. L. Reid, "Ordering Chaos: The Dunciad" (1974), in *Pope: Recent Essays by Several Hands*, esp. 681–84; see also John E. Sitter, *The Poetry of Pope's Dunciad*, 63; and Maynard Mack, "On Reading Pope," *College English* 7 (1946): 263–73; whom Sitter quotes: "In the *Rape of the Lock* it [satire] is done with tenderness, a sense of the endearing charm of mortal foibles, for one does not impale a butterfly upon an ax; but in the *Dunciad* it is done with indignation, for one does not survey the dry rot in a whole society through the rainbow wings of sylphs," 273.
28. *Prose Works*, 2:196.
29. *Corr.*, 3:164–65.
30. *TE*, 5:136–37 n. 283.
31. *Corr.*, 3:165.
32. *Swift's Rhetorical Art*, 62.
33. *The "Art" of Rhetoric*, 1.2.2.
34. *TE*, 5:xxiv–xxvii.
35. *Corr.*, 3:165 n. 4.
36. *TE*, 5:119 n. 149.
37. *Pope's Dunciad: A Study of its Meaning*, 62; Williams discusses important aspects of the poem relevant to Pope's rhetoric that I see no need to repeat. His discussion of genre, verbal distancing, and allusion through "double exposure" are particularly illuminating in this regard. His first three chapters cover the 1728 Dunciad and notes variorum.
38. *Institutio Oratoria*, 8. Preface. 22–24; see *TE*, 1:274 n. 309.
39. For further discussion of Pope's puns, see W. K. Wimsatt, Jr., "One Relation of Rhyme to Reason: Alexander Pope" (1944).
40. *Critical Works*, 2:347.
41. "Yet Mr. Dennis's Works afford us notable Examples in this kind. *Alexander* Pope hath sent abroad into the world as many *Bulls* as his Namesake Pope '*Alexander.*'—Let us take the initial and final letters of his Surname, viz., A.P——E, and they give you the Idea of an *Ape*.—*Pope* comes from the Latin word *Popa*, which signifies a little Wart; or from *Poppysma*, because he was continually *popping* out squibs of wit, or rather *Po-pysmata*, or *Po-pisms*. DENNIS" [irregular quotation marks removed], *TE*, 5:67 n. 61.
42. *Prose Works*, 2:209.
43. *An Essay concerning Human Understanding*, 2.33.6.
44. *An Essay concerning Human Understanding*, 2.33.16.
45. *TE*, 5:104 n. 54.
46. *Pope's Dunciad*, 33.
47. The word *fire* or *fires* occurs at least twelve times: B 1.144, 1.186, 1.235, 1.251, 3.66, 3.219, 3.239, 3.260, 3.312, 4.494, 4.633, and 4.649. Not surprisingly, the word does not appear in Book 2, in which mud, water, and urine would probably extinguish any hopes for the image.
48. See the map in Williams, *Pope's Dunciad*, 34–35. In his *A Preface to Pope*, 1976 (London and New York: Longman, 1983), I. R. F. Gordon describes the awful destruction: "The Fire of London raged for four days from 2 to 5 September 1666 and consumed all save the north-eastern and extreme western

parts of the City. The Royal Exchange, the Custom House, the Guildhall, the halls of forty-four of the Livery Companies, St. Paul's itself, and eighty-seven of the parish churches, besides about 13,200 houses, were burned down. Barely one fifth of the City was left standing. Thus the medieval City, which had changed so very little over several hundred years, had to be almost completely rebuilt," 32–33.

49. *TE*, 5:63 n. 27.

50. Maynard Mack, *Alexander Pope*, 41; Mack reports that on the wall of this house hung a plaque that read: "Here, by the Permission of Heaven, Hell broke loose upon this Protestant City, from the malicious Hearts of barbarous Papists, by the Hand of their Agent Hubert, who confessed, and on the Ruins of this Place declared the Fact, for which he was hanged, viz. That here begun that dreadful Fire, which is described and perpetuated on by the Neighbouring Pillar," 41. Papist and patriot, Pope again realizes the poetic possibility in this ironic inversion.

51. *Alexander Pope*, 32.

52. *An Essay concerning Human Understanding*, 3.10.34.

53. *De Oratore*, 3.16.61.

54. *Institutio Oratoria*, 2.15.2.

Works Cited

Addison, Joseph. *The Spectator*. 1711–12. Ed. Donald F. Bond. 5 vols. Oxford: Oxford University Press, 1965.

Aden, John M. " 'First Follow Nature': Strategy and Stratification in *An Essay on Criticism*." *Journal of English and Germanic Philology* 55 (1956): 604–17.

———. *Something Like Horace: Studies in the Art and Allusion of Pope's Horatian Satires*. Kingsport, Tenn.: Vanderbilt University Press, 1969.

Adler, Jacob H. *The Reach of Art: A Study in the Prosody of Pope*. University of Florida Monographs. Humanities no. 16 (1964).

Aristotle. *The "Art" of Rhetoric*. Trans. John Henry Freese. Vol. 22. Loeb Classical Library. 1926. Cambridge: Harvard University Press; London: William Heinemann, 1982.

———. *The Poetics*. Trans. W. Hamilton Fyfe. Vol. 23. Loeb Classical Library. 1927. Cambridge: Harvard University Press; London: William Heinemann, 1982.

Atkins, G. Douglas. *Quests of Difference: Reading Pope's Poems*. Lexington: University Press of Kentucky, 1986.

Barnard, John, ed. *Pope: The Critical Heritage*. 1973. London and Boston: Routledge & Kegan Paul, 1985.

Bate, Walter Jackson. *The Burden of the Past and the English Poet*. 1970. New York and London: W. W. Norton, 1972.

———. *Criticism: The Major Texts*. 1952. New York: Harcourt Brace Jovanovich, 1970.

Beaumont, Charles Allen. *Swift's Classical Rhetoric*. University of Georgia Monographs, no. 8. (1961).

Blair, Hugh. *Lectures on Rhetoric and Belles Lettres*. Ed. Harold F. Harding. 2 vols. 1783. Carbondale and Edwardsville: Southern Illinois University Press, 1965.

Blanchard, Rufus A., ed. *Discussions of Alexander Pope*. Boston: D. C. Heath, 1960.

Bloom, Harold. *The Anxiety of Influence: A Theory of Poetry*. New York: Oxford University Press, 1973.

Bogel, Frederick V. "Dulness Unbound: Rhetoric and Pope's *Dunciad*." *Publications of the Modern Language Association (PMLA)* 97 (1982): 844–55.

Boileau-Despréaux, Nicolas. "Le Lutrin." In *Contexts 2: The Rape of the Lock*. Ed. William Kinsley. 131–44. Hamden, Conn.: Archon Books, 1979.

Booth, Wayne C. *A Rhetoric of Irony*. Chicago and London: University of Chicago Press, 1974.

Boswell, James. *Boswell's Life of Johnson*. Ed. George Birkbeck Hill. 1934. Revised L. F. Powell. 6 vols. Oxford: Clarendon Press, 1964.

Broadbent, J. B. "Milton's Rhetoric." *Modern Philology* 56 (1959): 225–42.
Brower, Reuben A. *Alexander Pope: The Poetry of Allusion*. 1959. Oxford: Oxford University Press, 1968.
Bundy, Elroy L. *Studia Pindarica I/II. The Eleventh Olympian Ode/The First Isthmian Ode.* University of California Publications in Classical Philology 18.1–2 (1962): 1–34/35–92.
Burke, Edmund. *A Philosophical Enquiry into the Origin of our Ideas of the Sublime and Beautiful.* Ed. James T. Boulton. 1958. Notre Dame, Ind., and London: University of Notre Dame Press, 1968.
Burke, Kenneth. *Counter-Statement*. 1931. Chicago: University of Chicago Press, 1957.

———. *A Grammar of Motives*. 1945. Berkeley and Los Angeles: University of California Press, 1969.

———. "Rhetoric—Old and New." *Journal of General Education* 5 (1951): 202–9.

Butt, John. "Pope's Poetical Manuscripts." Warton Lecture on English Poetry. *Proceedings of the British Academy* 40 (1954): 23–39.
Byrd, Max. *Visits to Bedlam: Madness and Literature in the Eighteenth Century.* Columbia: University of South Carolina Press, 1974.
Bysshe, Edward. *The Art of English Poetry (1708)*. Ed. H. Richard Archer et al. Introduction by A. Dwight Culler. Augustan Reprint Society 40. Los Angeles: Clark Memorial Library, 1953.
Cairns, Francis. *Generic Composition in Greek and Roman Poetry*. Edinburgh: Edinburgh University Press, 1972.
Callan, Norman. "Pope and the Classics." In *Writers and Their Background: Alexander Pope*. Ed. Peter Dixon. 230–49. Athens: Ohio University Press, 1975.
Cassirer, Ernst. *The Philosophy of Symbolic Forms*. Vol. 2: *Mythical Thought*. Trans. Ralph Manheim. 3 vols. 1925. New Haven and London: Yale University Press, 1955.

———. *The Philosophy of the Enlightenment*. 1932. Trans. Fritz C. A. Koelln and James P. Pettegrove. Princeton: Princeton University Press, 1979.

Chalker, John. *The English Georgic: A Study in the Development of a Form.* Baltimore: Johns Hopkins Press, 1969.
Cicero. *De Oratore*. Trans E. W. Sutton and H. Rackham. Vols. 3 and 4. Loeb Classical Library. 1942. Cambridge: Harvard University Press; London: William Heinemann, 1976.
[Cicero]. *Ad C. Herennium, De Ratione Dicendi (Rhetorica Ad Herennium).* Trans. Harry Caplan. Vol. 1. Loeb Classical Library. 1954. Cambridge: Harvard University Press; London: William Heinemann, 1981.
Congreve, William. *The Complete Works of William Congreve*. Ed. Montague Summers. 4 vols. 1924. New York: Russell & Russell, 1964.
Culler, A. Dwight. "Edward Bysshe and The Poet's Handbook." *PMLA* 63 (1948): 858–85.
Davenant, William. "Preface to *Gondibert*" (1650). In *Critical Essays of the Seventeenth Century*. Vol. 2: 1650–1685. Ed. J. E. Spingarn. 1-53. 3 vols. Oxford: Clarendon Press, 1908.

Dennis, John. *The Critical Works of John Dennis*. Ed. Edward Niles Hooker. 2 vols. Baltimore: Johns Hopkins Press, 1943.

Dillon, Wentworth, Earl of Roscommon. "An Essay on Translated Verse" (1684). In *Critical Essays of the Seventeenth Century*. Vol. 2: 1650–1685. Ed. J. E. Spingarn. 297–309. 3 vols. Oxford: Clarendon Press, 1908.

Dionysius of Halicarnassus. *Ars Rhetorica*. In *Dionysii Halicarnassensis Opera Omnia*. 5:225–414. 6 vols. Lipsiae [Leipzig]: G. T. Georgi, 1774–75.

———. *On Literary Composition, Being the Greek Text of the De Compositione Verborvm*. Ed. and trans. W. Rhys Roberts. London: Macmillan, 1910.

Douglass, Richard H. "More on the Rhetoric and Imagery of Pope's Arbuthnot." *Studies in English Literature, 1500–1900* 13 (1973): 488–502.

Dryden, John. *Essays of John Dryden*. Ed. W. P. Ker. 2 vols. Oxford: Clarendon Press, 1900.

———. *The Poems of John Dryden*. Ed. James Kinsley. 4 vols. 1958. Oxford: Oxford University Press, 1970.

———. *The Works of John Dryden*. Vol. 3: *Poems 1685–1692*. Ed. Earl Miner. Berkeley and Los Angeles: University of California Press, 1969. [To be completed in 20 vols.]

Dubrow, Heather. *Genre*. The Critical Idiom. Series 42. London and New York: Methuen, 1982.

Ehrenpreis, Irvin. *Literary Meaning and Augustan Values*. Charlottesville: University Press of Virginia, 1974.

Empson, William. "Wit in the *Essay on Criticism*." *Hudson Review* 2.4 (1950): 559–77.

Feder, Lillian. "John Dryden's Use of Classical Rhetoric." *PMLA* 69 (1954): 1258–78.

Fenner, Jr., Arthur. "The Unity of Pope's *Essay on Criticism*." *Philological Quarterly* 39 (1960): 435–56.

Fowler, Alastair. *Kinds of Literature: An Introduction to the Theory of Genres and Modes*. Cambridge: Harvard University Press, 1982.

Frost, William. "*The Rape of the Lock* and Pope's Homer." *Modern Language Quarterly* 8 (1947): 342–54.

Frye, Northrop. "Towards Defining an Age of Sensibility" (1956). In *Eighteenth-Century English Literature: Modern Essays in Criticism*. Ed. James L. Clifford. 311–18. 1959. New York: Oxford University Press, 1964.

Fussell, Paul. *The Rhetorical World of Augustan Humanism: Ethics and Imagery from Swift to Burke*. 1965. London, Oxford, and New York: Oxford University Press, 1969.

Garrison, James D. *Dryden and the Tradition of Panegyric*. Berkeley: University of California Press, 1975.

Garth, Samuel. "The Dispensary." In *Poems on Affairs of State: Augustan Satirical Verse 1660–1714*. Vol. 6. Ed. Frank H. Ellis. 58–128. 7 vols. Ed. DeF. Lord et al. New Haven: Yale University Press, 1963–74.

Goldsmith, Oliver. *The Works of Oliver Goldsmith*. Ed. J. W. M. Gibbs. 5 vols. London: George Bell and Sons, 1885.

Gordon, I. R. F. *A Preface to Pope*. 1976. London and New York: Longman, 1983.

Griffin, Dustin H. *Alexander Pope: The Poet in the Poems*. Princeton: Princeton University Press, 1978.
Group μ: J. Dubois, F. Edeline, J.-M. Klinkenberg, P. Minguet, F. Pire, and H. Trinon. *A General Rhetoric*. Trans. Paul B. Burrell and Edgar M. Slotkin. *(Rhétorique générale)* 1970. Baltimore and London: Johns Hopkins University Press, 1981.
Havelock, Eric A. *Preface to Plato*. 1963. Cambridge and London: Harvard University Press, 1982.
Hirsch, Jr., E. D. *Validity in Interpretation*. New Haven: Yale University Press, 1967.
Horace, *Ars Poetica*. In *Satires, Epistles, and Ars Poetica*. Trans. H. Rushton Fairclough. Loeb Classical Library. 1926. Cambridge: Harvard University Press; London: William Heinemann, 1978.
Howell, Wilbur Samuel. *Eighteenth-Century British Logic and Rhetoric*. Princeton: Princeton University Press, 1971.
———. *Logic and Rhetoric in England, 1500–1700*. 1956. New York: Russell & Russell, 1961.
Hughes, R. E. "Pope's *Essay on Man:* The Rhetorical Structure of Epistle I." *Modern Language Notes* 70 (1955): 171–81.
Jack, Ian. "The Elegy as Exorcism: Pope's 'Verses to the Memory of an Unfortunate Lady'" (1978). In *Pope: Recent Essays by Several Hands*. Ed. Maynard Mack and James A. Winn. 266–84. Hamden, Conn.: Shoe String Press, 1980.
———. "Pope and his Audience: From the *Pastorals* to *The Dunciad Variorum*." In *Studies in the Eighteenth Century IV: Papers Presented at the Fourth David Nichol Smith Memorial Seminar Canberra 1976*. Ed. R. F. Brissenden and J. C. Eade. 1–19. Canberra: Australian National University Press, 1979.
Jackson, James L. "Pope's *The Rape of the Lock* Considered as a Five-Act Epic." *PMLA* 65 (1950): 1283–87.
Jacobson, Howard. *Ovid's Heroides*. Princeton: Princeton University Press, 1974.
Johnson, Samuel. *A Dictionary of the English Language*. 1755. New York: Arno Press, 1979.
———. *Lives of the English Poets*. Ed. George Birkbeck Hill. 3 vols. 1905. New York: Octagon Books, 1967.
———. *Samuel Johnson*. The Oxford Authors. Ed. Donald Greene. Oxford and New York: Oxford University Press, 1984.
Keener, Frederick M. *An Essay on Pope*. New York and London: Columbia University Press, 1974.
Kennedy, George. *The Art of Persuasion in Greece*. Princeton: Princeton University Press, 1963.
———. *The Art of Rhetoric in the Roman World: 300 B.C.–A.D. 300*. Princeton: Princeton University Press, 1972.
———. *Classical Rhetoric and Its Christian and Secular Tradition from Ancient to Modern Times*. Chapel Hill: University of North Carolina Press, 1980.
———. *Quintilian*. New York: Twayne, 1969.
Kinsley, William. "The Dunciad as Mock-Book" (1971). In *Pope: Recent Essays*

by Several Hands. Ed. Maynard Mack and James A. Winn. 707–28. Hamden, Conn.: Archon Books, 1980.

Lanham, Richard A. *A Handlist of Rhetorical Terms: A Guide for Students of English Literature.* 1968. Berkeley, Los Angeles, and London: University of California Press, 1969.

———. *Literacy and the Survival of Humanism.* New Haven and London: Yale University Press, 1983.

———. *The Motives of Eloquence: Literary Rhetoric in the Renaissance.* New Haven and London: Yale University Press, 1976.

Leranbaum, Miriam. *Alexander Pope's 'OPUS MAGNUM', 1729–1744.* Oxford: Oxford University Press, 1977.

Locke, John. *An Essay concerning Human Understanding.* Ed. L. A. Selby-Bigge. Great Books of the Western World. Vol. 35. 83–395. Chicago: Encyclopaedia Britannica, 1952.

Longinus, Dionysius. *'Longinus' On the Sublime.* Ed. D. A. Russell. Oxford: Clarendon Press, 1964.

———. *Oeuvres Diverses du Sieur D*** avec le Traité du Sublime ou du Merveilleux dans le Discours.* Trans. Nicolas Boileau-Despréaux. Paris: Denys Thierry, 1674.

———. *On the Sublime.* Trans. W. Hamilton Fyfe. Vol. 23. Loeb Classical Library. 1927. London: William Heinemann; Cambridge: Harvard University Press, 1982.

———. *A Treatise of the Sublime, or, The Marvellous in Discourse* in *The Works of Monsr. Boileau Despreaux.* Trans. John Ozell. 2:1–88. 2 vols. London: E. Sanger and E. Curll, 1711–12.

———. *The Works of Dionysius Longinus, On the Sublime: or, a Treatise Concerning the Sovereign Perfection of Writing.* Trans. Leonard Welsted. London: Sam Briscoe, 1712.

Lord, Albert B. *The Singer of Tales.* 1960. New York: Atheneum, 1978.

Lovejoy, Arthur O. " 'Nature' as Aesthetic Norm." *Modern Language Notes* 42 (1927): 444–50.

McLuhan, Marshall. *The Gutenberg Galaxy: The Making of Typographic Man.* 1962. Toronto: University of Toronto Press, 1968.

Mack, Maynard. *Alexander Pope: A Life.* New York: Norton; New Haven and London: Yale University Press, 1985.

———. "The Muse of Satire" (1951). In *Collected in Himself: Essays Critical, Biographical, and Bibliographical on Pope and Some of His Contemporaries.* Newark: University of Delaware Press; London and Toronto: Associated University Presses, 1982. Also in *Yale Review* 51 (1951): 80–92.

———. "On Reading Pope." *College English* 7 (1946): 263–73.

Maddison, Carol. *Apollo and the Nine: A History of the Ode.* London: Routledge and Kegan Paul, 1960.

Maresca, Thomas E. *Pope's Horatian Poems.* Columbus: Ohio State University Press, 1966.

Monk, Samuel H. "A Grace Beyond the Reach of Art." *Journal of the History of Ideas* 5 (1944): 131–50.

———. *The Sublime, A Study of Critical Theories in XVIII-Century England.* 1935. Ann Arbor: University of Michigan Press, 1962.

Morris, David B. *Alexander Pope, The Genius of Sense.* Cambridge and London: Harvard University Press, 1984.

Muecke, D. C. *Irony and the Ironic.* The Critical Idiom. Series 13. 1970. London and New York: Methuen, 1982.

Myrick, Kenneth Orne. *Sir Philip Sidney as a Literary Craftsman.* Cambridge: Harvard University Press, 1935.

Olson, Elder. "The Argument of Longinus' *On the Sublime.*" In *Critics and Criticism, Ancient and Modern.* Ed. R. S. Crane. 232–59. Chicago: University of Chicago Press, 1952.

———. "Rhetoric and the Appreciation of Pope." *Modern Philology* 37 (1939): 13–35.

Ong, Walter J. *Orality and Literacy: The Technologizing of the Word.* London: Methuen, 1982.

———. *Ramus: Method, and the Decay of Dialogue.* 1958. Cambridge and London: Harvard University Press, 1983.

Parkin, Rebecca Price. "Mythopoeic Activity in the *Rape of the Lock.*" *English Literary History* 21 (1954): 30–38.

———. *The Poetic Workmanship of Alexander Pope.* Minneapolis: University of Minnesota, 1955.

Plato. "Phaedrus." In *The Collected Dialogues of Plato.* Ed. Edith Hamilton and Huntington Cairns. Trans. R. Hackforth. 475–525. 1952. Princeton: Princeton University Press, 1973.

Pope, Alexander. *The Correspondence of Alexander Pope.* Ed. George Sherburn. 5 vols. Oxford: Clarendon Press, 1956. [Corr.]

———. *Eloïsa to Abelard with the letters of Heloise to Abelard in the version by JOHN HUGHES (1713).* Ed. James E. Wellington. With notes and introduction. University of Miami Critical Studies no. 5. Coral Gables, Fla.: University of Miami Press, 1965.

———. *The Last and Greatest Art: Some Unpublished Poetical Manuscripts of Alexander Pope.* Ed. Maynard Mack. London and Toronto: Associated University Presses; Newark: University of Delaware Press, 1984.

———. *Pope's Epistle to Bathurst: A Critical Reading with an Edition of the Manuscripts.* Ed. Earl R. Wasserman. Baltimore: Johns Hopkins Press, 1960.

———. *The Prose Works of Alexander Pope.* Vol. 1: *The Earlier Works, 1711–1720.* Ed. Norman Ault. Oxford: Shakespeare Head Press, 1936.

———. *The Prose Works of Alexander Pope.* Vol. 2: *The Major Works, 1725–1744.* Ed. Rosemary Cowler. Hamden, Conn.: Archon Books, 1986.

———. *The Twickenham Edition of the Poems of Alexander Pope.* Ed. John Butt et al. 11 vols. London: Methuen; New Haven: Yale University Press, 1939–69. [TE]

———. *The Works of Alexander Pope.* Ed. Whitwell Elwin and William John Courthope. 10 vols. 1871–89. New York: Gordion Press, 1967. [EC]

Price, Martin. *Swift's Rhetorical Art, A Study of Structure and Meaning.* Carbondale and Edwardsville: Southern Illinois Press; London and Amsterdam: Feffer & Simmons, 1973.

Puttenham, George. *The Arte of English Poesie* (1589). 1906. Kent, Ohio: Kent State University Press, 1970.

Quintilian. *The Institutio Oratoria of Quintilian.* Trans. H. E. Butler. 4 vols. Loeb Classical Library. 1920–22. Cambridge: Harvard University Press; London: William Heinemann, 1979–86.

Reid, B. L. "Ordering Chaos: *The Dunciad*" (1974). In *Pope: Recent Essays by Several Hands.* Ed. Maynard Mack and James A. Winn. 678–706. Hamden, Conn.: Archon Books, 1980.

Richards, I. A. *Principles of Literary Criticism.* 1925. New York: Harcourt, Brace & World, n.d.

Rogers, Pat. " 'The Enamelled Ground': The Language of Heraldry and Natural Description in *Windsor-Forest*" (1973). In *Pope: Recent Essays by Several Hands.* Ed. Maynard Mack and James A. Winn. 159–76. Hamden, Conn.: Shoe String Press, 1980.

———. *Hacks and Dunces: Pope, Swift and Grub Street. (Grub Street: Studies in a Subculture)* 1972. London and New York: Methuen, 1980.

———. "Time and Space in *Windsor Forest.*" In *The Art of Alexander Pope.* Ed. Howard Erskine-Hill and Anne Smith. 40–51. London: Vision Press, 1979.

Ross, John F. *Swift and Defoe: A Study in Literary Relationship.* Berkeley: University of California Press, 1941.

Rubel, Veré L. *Poetic Diction in the English Renaissance: From Skelton through Spenser.* New York: Modern Language Association; London: Oxford University Press, 1941.

Sackton, Alexander H. *Rhetoric as a Dramatic Language in Ben Jonson.* New York: Columbia University Press; London and Bombay: Oxford University Press, 1948.

Schmitz, Robert M. *Pope's Windsor Forest 1712, A Study of the Washington University Holograph.* Washington University Studies (New Series): Language and Literature 21. Saint Louis: Eden, 1952.

Shafer, Robert. *The English Ode to 1660: An Essay in Literary History.* Princeton: Princeton University Press; London: Oxford University Press, 1918.

Shankman, Steven. *Pope's Iliad: Homer in the Age of Passion.* Princeton: Princeton University Press, 1983.

Shelley, Percy Bysshe. *The Selected Poetry and Prose of Percy Bysshe Shelley.* Ed. Carlos Baker. New York: Random House, 1951.

Sherburn, George. *The Early Career of Alexander Pope.* 1934. New York: Russell & Russell, 1963.

———. "Pope at Work." In *Essays on the Eighteenth Century, Presented to David Nichol Smith in Honour of his Seventieth Birthday.* 49–64. Oxford: Clarendon Press, 1945.

Sherburn, George, and Donald F. Bond. "New Voices in Poetry." In *A Literary History of England.* Ed. Albert C. Baugh. 933–49. 2d ed. Englewood Cliffs, N.J.: Prentice-Hall, 1948.

Shuster, George N. *The English Ode from MILTON to KEATS.* New York: Columbia University Press, 1940.

Sitter, John E. *The Poetry of Pope's Dunciad.* Minneapolis: University of Minnesota Press; London and Bombay: Oxford University Press; Toronto: Copp Clark, 1971.

Sonnino, Lee A. *A Handbook of Sixteenth-Century Rhetoric*. London: Routledge & Kegan Paul, 1968.
Spence, Joseph. *Observations, Anecdotes, and Characters of Books and Men, Collected from Conversation* (1820). Ed. James Marshall Osborn. 2 vols. Oxford: Clarendon Press, 1966.
Stone, P. W. K. *The Art of Poetry 1750–1820: Theories of Poetic Composition and Style in the Late Neo-Classic and Early Romantic Periods*. New York: Barnes & Noble, 1967.
Tillotson, Geoffrey. *On the Poetry of Pope*. 1938. Oxford: Clarendon Press, 1950.
Trimpi, Wesley. "Horace's 'Ut Pictura Poesis': The Argument for Stylistic Decorum." *Traditio* 34 (1978): 29–73.
Tuve, Rosemond. *Elizabethan and Metaphysical Imagery, Renaissance Poetic and Twentieth Century Critics*. 1947. Chicago and London: University of Chicago Press, 1965.
Van Doren, Mark. *The Poetry of John Dryden*. New York: Harcourt, Brace and Howe, 1920.
Vann Rennes, Jacob Johan. *Bowles, Byron, and the Pope Controversy*. New York: Haskell House, 1966.
Varey, Simon. "Rhetoric and *An Essay on Man*." In *The Art of Alexander Pope*. Ed. Howard Erskine-Hill and Anne Smith. 132–43. London: Vision Press, 1979.
Vickers, Brian. "The Atrophy of Modern Rhetoric, Vico to De Man." *Rhetorica* 6.1 (1988): 21–56.
———. *Classical Rhetoric in English Poetry*. London: Macmillan, 1970.
Vida, Marco Girolamo. *The De Arte Poetica of Marco Girolamo Vida* (1517). Trans. Ralph G. Williams. New York: Columbia University Press, 1976.
Wallerstein, Ruth C. "The Development of the Rhetoric and Metre of the Heroic Couplet, Especially in 1625–1645." *PMLA* 50 (1935): 167–209.
Warren, Austin. *Alexander Pope as Critic and Humanist*. 1929. Gloucester: Peter Smith, 1963.
———. "The Mask of Pope." *Sewanee Review* 54 (1946): 19–33.
———. *Richard Crashaw, A Study in Baroque Sensibility*. Kingsport: Louisiana State University Press, 1939.
Warton, Joseph. *An Essay on the Writings and Genius of Pope*. 2 vols. London: T. Maiden for W. J. and J. Richardson et al., 1806.
Wasserman, Earl Reeves. "The Inherent Values of Eighteenth-Century Personification." *PMLA* 65 (1950): 435–63.
———. "The Limits of Allusion in *The Rape of the Lock*" (1966). In *Pope: Recent Essays by Several Hands*. Ed. Maynard Mack and James A. Winn. 224–46. Hamden, Conn.: Archon Books, 1980.
———. "Nature Moralized: The Divine Analogy in the Eighteenth Century." *English Literary History* 20 (1953): 39–76.
———. *The Subtler Language: Critical Readings of Neoclassic and Romantic Poems*. Baltimore: Johns Hopkins Press, 1959. Chap. 4.
Weinbrot, Howard D. *The Formal Strain: Studies in Augustan Imitation and Satire*. Chicago and London: University of Chicago Press, 1969.
Wilding, Michael. "Dryden and Satire: 'MacFlecknoe, Absalom and

Achitophel, the *Medall'*, and Juvenal" (1972). In *Writers and their Background: John Dryden*. Ed. Earl Miner. 191–233. Athens: Ohio University Press, 1975.

Williams, Aubrey L. *Pope's Dunciad: A Study of its Meaning*. London: Methuen, 1955.

Williamson, George. "The Rhetorical Pattern of Neo-Classical Wit." *Modern Philology* 33 (1935): 55–81.

Wimsatt, Jr., W. K. "One Relation of Rhyme to Reason: Alexander Pope." *Modern Language Quarterly* 5 (1944): 323–38.

———. "Rhetoric and Poems: Alexander Pope." In *English Institute Essays for 1948*. 183ff. New York: Columbia University Press, 1949.

Yeats, William Butler. *The Autobiography of William Butler Yeats, Consisting of Reveries over Childhood and Youth, The Trembling of the Veil, and Dramatis Personae*. 1916. New York: Collier Books, 1967.

Zimmermann, Hans-Joachim. *Alexander Popes Noten zu Homer: Eine Manuskript- und Quellenstudie*. Heidelberg: Carl Winter, 1966.

Index

Addison, Joseph, 151 n.7, 156 n.17; *Spectator*, (no. 418) 89, (no. 339) 169 n.73
Aden, John M., 25
Ad Herennium. See Rhetorica Ad Herennium
Anne (Queen), 45; name foils of, 60; in *Windsor-Forest*, 48, 49, 64
Arbuthnot, John: *Three Hours after Marriage*, 110
Aristotle, 14, 126, 133; *Art of Rhetoric*, 20; on *enthymeme* (rhetorical syllogism), examples, and maxims, 34; on means of persuasion, 30–31; on modes of argument, 26; *Poetics*, 65–66; on style, 30

Blair, Hugh: *Lectures on Rhetoric and Belles Lettres*, 114–15
Bliven, Bruce: "Diary of a Worrier," 69
Bloom, Harold, 17
Bogel, Frederic V., 154 n.48, 171 n.22
Boileau-Despréaux, Nicolas, 91, 114; *Art poétique*, 93; *Le Lutrin*, 81–82; on the sublime style, 109, 168 n.64; translation of Longinus, 107, 141, 142
Bolingbroke, Henry St. John, Lord, 13, 147 n.1
Booth, Wayne C., 68–69, 170–71 n.11
Boswell, James, 67
Bridges, Ralph, 88
Broome, William, 38
Brower, Reuben, 83, 95, 156 n.27
Browning, Robert, 96
Bundy, Elroy L., 159 nn. 74 and 76; on Pindar's use of subjective foils, 152 n.16, 158 n.66; on the *priamel*, 159 n.70
Burke, Edmund: *On the Sublime and Beautiful*, 113–14

Burke, Kenneth, 15, 89, 166 n.35
Butler, Samuel, 17–18
Byron, George Gordon, Lord, 17
Bysshe, Edward: *Art of English Poetry*, 53

Cairns, Francis, 164 n.13
Caplan, Harry, 158 n.64
Charles I, 49
Chaucer, Geoffrey, 70
Cicero, 14, 133. See also *Rhetorica Ad Herennium*
Coleridge, Samuel Taylor, 21
Congreve, William, 59; *Discourse on the Pindarique Odes*, 54–55; *To the QUEEN On the Victorious Progress of HER MAJESTY's Arms*, 54
Courthope, William John, 165 n.24
Cowley, Abraham, 55; Congreve and the odes of, 54; and the Pindaric ode, 52, 53; in *Windsor-Forest*, 48
Crashaw, Richard, 157–58 n.55; *Delights of the Muses*, 55; *In the praise of the Spring*, 55
Cromwell, Henry, 39, 55
Culler, A. Dwight, 53
Curll, Edmund, 124, 129–30

Dacier, Anne (Madame), 71–72
Davenant, Sir William: preface to *Gondibert*, 78–81
Defoe, Daniel: "A True Relation of the Apparition of Mrs. Veal," 165 n.29
Denham, Sir John, 48; *Cooper's Hill*, 40, 43, 53
Dennis, John, 28, 110, 115, 132; "Observations Upon Windsor-Forest," 42–43; on Pope's punning, 127–28; preface to *The Court of Death*, 50; preface to *Miscellanies in Verse and Prose*, 44–45; "Remarks on the

Rape of the Lock," 127–28; "REMARKS upon MR. POPE'S DUNCIAD," 71–72; on the sublime, 113, 114
Dillon, Earl of Roscommon, Wentworth, 39
Dionysius of Halicarnassus, 14, 39, 55; and the Dionysius rhetoric, 45–46; Pope's use of, 46. See also Dionysius rhetoric
Dionysius rhetoric, 40, 49, 50, 56–57; influence of, 45–46. See also Dionysius of Halicarnassus
Donne, John, 93
Doren, Mark Van, 157 n.46
Dryden, John, 59–60, 79, 157 n.46; Epistle Dedicatory of the Rival Ladies, 52–53; MacFlecknoe, 130; Of Dramatick Poesie, 78; A Parallel of Poetry and Painting, 41–42; To the Pious Memory of Mrs Anne Killegrew, 53, 157 n.45; preface to Eleonora, 40, 55; preface to the Sylvae, 52, 53; and Sir William Soames, Art of Poetry of, 52, 77, 93; Threnodia Augustalis, 53; on translating, 91, 163–64 n.10
Dunciad, The, 20; in Book 4, 33; irony in, 118–22; logos of, 68; Martinus Scriblerus of, 120; masking in, 122–27; metaphorical interplay in, 130–31; poet persona of, 66, 68, 69, 116, 119; Variorum (1729), 75–76; and Variorum (1729) compared, 116–18
Dyer, John: Grongar Hill, 51, 52

Edward III, 49
Elegy, 92–94. See also Genre
Elegy to the Memory of an Unfortunate Lady, 69; and elegiac practice, 92–95; "the imaginary second person" in, 99; logos as appeal in, 95; pathos in, 88, 89; phantasia in, 97; poet persona of, 90–91, 96; reader's engagement in, 90–91, 92; rhetorical appeals in, 94; Sapphic sublimity of, 114, 115; tragic elements in, 89, 96–97
Eliot, T. S.: "The Hollow Men," 69
Eloisa to Abelard, 66, 69; apostrophe in, 104–5; conduplicatio (word repetition) in, 104; as elegy, 93; Eloisa's pathos, 88, 102, 103, 104; ethos in, 103, 105–7; metalepsis in, 104–5; pathos as appeal in, 89, 94, 105, 107; phantasia in, 101, 106; ratiocinatio (rhetorical question) in, 103–4; reader's engagement in, 90–91, 92; Sapphic sublimity of, 114, 115; sublimity of, 100; tragic elements in, 89
Elwin, Whitwell, 155–56 n.13
Essay on Criticism, An, 41, 42, 43, 53, 79, 123; as a deliberation, 21, 25; egressio in, 24; exordium in, 22; on false eloquence, 133–34; on formal beauty, 81; on Homer, 71; logos of, 32; maxims in, 34–35; methods of appeal in, 28–32; narratio in, 22–23; peroratio in, 25; poet persona of, 20, 21, 27, 29, 36; Pope's poetic tours described in, 37; probatio in, 23–24; refutatio in, 24; rhetorical bases of, 22, 23, 24, 26; rhetorical outline of, 22–25; rhetoricians noted by Pope in, 150 n.5; transparency and opacity of expression in, 29; as a six-part oration, 22
Eustathius of Thessalonica, 84, 87
Expression, oral and literate, 31–32

Fenton, Elijah, 141, 156 n.31
Fermor, Arabella, 66
Fowler, Alastair, 93, 164 n.15
Frye, Northrop, 15–16
Fyfe, W. Hamilton, 141, 144

Garrison, James D., 45–46, 159 n.78
Garth, Samuel: The Dispensary, 75, 78, 81–82
Gay, John, 124, 162 n.36; Three Hours after Marriage, 110
Genre: and poetic kind, 41; Pope's use of, 14; of Windsor-Forest, 43–44. See also Elegy; Pindaric ode
George I, 61
Goldsmith, Oliver: "Life of Thomas Parnell," 162–63 n.38
Gordon, I. R. F., 172–73 n.48
Gorgias, 168 n.64
Granville, Baron Lansdowne, George,

44, 45, 47; name foils to, 60, 64; in *Windsor-Forest*, 49, 56, 58–59
Group μ, 148–49 n.6

Havelock, Eric A., 153 n.32
Henry VI, 49
Hill, Aaron, 123–24, 126
Hirsch, Jr., E. D., 155 n.11
Homer, 88–89; distancing through light and shadow, 70–73; *Iliad*, 83–87, 160 n.10; literary use of appeals in, 30–31, 32; *Odyssey*, 109
Horace, 50, 69; *Ars Poetica*, 25
Hudson, John, 45, 141
Hughes, John, 166 n.42
Hughes, R. E., 151 n.11

Jack, Ian, 162 n.36, 165 n.28, 169 n.1
Jackson, James L., 162 n.29
Jacobson, Howard, 166 n.43
Johnson, Samuel, 17; on *ecstasy*, 92; on *elegy*, 93; on *Elegy to the Memory of an Unfortunate Lady*, 94, 95–96, 165 n.27; *Life of Cowley*, 38; *Life of Gray*, 74; *Life of Pope*, 21–22, 38, 43; *London*, 94; on *ode*, 50, 64; on Pope's poet *persona*, 67; preface to Shakespeare, 67 on *The Rape of the Lock*, 78–79, 120–21
Jonson, Ben, 93, 157 n.54; *To Sir Lucius Cary and Sir H. Morison*, 55
Juvenal: *Third Satire*, 94

Keats, John, 111
Kennedy, George, 46, 47, 153 nn. 30 and 31, 171 n.12

Lanham, Richard A., 70
Lansdowne, Baron. *See* Granville, Baron Lansdowne, George
Lardner, Ring: "Gullible's Travels," 69
Le Bossu, René, 154 n.42
Leranbaum, Miriam, 147 n.1
Locke, John, 130, 133, 171 n.24; on the habitual train of thought, 128–29; on rhetoric in *An Essay concerning Human Understanding*, 132
London, Great Fire of, 130–31, 172–73 n.48
Longinus, 14, 50, 168 n.64; on "the imaginary second person," 99, 159 n.79 *On the Sublime*, 88; on *phantasia*, 97; Pope's use of, 94; on psychological effects of, 16; on Sappho, 114–15; on sources of the sublime, 108–9, 112; the sublime of, 107–13; translations of, 141–44. *See also* Sapphic sublimity; the Sublime
Lord, Albert B., 31

Mack, Maynard, 131, 166 n.39, 172 n.27, 173 n.50
McLuhan, Marshall, 170 nn. 5 and 7
Marvell, Andrew, 93
Menander of Laodicea, 45
Mill, John Stuart, 28–29
Milton, John, 93, 106, 164 n.14
Monk, Samuel H., 16, 109, 113, 167–68 n.62
Morris, David B., 77, 162 n.30
Muecke, D. C., 118

Olson, Elder, 111–12
Opacity of expression. *See* Transparency and opacity of expression
Ovid, 115; *Heroides*, 100, 166–67 n.43
Ozell, John, 141, 142–43, 167 n.57

Parkin, Rebecca Price, 121, 171 n.14
Parnell, Thomas, 162–63 n.38
Passions: *ethos* and *pathos* as, 35–36, 154 n.42
Peacham, Henry: *The Garden of Eloquence*, 104–5, 165 n.32
Petre, Robert, Lord, 66
Pindar, 50, 55–56, 158 nn. 64 and 66
Pindaric ode, 50–56. *See also* Genre
Plato: *Phaedrus*, 29–30
Pope, Alexander: and alexandrines, 53–54; on allegory, 161 n.21; and his audience, 162 n.36, 169 n.1; empirical attitude of, 32–33; *An Epistle to Dr. Arbuthnot*, 90, 106; *An Essay on Man*, 13, 32, 36, 65, 134–35, 150 n.16; Homeric translations, 14, 32, 72–73, 83, 160 n.10; *A Key to the Lock*, 120; *Memoirs of Martinus Scriblerus*, 69; merits as a poet, 17; *Messiah*, 68; *Moral Essays*, 13; and Ovid, 166–67 n.43; *Pastorals*, 54; on *pathos* in Homer's *Iliad*, 94–95; *Peri*

Bathous, 20, 37–38, 45, 110, 111, 161 nn. 21 and 22, 167 n.55; and persona by, 28–29, 66–69; pictorialization in poetry of, 69–73, 83; poetical career of, 13; poetic *tours* of, 37, 121; postscript to the *Odyssey*, 141, 154 n.42; preface to *Works of 1717*, 88, 102; *psychagôgia* of, 15, 30; and puns *(paranomasia)* by, 127–28; on reason and the passions, 35–37; and representative meter, 38–39; rhetorical technique of, 14–15, 20; rhetorical use of titles by, 68–69; satirical use of names by, 159 n.72; *Spectator*, (no. 408), 35–36; on the sublime style, 110; *The Temple of Fame*, 55; *Three Hours after Marriage*, 110; translation of Ovid's *Sapho to Phaon*, 115; and triplets, 54; *The Universal Prayer*, 68; *Verses to the Memory of an Unfortunate Lady*, 93. See also *The Dunciad*; *Elegy to the Memory of an Unfortunate Lady*; *Eloisa to Abelard*; *An Essay on Criticism*; *The Rape of the Lock*; *Windsor-Forest*

Price, Martin, 120, 122–23, 125–26

Puttenham, George, 99–100

Quintilian, 14, 50, 68; on allegory, 119–20, 121; on *apostrophe*, 104; on eloquence and a virtuous life, 133; on *ethos*, 154 n.41; on following poets, 152 n.13; forensic model of, 22; *Institutio Oratoria*, 20; and irony, 118–21; on metaphor, 119, 171 n.16; on natural order of argument, 36; on orator's purpose, 25, 26, 27; on the *persona*, 27; Pope's use of, 27–28, 150–51 n.5; on *prosopopoeia* (personification), 152 n.17; on rhetorical *basis* (or *stasis*), 22, 151 n.8; on style, 127

Rape of the Lock, The, 20, 123, 128; Clarissa's speech in, 87, 120; dramatic design of, 76–81; dramatic irony in, 65, 122; epic allusion in, 75–76, 83–87; *ethos* in, 66–67, 87; *exordia* in, 73–74; *logos* of, 68, 83; metaphor in, 73–74, 84–85; poet *persona* of, 65, 66–69, 81–82, 83, 88, 133–34; transparency and opacity of expression in, 73–76, 77–78

Rhetoric, 14; and dialectic, 33; old and new, 15–16, 21–22

Rhetorica Ad Herennium, 56–57, 158 nn. 61, 64, and 67; on *conduplicatio* (word repetition), 166 n.34; on *ratiocinatio* (rhetorical question), 158–59 n.69

Richards, I. A., 19

Rogers, Pat, 155 n.6

Roscoe, William, 165 n.25

Ross, John F., 119

Russell, D. A., 91, 159 n.79

Sapphic sublimity, 89, 92, 114–15; in *Elegy to the Memory of an Unfortunate Lady*, 98; in *Eloisa to Abelard*, 107; Longinus on, 145–46. See also Longinus; the Sublime

Sappho, 114; *Ode to Anactoria*, 107, 115, 145–46

Schmitz, Robert M., 52

Scipio Africanus, 48

Shafer, Robert, 51, 157 n.54, 158 nn. 60 and 64

Shakespeare, William: *Hamlet*, 100–101; *The Rape of Lucrece*, 69

Shankman, Steven, 71, 72, 161 n.14

Shelley, Percy Bysshe, 149 n.15; *A Defence of Poetry*, 16–17, 19

Sherburn, George, 126

Sidney, Sir Philip: *An Apology for Poetry*, 16, 17

Soames, Sir William: and John Dryden, *Art of Poetry* of, 52, 77, 93

Sophocles, 50

Spence, Joseph, 55, 79, 150 n.16

Stone, P. W. K., 114

Sublime, the: *ecstasis* and *ecstasy*, 91–92, 164 n.12; eighteenth-century conceptions of, 107–15; emotion and, 112–14; Longinus on the principle sources of, 108–9, 112; style, 16, 109–10, 168 n.64. See also Longinus; Sapphic sublimity

Surrey, Henry Howard, Earl of, 48

Swift, Jonathan, 124, 162–63 n.38; and irony of, 118, 125–26

Tillotson, Geoffrey, 51, 82, 100, 101, 167 nn. 47 and 49
Titus Pomponius, 48
Transparency and opacity in expression: in *An Essay on Criticism*, 29; described, 69–73; in *The Rape of the Lock*, 73–76; in *Windsor-Forest*, 62
Trumball, Sir William, 48
Tuve, Rosemond, 168 n.64

Utrecht, Treaty of, 47, 48

Vida, Marco Girolamo: *De Arte Poetica*, 39
Virgil, 88–89, 130; *Georgics*, 55

Waller, Edmund, 52–53
Walsh, William, 53
Warren, Austin, 157 n.53, 157–58 n.55
Warton, Joseph: *An Essay on the Genius and Writings of Pope*, 162 n.32
Wasserman, Earl R., 40, 159 n.72, 161 n.21
Welstead, Leonard, 141, 143
Wilding, Michael, 163 n.40
William I, 47
William III, 61
Williams, Aubrey L., 127, 130, 170 n.2, 172 n.37
Wimsatt, W. K., 159 n.72
Windsor-Forest, 21, 68, 99, 107, 110–11; elements of festival panegyric in, 44–49, 50–51; a hermeneutic circle in, 43, 155 n.11; *name caps* in, 59, 61; *name foils* in, 60, 63; outline of, 47–49; poet *persona* of, 63–64; *priamel* (or *praeambulum*) in, 59, 159 n.70; prosopopoeia (personification) in, 63–64; *ratiocinatio* (rhetorical question) in, 59; reader's engagement in, 90, 92; rhetorical appeals in, 57; rhetorical design in, 56–57; 1712 holograph, 52, 58, 61; subjective rhetorical foils in, 58–59, 60; themes of restoration and limitation in, 61, 159 n.78; transparency and opacity of expression in, 62
Wycherly, William, 46–47

Yeats, William Butler, 28–29